This Old House
By the Lake

by

Judith Petres-Balogh

TRAFFORD

National Library of Canada Cataloguing in Publication

Balogh, Judith Petres, 1933-
    This old house by the lake / Judith Petres Balogh.
ISBN 1-55369-741-3
    I. Title.
DB958.6.B34A3 2002   943.905'4'092   C2002-903246-6

TRAFFORD

This book was published *on-demand* in cooperation with Trafford Publishing.
On-demand publishing is a unique process and service of making a book available for retail sale to the public taking advantage of on-demand manufacturing and Internet marketing. **On-demand publishing** includes promotions, retail sales, manufacturing, order fulfilment, accounting and collecting royalties on behalf of the author.

Suite 6E, 2333 Government St., Victoria, B.C. V8T 4P4, CANADA
Phone   250-383-6864   Toll-free   1-888-232-4444 (Canada & US)
Fax   250-383-6804   E-mail   sales@trafford.com
Web site   www.trafford.com   TRAFFORD PUBLISHING IS A DIVISION OF TRAFFORD HOLDINGS LTD.
Trafford Catalogue #02-0554   www.trafford.com/robots/02-0554.html

10   9   8   7   6   5   4   3

PROLOGUE

When I was young, my generation went through "phases". Some of these phases were our own; others belonged to the children we produced along the way. In either case, we prayed piously for each to pass. The sooner, the better. Later, as prices rose, suburbs grew and psychology became a household word, these phases acquired deeper meanings, respectability, and total acceptance. They were also renamed, and were now referred to as "passages." As the name implies, these too passed eventually and as a reward for enduring them all, we could look forward to a peaceful Golden Age with cookies baking in our ovens and grandchildren romping around the house. White-haired and at peace with the world, we would preside over holiday tables, exuding benevolent wisdom, enviable charm and happy contentment. The work of our life successfully done, all the passages safely behind us, we would gently and gracefully fade into the golden sunset.

These were reasonable expectations. There was nothing extravagant in the plan and it would not have broken the federal budget to achieve them. But fate, in its bottomless perversity, had a different denouement for us.

In the second half of the seventies, after a divorce and after seeing my three grown children settled, I was hired by the US Department of Defense as a teacher for the dependents of the military. I was stationed in Germany, where in due time I married a second time, then earned two master degrees, one in special education (of the gifted) and one in school administration. I was nearing my sixtieth birthday, but life was never better.

But, as in all good stories, conflict entered. There were ominous clouds gathering on the horizon effectively blurring the golden sunset we took for granted. The Storm finally broke and the Gulf War became a reality, but which mercifully did not last as long as was initially feared.

The preceding paragraphs contain enough material for a novel about the length of War and Peace. But the topic of this tale is limited to a short period of time just after the war, and the events following it. Our life changed fundamentally, and we experienced what surely is the grandmother of all passages.

Our rejoicing about the war being over was marred by a new worry, more personal in its nature than the war itself. Rumors were rampant and contradictory, but one basic issue was undeniable: the US military forces in Europe were heading for a major downsizing in the near future. Obviously, that meant fewer dependents, hence fewer and smaller schools. It did not take three college degrees to figure out that many of us were facing unemployment at an age when we were no longer marketable.

Our huge staff was not part of the Department of Education; we were employed by the Department of Defense. Hence at my retirement the years I was teaching in Ohio would not be calculated into the total years of service I had to my credit. I worked only for a period of thirteen years for DoDDS (Department of Defense Dependents' Schools), and so I was not even eligible for retirement yet, and even if I were, the benefits would be ridiculously low. As far as retaining my job, my seniority was not impressive either.

I spent the years at DoDDS teaching the gifted in special programs at one large school, and setting up enrichment programs in six others. During the last three years I was part of the administration in the position of Educational Program Manager, or EPM, as I was called.

The turnover rate was brisk in these overseas schools, because a large percentage of the teaching staff was made up of military spouses. When the military tour of duty was completed and the husbands were transferred, usually back home to the USA, the wife-teachers followed them. Few of the educators lasted longer than four years. In view of this, I appeared to have a lot of seniority. However, the rest of the educators, and especially those in administration, were not military dependents and the majority had well over twenty-five years of service to their credits. It was obvious and fair that when the trimming started, DoDDS should retain those with venerable seniority.

But these noble considerations did not ease the worries about my position. My husband, with the inelegant title of "non-resident alien" in people skills, and was computer literate at a time, when a great many people in Europe did not know how to turn on the CP. Having lived a little over a decade in Europe, I was also fairly familiar with the continental way of thinking and dealing. I hoped that some of the American companies expanding into the old continent could use my skills. Some said sweetly and pointedly that they are not hiring the 'elderly" (being an ocean away from our judicial system, they felt that a little discrimination could not hurt them). A few said, "We'll keep you in mind", but the majority never even responded. So much for the planned career changes we were encouraged to seek.

The school year rumbled to its end, made unforgettable by grave speculations, wild rumors and an intolerable degree of anxiety. September and the new school year brought all sorts of promises, but no solutions. Stress-related illnesses were epidemic.

Our personal worries increased. The lease on our rented house was expiring, and we had to make a decision soon if we did not want to lose thousands of dollars. Finally I called the Regional Office and explained that we have serious commitments and I must have some information in order to make a rational decision. While I did not expect that the problem of my lease would be on their priority list, it helped me little to hear that the Office was not in a position to promise anything. However, they were satisfied with the plans they were making for us. When I inquired what these plans might be, I was told not to worry. However, I am past the age when Big Daddy may make the decisions for me without consulting me first, so I pressed on for some details. "There is a chance that some of the educators might have to relocate," the spokesperson hinted as if mentioning a passing idea before he hung up on me. "To Japan, or Sicily or Central America." He listed these places with a faint tremble of excitement in his voice, as if he were planning the vacation of my life. This concluded our interview. Saint Rita, merciful saint of all impossible situations, can't you see that I cannot work in Japan and sleep in Germany, where my husband's job would keep him at least until the beginning of next year? Can't you intervene for us? The receiver in my hand buzzed stupidly. Saint Rita was otherwise occupied and wasn't listening either.

In November the superintendent appeared at our school. It was one of her scheduled visits, but Joyce, (the assistant principal) and I paid little attention to it. We were habitually ignored by her, and were used to our blessed anonymity.

The superintendent was a beautiful woman in a cold, detached way, and she was definitely one of the best-dressed women I ever knew. Her main purpose for coming periodically to our school was to evaluate the performance of our principal, and she paid scant attention to Joyce or me. When the principal sent for us with the message that the superintendent wanted to see us, we immediately had the foreboding of bad news.

"This is to cap off a perfectly awful day," Joyce mumbled. "Did you maul a parent recently?"

"Not during my waking hours. Did you?"

"Negative. Maybe she just wants to express her thanks for our unfailing dedication." We both laughed. We were not particularly spoiled by appreciation.

The superintendent was elegantly and expensively understated. Her flawless figure was packaged in the finest gray woolen suit and a mauve silk blouse. Every hair was in its perfect place and her accessories were exquisite. She stood up as we came in, and leaned her slim, tall frame against the principal's desk. She did not offer us a seat.

Instinctively I smoothed my straight hair and wished I had worn heels. Joyce and I, tired and not very impeccable after playground and lunch duties, stood like two misbehaving children in front of her. Did she expect us to genuflect?

"Well ladies, I have actually very little to say," she said with a melodious voice, just this side of sugary. "As you know, the draw-down has started and it goes faster than anticipated. It is also more massive than expected. At this point we don't know what will happen at the end of the school year. Nobody's job is secure, not even mine. All I can tell you that Judith's job is history. We are eliminating all EPM positions. Joyce, your job will be intact, but you won't be in it. We are moving someone with more seniority into this slot. That is all, ladies."

We were dismissed. I was kinder than this to students who were suspended for misbehavior from school. I was kinder than this when I had to tell a teacher that his or her performance was badly in need for major improvements. I was kinder than this when I told my first husband that I wanted a divorce. With a remarkable economy of words, we were told that it was all over. Our careers were in the basket and in a way so were our lives. Joyce was a single parent supporting two small children and I was very close to retirement age, married to a "non-resident" alien. Joyce and I were stranded a continent away from our families and from our supporting network, and had no real options to fix our lives.

As soon as the superintendent was gone Christine, the principal, came up to our office and hugged us silently.

Christine is tall, black, charismatic, generous and not only very beautiful, but also flawlessly good and happy, securely enveloped in what is sometimes called 'chic', or 'class', or "style". This special aura of hers is rooted in love and understanding, tolerance. It is something that cannot be learned; one either has the luck to be born with it, or be always without it. She has it in abundance. She also has something that my husband calls "stage presence"; wherever she appears, she cannot be ignored. Without ever trying, she always manages to be the principal figure in the gathering, and people always want to be near her. Her most outstanding features are her huge, gorgeous eyes, so expressive that they seem to have a life of their own. Hera, wife of Zeus, would have killed to have such eyes.

Christine has a superb talent to mimic almost anyone. At the end of a terrible day she used to make the day good again by relating her encounters with children, teachers, parents, and giving perfect and hilarious interpretations of the people who crossed her path that day. In a short while Joyce and I were usually reduced to helpless laughter and the tensions, frustrations and exhaustion vanished from us. Christine also has a beautiful voice. She could mesmerize students of all ages when she gathered them for a story hour, and she brought down the house and stole the show from the principal actors, when in Frankfurt, Germany she sang on stage the role of Bloody Mary from South Pacific. Both of us loved her. Without her we could not have survived those difficult years.

But this time she did not speak, and did not attempt to imitate the superintendent's sweet voice or clipped style. Hugging us silently, she tried to reassure us. Although childless and years younger than I, she gave the solid, warm assurance only a loving mother can give.

The superintendent promised that after all the teachers will have been relocated, and if there were any teaching positions left vacant, we could be considered for these, Chris told us. This scared me more than relocation. I was sixty and have not been in a regular classroom for more than a decade. Besides, I was promoted from the classroom to special education, and from there into administration at a considerable cost in hard work, expense and plain sweat, and had no desire to go back to a situation which I left after serious considerations. After twenty-five successful years in the classroom, I was burned out and was astute enough to know that a change in position was necessary. Children deserve the fresh energy, which I no longer had. Due to a slip of tongue children sometimes called me "mom" during instruction. When the slip turned to "grandma", I knew my time in the classroom was over. Children, mimicking society at large, prefer the young.

We spent that Christmas in Hungary. The purpose of our visit had an official slant. After the fall of Communism in Hungary, my husband was notified that he might reclaim the property, which was confiscated from him, when he chose political exile in the seventies. The property stood empty for a quarter of a century. Because nobody in his right might wanted it, the State generously agreed that we could have it back. My husband's presence was required for the completion of the paperwork. My grandmother, well known to have a worn phrase for every situation in life, used to say, "Walk with confidence and keep your mind and your eyes open, because you do not know when destiny will bump into you." We certainly had no inclination of bumping into anything, least of all our destiny, on that cold, foggy morning when we started the thousand-kilometer track toward a country that just emerged from Communism. We were glad at the prospect of getting away for a few days from our incessant worries about our future, and had no deep thoughts about anything else.

The property is located in Zalaszabar, a village so tiny that it barely shows up on local, greatly enlarged maps. We inspected our "mansion" during the previous summer and despaired. If there is such a thing as "punishment by real estate", this concentrated piece of disaster surely was it. Ever conscious of the environment, we immediately hired a crew to clean up and cart away the accumulated rubbish, in order to make it look less like the municipal garbage dump of a middle-sized city. Having done our civic duty and hoping in vain for an earthquake to take care of the rest, we fled to spend the rest of the summer in a civilized place. I am not the pioneer kind.

Nevertheless, we had to return to it once again, because the papers had to be signed. It was a bleak day when we arrived. Ill-humored birds sat brooding on the branches. Low, black clouds, the color of old pewter, banked above the hills, and there was mud everywhere. The house was as cold as a medieval church and there was no indoor plumbing.

We walked around the place trying to work up some enthusiasm and attempted to look at it creatively, like those remarkable people, who make wonderful homes out of old sawmills, wine-cellars, railroad stations and factories that were already outdated during the Industrial Revolution. We knew about people who restored castles that were destroyed in the twelfth century either by earthquakes or invading hordes, or both, and were eroding ever since.

We tried sincerely to discover some romantic charm emerging from the wreck, but failed to see anything but an ugly old house, lacking personality and creature comforts. It was a boring, ugly building, not a romantic ruin with unlimited architectural possibilities. And while the rooms were large enough, the house was far too small, consisting of three rooms and a shed. These opened from a generously wide hallway, which was as long as the entire front of the house. Only a person suffering from a case of acute megalomania would call it a mansion. The floors were quietly rotting away, the north wall was ready to cave in and the electrical system looked so frail that we decided against trying to turn on the switch. It only had three impressive features: the walls were over a yard thick; two of the rooms had massive exposed beams on the ceiling; and the door of the outhouse, (located about fifty paces from the house) had a vent in the shape of a heart. I am still trying to solve the association between the heart and the alimentary canal, but I remain mystified. Perhaps an ancestor had a weird sense of humor, which was somehow lost on later generations.

Actually this was not my first encounter with an artistic heart at a place I least expected it to be. I have seen such a heart-shaped "vent" once before, in the castle museum of Erbach, Germany, where an actual chastity belt was displayed on the shelf. It was a horribly wicked implement; its design very much like a sanitary belt, complete with what looked like a pad. Ah, but there was the rub, — no pun intended, because almost the entire devilish contraption was made of cast iron. I suppose it takes a woman to fully comprehend the horror of it. Up to that time I only half-believed that such a thing really existed, or that women were made to wear them while their husbands, with the key to it in their pockets, took off to fight in the Crusades. (And whatever happened if they left their wives pregnant and were not back by the date of the delivery? Did she call the locksmith before the midwife? Or were midwives of the times accomplished lock-picks?) At any rate, this satanic device too had a heart-shaped vent to facilitate to a degree some of nature's necessities. If that is not pathological, I surely don't know what is.

So we stared at each other, this house and we; it was not love at first sight, to be sure. The irony was that the location of the village, adjacent to a natural reservation and near the shores of the Lesser Lake Balaton, is lovely beyond words. It is surrounded by gentle hills, covered with ancient vineyards, forests of lime trees, and on most days everything is softened by a blue haze, a gentle gift of the two lakes, the Balaton and the Lesser Balaton. The bad news is that little of this can be seen from the house, which was quietly begging for a dignified end by a demolition crew. In my intense preoccupation while trying to see something that was not there, I failed to see the gleam in my husband's eyes. I thought his eyes were misty on account of the cold.

As soon as we took care of the formalities, we fled back to Budapest and to the Intercontinental, where room service was a fact of life, and I soon forgot the sheer horror of an outhouse in December. Even the heart-shaped vent could not compensate for the agony endured there.

The post-Christmas snow was washed away by the rains of January. My husband was retired and received the obligatory wristwatch, a tidy severance pay, and we were feasting on the last morsels of exotic foods found in the fancy basket his company gave him. In our school system a general shuffling of personnel took place that reminded us of playing musical chairs, but for a while hopes rose again. It looked like something positive was happening after all. People were relocated, EPMs promoted to become principals or assistant principals and the sense of relief was palpable all around.

Then in February the regional director called a big meeting at the end of the instructional day in a high school nearby. Teachers and administrators of four schools attended; the reps of the teachers' union were there, the top brass from the military, and many concerned parents. I arrived a bit late, having had a problem with one of the departing school buses, and sat down near the door.

"I am sorry to say," said the Director with questionable sorrow in his voice, "but there is still a handful of people for whom we could find no positions. Most teachers have been placed, but we could not do the same for our administrators. Because of the draw-down we'll have far less schools, and the ones we'll maintain will be many times smaller than before. There just aren't enough openings for all the principals, assistant principals, not to mention the EPMs. Those, who were not assigned positions as of now, are "excess". We are deeply sorry, but those individuals, who were not placed or promoted as of today, will not have a job next September."

He spoke some more, but I heard enough and slipped out quietly the same door I came in. The months of insecurity and guessing were over. I could forget about the endless emotional roller coaster ride, the merciless swings between hope and despair. I am "excess", and not a favorite daughter of DoDDS. They could not even find a teaching position for me. In a few weeks they will hand me the obligatory mug, which all departing educators receive, and that would be the end of my career.

In my bottomless bitterness I completely ignored the fact that just a few weeks ago the idea of having to teach in a regular classroom again, scared me senseless. I could only see my own failure now, and was irrationally and intensely hurt. Darker thoughts came. Why me? Was I not good enough for a promotion that others with less experience and less distinguished track records received? Did they pass me because I did not make the grade? Tears would not come, but I spiraled down into a dangerous black hole of pain. Why did I ever believe that what I did counted? Why was I so convinced that I was good at what I was doing? Whence came the conviction that the system needed me, and that my dedication was important to anybody? I was a zero, and things would go on splendidly without me. I hung my head in shame and humiliation.

I sat in the car for a while, waiting for the hurt to subside, to find a promising note, a shred of hope, something I could use as a lifesaver. But my mind did not function in the old, methodical way it used to. Somewhere in a rational corner of my mind there was the knowledge that all this was not really personal, that indeed I was not singled out, that I was not the only one losing the job, and that even those, who were now clinging to their positions like birds in a storm to a tree branch, would sooner or later lose it too. But irrational pain took over and I sunk into despair, shame and self-pity. The meeting was over by now, and people started to leave the building. I put the car in gear and rolled out of the parking lot. I was ashamed to face the others and tried to avoid even Joyce and Christine.

That evening my husband and I took our drinks up to the gallery, which was our favorite place in the house. The rain was beating against the clerestory windows and the wind howled outside among the pine trees as we sank into our reading chairs. It was cold and wet outside, but here the shelves were lined with hundreds of books and the contented houseplants shimmered in the soft light of the lamps. I sighed as I sipped my smooth Sandeman. This was my world, my secure haven. Although not our own, a thousand memories made it into a real home for us. I almost smiled, but then remembered the Verdict. The glow died.

"I know, how you feel," my husband said quietly. "This situation is a real bitch. But we are not going to crumble, are we? No one has the right to play games with our lives and we won't be victimized any longer. From now on, we'll take charge of our destiny. I have a plan and I know it will work."

It was wonderful to hear positive plans. The man of the house has spoken, and he would yank me out of this unreasonable stupor and depression. There are many noble and emotional reasons to marry and to stay married, but carrying the load in tandem is no mean benefit of the union. He often told me that life is a two-person problem that only a fool would attempt to solve alone. His voice carried self-assurance and I already felt much better.

"We need to analyze the situation rationally," he continued in the calm manner he always uses whenever he is not being romantic. "Our first problem is that we'll be soon without two very comfortable incomes. In other words, we won't have much to live on, or at least not in the manner we are accustomed." I nodded in agreement. The wonderful trips we both loved would no longer be part of our life. We could live without champagne. New Year's Eve in Paris, skiing in the Alps, cruising the Greek islands, or spending Easter in Italy would have to go. The big house, the cleaning woman, probably one of the cars. Summer brunches at the *Ente von Lebel,* or at the Casino at Wiesbaden would have to be history. We might not even be able to afford the Officers' Club. I could learn to live without a hairdresser and the weekly cosmetic sessions. Yes, there were many areas in our life, which we could trim down, or eliminate completely. As long as I still had them all, the prospect did not even look particularly austere.

"Our second problem is that we do not own a house, nor can we buy one from our depleted funds. In plain language, we don't have anywhere to go." He filled my glass with sherry again, then sat down in his chair.

"But we have that apartment in your daughter's house, right here in Germany," I objected.

"Indeed we do, and we won't give it up. But it is far too small for long-term staying, and we couldn't afford anything bigger. And as I said just now, our combined incomes would not be nearly enough to cover the expenses of the simplest of life styles in Germany year round." I knew he was right, but felt that somehow I must argue to retain the status quo.

"These are givens, which force us to consider the third problem," he continued patiently, effectively cutting me off before I could start my argument. "We must find a place on the globe, where we could live comfortably on our new, downsized income. We don't want to give up too much, just because we are retiring." He was right, although we already discussed most of it and none of the above was great, or even novel news. And none of it gladdened my heart.

"Please, try to take my suggestion calmly and don't explode before I say all I want to say. I thought about the problem and weighed the only possible solution carefully. And I am in full possession of my intellectual faculties." The long preamble was not like him. Suddenly alert, I sat bolt upright in my chair while all sorts of alarms were going off, triggering vast quantities of fight-or-flight hormones, activating the cardiovascular system, the muscles, and everything else that could be used in a real emergency. My system was ready to receive the punch.

"We'll renovate the house in Hungary and we'll move into it," he announced calmly. Very carefully I placed my glass on the reading table and screamed, not so calmly, "We'll do WHAT?"

"Keep your voice down, because you'll frighten the plants. That house is not as bad as you think it is. Basically it is of sound construction, is large enough for a start, and it has possibilities for extension. I made many computations after we returned from Hungary, included every expense I could think of. I came up with a figure, which we could easily afford. Believe me, it will be a drop-dead, ass-kicking house. In all honesty, where on earth could you acquire a house, any house, for such a low price?"

"Only in Zalaszabar," I answered with less grace than I intended. He was obviously excited by the idea, and chose to ignore my bad mood and heavy misgivings. He had it figured out to the last detail, and his enthusiasm was almost, but not entirely infectious.

"Ever since January I haven't a thing to do, and am eager to get busy with a good project. We could start working on it as soon as you agree."

"I wasn't officially fired yet," I reminded him.

"You will be," he reassured me. "But the way your outfit is doing things, you might still be there next September. However, by the time the ax falls, our house will be ready. Don't you agree that it would be a vast improvement over having to live on welfare?"

"Definitely. But what will we do for money as far as renovation and addition is concerned?"

"I told you, the cost will be far less than I first imagined. As a matter of fact I had to redo some of my computations because I couldn't believe how ridiculously low the cost would be. Darling, you suffer from a chronic poverty-complex, but you know well enough that we have enough money, and some to spare. This project won't bleed us white." Whenever he is vexed with me, he calls me "darling" or "dearest".

"After which the savings account of my preschool granddaughter would appear enviably grand in comparison to ours."

"Don't dramatize. You know it is not as bad as all that. Besides, we'll have your salary for a few more months. My severance check and retirement benefits added to your severance pay from DoDDS would resuscitate our savings account. Also, if they hand you the walking papers, they either have to early-retire you, or give unemployment compensation or something. Life is so inexpensive in Hungary that once we are settled there, we could save more than half of our monthly incomes; yet, live as luxuriously as God would in France. So where is the problem?"

But there were plenty of problems and he too was aware of them, despite the grandiose pretense that smooth sailing was ahead.

Other people have lost their jobs and survived it. Of course, not all of them were as close as I, to retirement, with so few years to their credits, and not all of them were stranded on another continent. And not all of them had the political and emotional considerations I had to face in addition to losing the job.

Problems and images surfaced, not in any significant order, but in a random fashion. I had no other answer to them except the rising lump in the throat. How do we build there? How do we get our household stuff across two borders? What are we to do about customs duty? What about citizenship? I'd never give up mine, but could I live as an American in Hungary for an extended time, or perhaps forever? For heaven's sake, as late as last Christmas, I still needed flag orders from the military to enter Hungary and I had to go through an intensive lecture before and a debriefing after I returned! How do we go about moving there? And above all, what about my family? I have three children and their spouses, four grandchildren, a mother over eighty and a sister with her four children whom I dearly love, and a host of other relatives and friends. Could I stand the separation from them all? Must I make a choice between the man I love and the family I love just as much?

And could I give up the customs, the traditions, and the culture that I cherish? The huge family reunions and holidays, the turkey and the pumpkin pie, the Fourth of July picnics with the compulsory chocolate cake with white frosting, decorated with alternating stripes of blueberries and strawberries. Shared jokes that cannot be translated into another language, and the easygoing fellowship of the neighborhood. A sense of freedom and pulsating energy. School marching bands and baseball games. Outdoor art shows and strawberry and maple syrup festivals. The pastor greeting his flock at the church door. Supermarkets and smiles everywhere. And those unbelievable libraries and bookstores that are unique in the world! The wonderful sentence that makes a world of difference in our lives: "no problem, Ma'am". Truck drivers, the last knights on this planet, and kids in ghoulish outfits shrieking trick or treat. Thousands of twinkling Christmas lights everywhere. The last fourteen days of shopping before Christmas. The television program that is interrupted with the important message that Santa was sighted on the radar as he flew over Newfoundland. And the estimated time of his arrival given. People, who may be courteous, outspoken, funny or rude, but people with whom I can communicate not just because we speak the same language, but because we share the same background, the same cultural literacy.

I never gave up hope that despite my husband's foreign background we would end up living back home in the United States.

For a brief moment I stopped to consider these memories and emotions. Could they be the first signs of homesickness? As far as I can tell, homesickness appears when two main factors are present: love of a place and the inability to live there.

For homesickness to appear, first one must have a deep attachment to a place, its people and culture, regardless whether the place in question provided a wonderful life, or merely rags and bare subsistence. The roots of this sense of belonging, (some would even call it love), reach back into earliest childhood and its reasons and scope are difficult to estimate. Then if for some reason one must leave this place, there remains a constant yearning for it. This is not yet true homesickness, because the road back to it is not yet blocked.

The true sickness starts when this place, for some reason, is out of reach. Many famous émigrés and expatriates, including Sophia Loren and Anna Pavlova, suffered deeply from it. The two grande dames , both beautiful, talented, successful, rich, admired, loved, and both of whom reached the maximum of their potentials, fulfilled their goals, and had everything that common mortals only dream about, knew homesickness. All the riches and glitter did not compensate them for a place which was at the center of their being.

But there is also a special kind of homesickness, which yearns not so much for a place, but rather for times past, and for lifestyles gone. Marcel Proust and Tomasi de Lampedusa explored these hungers, and so did John Ciardi in his poem, "Talking Myself to Sleep at One More Hilton." (*This Strangest Everything*, Rutgers University, 1966) The two yearnings, one physical, the other more elusive, are often so intertwined that it is hard to see the boundaries; one sharpens the pain caused by the other.

But Americans usually are not prone to this particular brand of malady. Even by the wildest stretch of romantic imagination, they cannot be labeled nomads, but undeniably many of them are forever on the move. During their mobility they haven't the time or the inclination to form deep attachments to a place, or even to people, which is the reason for a quintessentially American brand of solitude. I met youngsters who attended eight schools in twelve years, and these were not just isolated cases restricted to the military way of life. I met military wives who were afraid to form friendships, because they knew that in a couple of years they would have to move on, and the pain of farewell would be too intense. It was safer not to get involved. But this particular brand of solitude is not homesickness; as a matter of fact it is the very agent that prevents it. We are also shielded from this special pain by the very homogeneous nature of our society. By the close of the millenium an Ohioan does not feel out of place in Indiana, Maine or Colorado. Home is everywhere between our shores, and the adjustments to be made at a new location are minimal. When the place of attachment stretches fifty states wide, the emotion weakens. And let us face it, there are few, if any, who would find it impossible in the USA to visit the home where they grew up, barring those places where highways and shopping centers cover the sites of the old homesteads.

But, and this was a new and disturbing realization, I would be a prime candidate for homesickness. I do have the strong attachment to my home, and the new circumstances would be such that I could not hope to return to what I love. Not if I make the decision that is expected of me now.

"No. NO. It is impossible. I can't," I whispered close to tears. The adrenaline subsided and all I felt was just infinite weariness.

"Yes, you can. We really have no other options. And believe me, it won't be as bad as you fear. Hungary is a place where our income would be more than adequate. We would actually be quite rich. You speak fluent Hungarian," he pointed out, "and therefore, it would not be such a hardship for you to live there as it would be for me to live in the USA."

"But you do speak English," I objected weakly, knowing that my argument was not strong enough.

"Yes, I do. Like a little kid. And I'm too old to grow beyond that. I could never really make the language of literature my own any more, and you know that neither of us could live without that." And teachers have been telling me all my life that speaking several languages is an advantage! Now I have to give up my family and a lifestyle, just because I am fluent in another language, and therefore presumably I could adapt easier in a new environment.

He reminded me that my three children from the first marriage each ended up living in a different state of the union, so even if we lived in the States, I would not see them any more often than once a year. And, he added, Hungary is not any further from the USA than Germany is, as the crow, or in this case as the seagull flies. I was still fighting that lump in my throat and could not find the voice to explain that besides the geographical, there is also a psychological boundary, not easily defined. Although we lived in Germany for more than a dozen years and saw much of Europe during vacations and the weekends, we always returned to home base, where I was once again, so to speak, in the United States. I taught American children in an American school, Sundays we attended the chapel on the base, after which we would go for a lavish brunch at the Officers' Club, where we met American friends. I piled American groceries into my shopping cart at the commissary, and my address, near Frankfurt Germany, was APO N.Y. American doctors took care of us, and I read the Stars and Stripes at the breakfast table, home-delivered by American schoolboys. More than half the houses in the suburb where we lived, were occupied by families of American military men, and on summer evenings friends would saunter across the gardens in the back of the houses for a pre-dinner cocktail and a chat. Once by accident I dialed the wrong number, and an American voice answered the phone. I might as well have been in Ohio. Because of these things, while living in Germany it did not feel as if we lived abroad. Hungary seemed vastly more distant. Moving to Hungary would really make me an expatriate. There I would really be living abroad and in isolation.

But he was flying high and already made up a budget for us, and assured me that I could continue visiting my family once a year as I had done in the past.

"Would I have to swim to get there?"

"Only during the odd years, when the First of January falls on the Second. And in a pinch, you could always fly your broom."

My family was calm enough when I shared our plans with them. Mother, small and fragile, spoke calmly into the telephone that echoed and hummed through the transatlantic lines. "Darling, do as you think is best. My prayers are with you." She was cheerful; I was near tears.

My children thought the idea was hilarious. Christina combed the bookstores and mailed me stacks of books on how to make soap and beauty aids, how to can and how to freeze the summer's bounty. Andrea sent me a T-shirt with Toto and the words, "I don't think we're in Kansas anymore." My son suggested that I learn how to make smoke signals. My sister suggested that we all pitch in and buy an airplane.

I shared our decision with Joyce, and she listened thoughtfully.

"You are not sure, are you, that this is a wise decision?" As always, she was right. I accepted it with my intellect, because I understood that this was the best solution, perhaps the only option we had, but I was fighting it emotionally and kept hoping that soon I would wake up from this nightmare and everything would be as it always was.

Of course, there was no waking up. Since our lease was up in April and our hopes were dashed as far as my employment after the current school year was concerned, we decided to start remodeling in Hungary at once. The decision seemed simple enough, but the implications were enormous. Again, I panicked.

"I can hear your blood-pressure rising," complained my husband. "We haven't even started yet, so keep calm. You haven't my permission to lose your head just yet."

Before I could change my mind, he found a small apartment for me next to our school, where I could stay during the workweek, and he left for Zalaszabar the same week to start doing things to that wreck. There was no turning back.

CHAPTER ONE

From the time my husband left, I stayed all week in my miserable and cramped little attic apartment, enjoying the only advantage there was: I could walk to the school building where I worked. On Friday I drove the fifty miles to our suburban home, to pack, and to make monumental decisions of what to take and what to pitch. Meanwhile, a thousand kilometers away, my husband, like a lonely pioneer, was facing gigantic and often ridiculous problems while trying to a build a home for us.

To begin with my task, I packed a big, cedar-lined travel chest, the size of a family deep freezer, and filled it with bed sheets, comforters, towels, pillows, pots and pans and other essentials, such as a bed canopy, scented candles and some choice books. I also wrapped a king size mattress in yards of plastic, and had the two bulky things hauled to the railway station to be shipped to Hungary. A man, who must live among crumbling ruins without indoor plumbing, deserves some of the comforts of home.

The house in Hungary had no telephone. As a matter of fact, there was none in the village, except an ancient model at the post office, which could only be used on weekdays during business hours, from ten in the morning until one in the afternoon, provided it worked. Unfortunately, that was also the time when I worked, and since I was very seldom at my desk, he often missed me with his call, even though the entire school was alerted, and everybody made it his business to find me. Sometimes we were lucky and could talk for a few minutes. He told me that he talked with immigration and customs officials and they all told him a different tale, because most people who come to them want to leave Hungary and not come into it. They have no experience with people who want to settle there. Everybody was very kind and utterly ignorant. However, the good news was that he did hire a mammoth of a truck with a trailer and two drivers from a large exporting-importing firm that understands all about red tape. Bricklayers, stone masons, carpenters, roofers, plumbers and electricians were all lined up. And yes, he did get my two "packages" and he was shocked at the size, and at the shipping expense. He reminded me that we were in the saving mode, and that I am to curb my extravagant notions. The good news was that he did not have to pay customs duty on it, because the officials had no experience with such a strange shipment, and they decided to let it go. And he missed me.

He sounded upbeat and years younger; his voice was alive with excitement, but I had misgivings. The old house in Hungary consisted basically of three rooms. Construction on the addition hasn't even started yet. In Germany we were living in an eight-room house with half a dozen utility and storage rooms, a double garage and a shed for garden furniture and tools. I expressed some concern, because I had trouble visualizing how it would all fit, even if we were to stuff our worldly goods warehouse fashion into the three rooms, until the house was completed. And how could the floors be replaced and the walls painted if the rooms were packed with crates and furniture to the ceilings?

"Don't worry, it will all be resolved," he answered breezily and it should have reassured me, but it did not. I am not a man-hater and nobody ever called me a wild feminist, but I do know that the mind-set and thinking mode of the male is totally different from that of the female. Through some mysterious genetic design, (some would even call it an error) the male becomes absolutely useless in a real crisis involving the nest. Without doubt, men possess practical minds, yet in some situations they appear in a transcendental state, ignoring the important details and facts, and they are not able to comprehend the unexpected, and (in their opinion) totally unwarranted nervous break-down of their wives in the middle of spring house-cleaning. They have not done anything wrong really, unless you count bringing home the boss and five other colleagues for dinner. Unannounced. See what I mean?

As far as they are concerned, things will be resolved and the female is not to worry about a thing. Not unless the house is already on fire. Nancy Reagan, compared to me, is just a beginner in the ways of riveting eyes adoringly, but unlike her, I do draw the line somewhere. In this case adoration stopped when the man in my life could not comprehend the spatial problem of placing the furniture of eight rooms into three. I became progressively uneasy and vocalized with great and increasing emphasis my need for detailed plans. I might as well have asked for the stars.

Fortunately, there was no time left to indulge in worrying. The school kept me busy all week and the weekends were no recreation either. There was the washing, shopping and some food preparation to be done; but packing up for moving was the real reason of my weekend trips to our abandoned home.

As D-Day was approaching, I was getting adjusted to the mad pace. My husband, before he left, bought one hundred cartons from the local moving company, which was to load the Hungarian van on moving day. It was his naive hope that everything would fit into them with space to spare. I filled them all in two weekends, but the house still looked very much lived in, so I called for seventy-five more cartons. A week later, when I called again, they started to regard me with that mixture of pity and awe usually reserved for ladies who keep a hundred cats.

I spent long hours, late into the night, sorting our belongings. And the things I found! The heavy, honey-blond braids of my daughter when overnight she grew up to be a big girl and cut the childish hair…a picture of two birds kissing, entirely made up of nails pounded into a piece of wood. It was a Valentine from my eight-year old son. The tiny handprint in clay, my first granddaughter's first gift to me. Delicate handkerchiefs, embroidered more than sixty years ago by my mother for her trousseau. A dried rose from my daughter's wedding bouquet… It takes a very long time to pack up memories. I was also packing about two thousand books along with china, crystal, silver, paintings, clothing, and kitchen things to do justice to a gourmet restaurant. As the house became bare, the treasures and memories of a very exciting life were wrapped in tons of tissue paper and miles of bubbly plastic. By the end of March I was verging on total physical exhaustion and fell asleep before I hit the pillow. I made a solemn vow that the only move I'd ever make in the future would be to the cemetery, because nothing has to be taken along, and all the work is done by others.

The last phone call from Hungary did not sound encouraging. The foundation for the addition was laid, but before the walls could be erected, the skies opened up and it looked like Zalaszabar was in for the biblical forty-day rain. The construction crew sought dry shelter elsewhere and all work stopped. For the first time, my husband hinted at difficulties in Paradise. It was impossible to get the stonemason, or anybody else involved in the construction, to appear on site at the promised time. Things were a bit slow, he admitted grudgingly. Buying the required material also posed unaccustomed problems. Not having a phone was the worst. He spent many futile hours on the wheels, trying to find things needed by the workers.

At any rate, it won't be possible to off-load the contents of the moving van at the house, because it won't be anywhere near ready, he told me long distance. Sensing in my voice the hysteria he so feared, (and I didn't even plan to say "I told you so"), he quickly added that everything was under control, and he made arrangements for the storage of our household goods. Before I could take a deep breath to start my arguments, he told me that not only do we have three perfectly good rooms in the house, but his sister, who will be our neighbor, generously offered a room in her house for our more valuable items, her garage for the things that won't mind mold and mice and her barn for the things that can stand the assaults of Mother Nature through every crack in the wall. In addition, he rented an empty house in the village, which is actually unlivable, but would serve excellently as a furniture storage place.

Cheered by cheering me, he explained with new vigor that all I had to do now is go over the cartons I already packed, and decide how to route them among the five locations where they would be stored for eternity, as far as I could make out. No big deal, he said lightly, you could do it in half an hour. Marking them would facilitate the off-loading. Yes, no big deal, as far as he was concerned. Anyhow, how difficult is it to delegate jobs across one thousand kilometers to a willing and adoring wife? Nancy Reagan, take note. The only difficulty was that I lost track of what I packed into those twenty dozen boxes.

There I was, knee deep in the shambles of a partially dismantled home of eight rooms, perennially short of cartons and with the uncanny feeling that this adventure would have more surprises for me than what I bargained for. However, I took fat marking pens in five colors and obediently strained my memory about the contents of the mountains of boxes and marked them all in good faith.

I recalled with compassion the story of a good friend of mine, a professional military wife. (Strange as it may sound, there is such a thing.)

Her lot in life was to habitually take care of everything that is involved in a transfer from one military base to another. Having done it more times than she cares to remember, she developed infallible techniques and mastered reliable coping behavior. She became a real pro in moving, although not happy about it. Usually her husband, a high-ranking officer, left weeks before the movers came. He was a Very Important Person and needed to take over a command some place or another, while she did the packing, the checking-out procedure (not a good topic for a sitcom), the shipping of household goods, the car, cat, dog and of course their three kids.

When she was moving from their current overseas post back to Texas, blasphemously she sported a bright red tee shirt with the words, "I'm moving. Where the hell are you?"

But the Olympic gods, who historically detested uppity airs and swiftly punished such behavior, had their revenge. She should not have tried to drag her top brass husband into her sordid little affair of moving. Military husbands have more important things to do and that is how it was from the time the first Roman centurion was transferred from the Campagna to Trier. Military wives move. That is what they do. Amy should have known this. After all she was labeled all her life a "dependent", which in military jargon means that she took care of their lives so that he could take care of his battalions.

It so happened that the packers that day worked with diabolical speed. This did not ruffle her. Trained in all eventualities that could occur during a move, she already had two suitcases packed with their bare essentials to tie them over until their departure. She placed the suitcases in one of the already emptied bathrooms and stationed her son at the door to guard. Her mind at ease about the safety of the changes of underwear, she followed the packing demons and cringed as they taped the legs of her period furniture as if they were the extremities of Egyptian mummies and begged them not to pack the garbage, or at least not into her Chinese Chippendale. It was a nightmare in fast-forward, but by early afternoon she was free to move into the hotel for "transient dependents".

Several hours later she called me, and screamed incoherent fragments, peppered by mostly unprintable profanities into the telephone. She is such a perfect lady that this was completely out of character, and it scared me. Before this, the worst oath she ever uttered was "ding-dong". Could it be that finally she reached her limits and snapped? It took some time until she got a grip on herself and told me that for a second her son wandered away from his post. During that one, single, unguarded moment one of the demons grabbed the two suitcases, and now they were on their way in a sealed container toward Bremerhaven and the cargo ship.

"This isn't like you, poor darling! You must be totally exhausted, " I soothed her in my best supportive tone. "Try to calm down; have a drink or a piece of chocolate cake. Tomorrow, first thing in the morning, trot over to the Post Exchange and get some underwear and toiletries to help you through until your flight. You had bigger losses than four toothbrushes and never acted like this before!"

"The hell with the underpants and the toothbrushes," she screamed. "My purse was in on one of those suitcases with our passports, travel orders and all my money!" I could sympathize with that. But I learned my lesson, and decided to do most of the packing on my own, even if it would kill me. Which it very nearly did.

My husband arrived back in Germany during the weekend before our scheduled move and was in extremely good spirits. He was full of plans, anecdotes and ideas, and obviously enjoyed all the organizing and supervising. This was fortunate for both of us. He did not have time left to brood about his retirement, which can be devastating for some men, which in turn is very hard on some wives.

The game plan for the last phase of the move was perfectly worked out to the last details. During the week we would stay in our suburban home. While I worked, my husband would take care of such things as the post office, the bank, the gas, phone and electric companies, disconnect the electrical equipment and the chandeliers, pack up the contents of his own desk and file cabinets.

The moving van with the two drivers would arrive on Wednesday evening and we'd take them to eat supper at a local *Gasthaus*. They would sleep in the guestrooms, but use their own sleeping bags. I would take Thursday off from work, but would be back in school on Friday, that being the last day of school before the spring break and bound to be hectic. The cabinetmaker and the team of movers, who would, respectively, disassemble our huge wardrobes and the kitchen cabinets, then load the van, would all report on Thursday morning. After the van will have left on Thursday afternoon, my husband and I would drive to my attic apartment and spend the night there.

Saturday morning, we would return to the now empty house with a cleaning crew and a hired van. We would haul the unwanted furniture and other stuff to the city dump and after the customary inspection by the landlord, we would return the keys and leave at noon for Hungary to keep our rendezvous with our household goods on Monday at Zalaszabar. I would spend the week of spring break in Hungary arranging things as best as I could, then fly back on Sunday to Germany to be at school on Monday morning.

I was proud of the plan, which was worked out with the precision of a military maneuver. It was flawless, left-brained, and I was never far from my notebook, where I checked off each item that was completed. Nothing could go wrong, right? Wrong.

I rushed home two hours earlier on that last Tuesday before our move. There was still a great deal to do, in particular my husband's list was not getting noticeable shorter. The chandeliers still bathed the demolished house in a soft glow, and his half of the study was untouched. It would take an act of God (perhaps) for me even to near his desk and file cabinets, let alone touch them, or pack their contents. I decided to become a bit more forceful about his tasks that night, since time was running out.

But I was happy all the way home from school. He was waiting for me and together we would tackle the job easily. The lonely, miserable times were over. Most important of all, we made good decisions, worked at shaping our future and knew where we were heading. While everybody else was still busy wringing hands, and praying to the employment god and the State Department god, we did something positive. When the final crash came, it would not find us floating on an ice floe with bare bottoms and not even an umbrella over our heads. I felt such a sense of freedom that I sang all the way home, although my singing voice was often compared to never mind what.

As I was ready to pull into our elegant cul-de-sac, the song froze in my throat and I stared with disbelief, hoping that it was only exhaustion playing tricks on my optic nerves. A monstrously huge van and trailer (93 cubic meters of it) was backed into our quaint little street. This overgrown *Hungarocamion* took up the entire front of our townhouse AND that of our neighbor's. It was so tall that in the slanting afternoon sunlight its shadow darkened the upstairs windows. I have seen countless such things rumble on the highways, but somehow standing still next to the rose gardens and lacy pergolas, it appeared not only ridiculously incongruous, but also a great deal larger than what I remembered. I braked and waited for the vision to go away, but it refused to dissipate. It would have probably taken a herd of elephants to budge it. I backed out of the cul-de-sac and parked on the street, wondering if somehow I confused the date. But I knew all along that this was definitely not Wednesday.

The drivers of this frightening behemoth, two wonderfully friendly men, bursting with energy, high spirits and sheer masculine good looks, were having a blast with my husband in the living-room among the boxes, crates and rolled up carpets. The three of them were sharing the food the guys brought from Hungary. A big pot of spicy boar stew, quantities of green peppers and fresh bread were spread on the alabaster coffee table. The entire house was filled with the tantalizing fragrance. My husband was popping champagne bottles; they were deep in politics and there was a definite male bonding in the air. Nobody did anything that looked even remotely like packing. Not that I expected the drivers to do it. I did not even expect their presence, but I did hope that my husband would have at least attacked the study. The big question was: why did they arrive a day earlier and keep us from doing our work? But there was no point in expecting a rational answer from three boar-eating, champagne-drinking men at this stage. The world seemed at a standstill, but everybody was having a good time.

The guys came earlier to give us plenty of time to load, my husband explained later. Once again, I was not to worry, because everything is going according to plans, or even ahead of plans. Looking at the three of them I had very grave doubts about that. I was also wondering how my neighbors would react when they find their doorway and garage blocked by a monster straight out of a horror movie. The two drivers did not look as if they were in any condition to handle a child's tricycle, let alone this thing that probably had about thirty-five gearshifts. I had no idea how they managed to turn it into our narrow street in the first place. There was one-eighth of an inch to spare on either side of the flower-bordered drive. I was the only one who was sober, but it helped little under the circumstances.

At nine that evening everybody was hungry again. I had not planned anything for the four of us, and had no other choice but to go out to eat. (Germany at that time had not yet discovered the miracle of home-delivery foods.) I would have liked to stay home, but I was the designated driver, so there was no room left for arguments. I had a splitting left-brain headache at the thought of my carefully designed schedule being washed away by more champagne and a long dinner eaten leisurely, three villages down the road. While doing a renovation job on my face before we left, I was designing the invitation card for the solemn event of my canonization. Right on cue, my husband came into the dressing room to give me a hug and asked, "Aren't you happy? Aren't these capital fellows? My, you look gorgeous!" and with that he whirled out again. The man acts as if we were heading for the Viennese State Opera House for the Christmas Ball, I thought incredulously.

After we returned, I did as much as I could to advance the ordeal of packing and seriously considered ways in which I could rip the fixtures from the walls. I pack when I must, but I can't disconnect things. Men's tools are mysterious and complicated. Many years ago one of my daughters and I were helping my son to install something. Standing on the ladder, he called down for a level. My daughter promptly handed him a wrench, but I corrected her saying that he did not ask for a screwdriver. Since then my daughters, without my interference or help, changed their personalities enough so that they consider a screwdriver and a battery-operated drill to be part of every woman's must-have kit right next to the moisturizers and the nail polish, but my own handy-woman's skills remain technically challenged. At midnight the three guys were still saving the world, in which apparently there was no time allotted for moving.

Wednesday was a repeat performance of the day before. The guys weren't even creative enough to change the brand of champagne they were drinking. I took a deep breath, and decided to stay calm. After all, I was not the only one who had an interest in this moving project. If they were not about to consolidate their efforts on their own initiative, and continued their alcohol marinated male bonding, no amount of nagging on my part could change them. I might as well save my last three nerves for a real emergency, which was surely looming on the horizon.

To be fair though, like a lover trying to find signs of her mate's indiscretions during her absence, I investigated the house and found that the desk and the cabinets were actually emptied and some of the chandeliers were dismantled. There were also many more empty bottles than was decent to consume in broad daylight. Other than that I found no other traces of either sin or virtue. I fell asleep that night to the sweet music of pounding, shoving, crashing and very creative expletives as the three guys buckled down to accomplish some serious last minute jobs.

I got up at four on Thursday morning. The two drivers were snoring in the guestrooms and my husband did the same in our bedroom. His answer to my wake-up call was that surely I must be jesting, he just went to bed a minute ago. We had a little fruitless Shakespearean conversation about larks and nightingales, but I admitted defeat. At that hour he could not have made the distinction between a well-developed Pterodactyl from the Jurassic period and a common house sparrow, so why bother with the songbirds of Romeo and Juliet?

It was hopeless to wait for their graceless awakening, so I reverted to the all-time remedy, and made lists. It gave me a sense of security to stick numbers on the doors to show in which order to empty the rooms, and how to load the crates into the van in accordance with the revised routing plan.

It was still pitch dark outside and heavy rain was pouring. I don't mean a sad little drizzle down the windowpanes, like farewell tears at our departure. What we had was big, heavy-duty rain, straight out of Noah's times. It was a steady downpour: the sheets of rain twisting in the wind, like heavy, dark draperies. The wet roofs of our neighbors glistened with steely gray malevolence as the indifferent early morning light started to spread feebly over the rain-soaked world. How well would the plastic wrapping protect the paintings, the upholstery, and the rugs? Would everything get moldy in the tightly packed, damp van from Thursday until the following Monday? I was not a happy packer.

Thanks to my noisy administrations and my frequent and loud pleas to St. Rita, everyone was up by 5:30 and I had the privilege of cooking a substantial breakfast in a practically demolished kitchen. Our drivers asked for "about" four eggs each for their omelets and as I broke a dozen eggs into the pan I should have had a premonition that this would be my fate for the coming years. However, usually more rational than spiritual, and not acquainted with life and customs behind the no longer existing Iron Curtain, I had no deep thoughts about the huge breakfast that morning. All I felt was a sense of relief that serving an even dozen of eggs I would be spared the problem of what to do with a few eggs left over in the carton.

Fortified by breakfast and coffee (instead of champagne), finally the men were able to do some real work. The cabinetmaker arrived, dismantled the heavy pieces and placed the screws, hinges and such in carefully marked bags. The two drivers were busy disconnecting the washer and the drier. Perhaps after all, we'll make it, I told St. Rita. If only the loading crew too would show up. We called the company every five minutes, but they must have left town, because no one answered. Our drivers started to get nervous; they had a long trip ahead of them and did not calculate into their plans long delays right at the start. Silently and with amazing precision they started to load the van. I was upset; it was not their job to do. Two exhausted drivers up in their cab, driving eighteen wheels for a thousand kilometers at night, and in heavy rain, is a very bad idea indeed.

Shortly after nine the loading crew finally arrived. The team consisted of two Turks, a Yugoslavian and two gay men of undetermined nationality, who were totally absorbed in each other, ignoring the rest of us, and also the work ahead of them. At ten my drivers were hungry again, and since I can't stand people looking on while others are eating, I invited the loading crew to join us. This hardworking international team, which already worked for almost an hour, sat down and breakfasted on 25 rolls, an entire salami, two pounds of cheese, two dozen hard-boiled eggs, a dozen cartons of yogurt, tomatoes, peppers, chips and a plate of donuts.

At 1400 hours I set the table again and the loading crew, inspired by the memory of their breakfast, quickly slid their modest baloney sandwiches back into their bags. Then, like seriously starved men, they dug into our huge bowl of stuffed cabbage, plates of cold roast beef, potato salad, two loaves of bread, a basket of fruit and a chocolate cake. Our two lovers moved away from the table and sitting on the oak steps leading upstairs, fed each other. This was the first time in my life of sixty years that the simple act of eating the very robust and virtuous stuffed cabbage appeared so sensual that I was embarrassed to look at them. Their performance rated a fat X. Perhaps even an XXX. And that was before they licked off the sour cream from each other's lips.

After this midday repast our two drivers moved the packed trailer out from the cul-de-sac and parked it somewhere near a field. The loading of the truck started. It was still raining and also hailing, at least intermittently. The house was cold and we were getting tired; the loaders showed signs of boredom. They would have preferred to shove it all in, on a first come, first shoved basis, and gave me the evil eye when I ordered them otherwise. But since it was I, who would suffer through the unloading in Zalaszabar, I did not let them out of sight. It was probably fortunate that I did not understand their mumbling in languages quite foreign to me.

At 1700 hours the packing crew expressed their deep regrets of having to stop working. Their Union would be very unhappy if they worked past the magic hour. So they said Aloha, or Arrivederci, or whatever it is they say in Turkish. We pointed out that they arrived two hours late and spent two hours eating. Shrugs and many a "so sorry" followed, but unfortunately, they still wanted to leave and that was that. They smiled a lot, apologized profusely and handed us the bill, which was twice the amount agreed upon. They added very creative items to it, for example, they charged fifty DMs per hour for the privately owned car in which the five of them came to work and was parked all day on the street..

"You see," said the Turk, "during the time it is parked, the car does not earn any money. So, you must pay for the wasted time and the lost income. Can you see that?" We could not see this and did not pay. I must remind DoDDS to pay for my idly parked car while I work at the school…

After a rather colorful and high-volume argument with the head of their company, the packers left with the originally agreed amount, and we were left alone with the drivers, who, bless their soul, continued to pack without a word of protest. Yet, despite the friendly tone and easy comradeship, the tail end of the loading went slower than we anticipated. We missed the five men, and our bodies just about reached the tolerance level for stress. That architectural wonder of our house was built on five levels and if I never see another step again for the rest of my life, it will suit me perfectly. Even without carrying heavy loads, those oak stairs could give pains to the legs and hips that the Grand Inquisitor forgot to invent.

As the last light faded in the spring evening, the last box was shoved in, but we were too tired to talk. The drivers were very anxious to leave, so they declined our invitation to go out to eat, and would not hear of spending another night at our house. There was no holding them back, because they were on a very tight schedule. Using leftovers and a pinch of imagination I offered a bite to eat, and then they disappeared into the bathrooms to take their showers. Refreshed and once again buoyant, they left with our good wishes, to couple the truck to the trailer, and then be off on the long journey.

In preparation for driving over to my attic apartment, fifty-some miles away, we loaded the two cars with what was left behind in the house, including our hunting guns. The house, which we loved so much, was now totally empty, except for the vacuum cleaner, cleaning tools and detergents we stored for the cleaning crew that was expected on Saturday.

We walked through it one more time, hand in hand, not saying much. We both had a very difficult and hard life before we met, and it was here for the first time that we were completely happy and free of worries. It was our first real home together, and every room, every corner was heavy with memories. We loved the place, and there was intense pain at the thought of having to leave it.

We ended up in the kitchen, where my husband had cooled a bottle of my favorite champagne and handed me a bouquet of red roses as a farewell present. I was misty-eyed, just like any woman would be in my place. Here was my man, who in the midst of all this turmoil found the time and energy for a romantic gesture. Small wonder that I was willing to go with him to the end of the world. Or to Hungary, if it had to be.

And it was here, while clinking our glasses and counting our blessings that we saw, almost simultaneously, the pack of documents placed carefully on the windowsill. These papers were needed for our household goods to pass through the borders of Germany and Austria, then into Hungary. In their exhaustion, the drivers forgot them.

It was the ultimate script for a bad movie, and although the situation was more slapstick than anything else, nobody was laughing. As a matter of fact, at least one of the actors was about to lose her mind and to start screaming like a banshee. But for the first moments our only reaction was speechless disbelief. How could they forget the thing that was about as important as the ignition key?

"Don't worry," said my knight in true Medieval Knightly Fashion, as he was coming to his senses. "I'll catch up with them. When did they leave our house? Twenty minutes ago? Not even that much. But they had to first couple the trailer to the truck, which is so overloaded that it can hardly move more than 40 miles an hour in this rain. Stay here and mind the phone, I'll catch them and be back in no time."

With that he grabbed the papers and took off in the pouring rain. He had our four guns in the backseat of his car and thinking about it, I really got sick. The guns were registered in my name and the papers were in my purse. I visualized an accident, which was awful enough in itself. But then I imagined the reactions first of the German *Polizei* on the scene, followed by the American MPs, who would find four guns in the car of a man, who was speeding on a rainy highway, in a car decorated with overseas US military license plates, had no firearms registration, and who on top is not a citizen of the USA, Germany, or any other country on the globe. Telling them that he was chasing a van with Hungarian license plates would have hardly improved the situation. I had visions of both of us spending the next quarter of a century on bread and water in a prison, reserved for gun smuggling terrorists. And that was one of the less frightening scenarios I could conjure up.

I was standing in the totally empty house, brooding over these dark thoughts and contemplating how to spend the next hour, when someone rang the doorbell. In the doorway, cheerfully dripping rainwater over the tile of the entrance floor, stood the younger driver.

"What are you doing here?" I stammered by way of greeting.

"We had trouble coupling up the trailer. It took a bit longer, because there was so little room to do it," he explained patiently. "We were just about ready to leave, when we realized that the papers were left in the kitchen. We were scared that you already left; in which case I was ready to break the window to get in. But all is well that ends well. If you'll kindly let me have the packet, we'll be on our way."

There is really no gentle way of telling a tired person, who was loading (with a hang-over) furniture and crates all day, and who was facing a three-day ordeal, that the papers without which he could not haul household goods across three border checks, was by that time near the vicinity of the Frankfurt airport. How were we to know that they never left our village? Before he could break down sobbing and embarrass us both, I promised him to get those papers in no time. I had a snazzy sports car parked on the street that could easily catch a helicopter, let alone the Tracker with its four cylinders and put-put engine. The Tracker was no match in a race.

I told the driver to stay at the house and mind the phone in case we need to call. Since my husband accidentally took both sets of house keys, the driver had orders not to leave the house, because he could not get back in after he slammed the door.

"But my pal is waiting for me in the field," he argued forlornly.

"This is hardly the time to worry about social etiquette," I snapped. "If he is curious what happened to you, he can walk here. I'll catch up with my husband, flag him down and we'll be back in half an hour." I knew that he did not believe me, but I could not stay and comfort him. I grabbed my keys and flew out the door.

Here is the situation: it is raining hard, visibility is zilch, the roads are slick and I am chasing a husband, who is chasing (with the guns in the backseat) an oversized transport van, which never left our village, but was parked a half mile away, near a sodden field, in the opposite direction from where we both took off to catch it. Meanwhile, one driver is sitting in the rain wondering about his buddy, while the other is staring at a telephone that would not ring.

So I was speeding down the *Autobahn*, which at that hour and because of that weather, was luckily quite deserted. There are no speed limits on most German expressways, but only a fool would speed in that weather. The Frankfurt *Autobahn* had two fools speeding that night. The rain was coming down hard and I tried not to think of my wide tires and the very real danger of aquaplaning. From time to time I had to remind myself to loosen the grip on the steering wheel, because my wrists were getting numb from clutching so tightly. My eyes were burning from staring through the veil of rain, my body was aching at all the wrong places and I was getting terribly sleepy. Fifty miles later, as I passed the exit that would have taken me to my attic apartment, I knew I would never catch up with my husband. I do not know how he did it, but he was way ahead of me. I drove one more exit, then turned and backtracked to my apartment. The chase was becoming futile and ridiculous, and it is my conviction that at times the only way one can win is by giving up the impossible. Quit beating a dead horse; get off of it, is my motto.

As soon as I arrived at my attic, I called the house and faced yet another ridiculous frustration. It so happened that almost at the same moment when I called, so did my husband. Of course he had no reason to believe that I was not at the house, and almost hung up when a man answered, thinking he had the wrong number. It was precisely at that moment when I too called the house. Because during our working life we relied heavily on the phone, we had two lines and each had two extensions with very long cords, so we could drag the phones all over the house. This is why we could call the house at the same time. We never thought that this arrangement is particularly unusual, but the driver, coming from a seriously under-phoned country, was nonplussed and could not grasp the wonder of two independent phone lines in a private home. When my husband called, the driver picked up the phone in the kitchen, where he was standing, but when the other phone started to ring, he thought it was the doorbell, and rushing there to answer it, almost disconnected my husband. Not finding anyone at the door, he picked up the phone again, while the other phone kept on ringing stubbornly, because I assumed that the fool would not have left the house. My husband, who could also hear the other phone ringing, tried to explain what to do. Finally, while my husband was stuffing his dwindling supply of coins into the phone, the driver recovered his wits, carried the phone from the kitchen to the hallway, picked up that receiver too and a three-way conversation of sorts was established. We had to act quickly, before we got disconnected, due to his shortage of coins.

I suggested that my husband and the drivers meet halfway on the expressway at the huge truck-stop between the airport and the exit to the road where my apartment was located. Then the drivers could move on east with their papers and my husband could be at my place in ten minutes, especially the way he drove that night. I thought it was a good plan.

The driver had no idea what truck-stop and what exists I was talking about. He made the trip on the average every ten days, sometimes more often. He was a very bright fellow, acting very stupidly.

"I don't know what you mean," he complained unhappily. "I don't know of any truck-stop for the next two hundred kilometers."

"How about the airport exits?"

"What airport?"

"Frankfurt airport. You drive past it when you come here and can't miss it, since half the time you think the planes might land right on top of your van."

"Never saw it."

I could not believe that a basically intelligent man could be so dense. Just as my husband's last coins were swallowed, the horrible truth was revealed. They never drive on the expressway, on which we both chased them! Although it is the shortest and most logical way to Hungary, they always drive the long, tortuous way, through Czechoslovakia.

"Trucks are not permitted to drive in Austria on the weekends or during the night, the fees at the toll booths are very high and so is the price of gasoline. Also the Austrians make a sport of hassling us, and making us wait sometimes up to two days. We never have any trouble with the Czechs. So we always drive that way."

There was but one way to solve the problem and I hated to say it: my husband had to drive back the long distance to our house, give them the papers then backtrack once again the 50 miles to my apartment.

I did the only sensible thing there was to do: took a shower and went to bed. But I knew he was just as tired as I was, and at this very moment was still fighting the rain and the slick roads. I was worried and sleep would not come. Sometimes around midnight he called from the house. He handed over the papers and the guys were gone. However he was so exhausted that he could not face another 45 minutes on the road. He'll stay at the house and sleep on the floor, he told me. There were some blankets in the car and that would do.

I hung up relieved that at least he was safe and after all, we would both get a few hours of sleep before a difficult day. I slept, but he did not. Being a born neatnik, he decided to vacuum-clean the carpet before he slept on it. To make a long and awful story short: during the very first minute of his household chore the belt of the cleaner busted, something else broke, and my husband disappeared in a choking cloud of dust and profanities. He had to go back in the rain to get his tools from the car, to repair the cleaner, then take another shower. It was around three o'clock when at long last he bedded down on the floor.

Come to think of, he never thanked me for my excellent foresight for having a spare belt for the vacuum cleaner handy. Since it is not really my style to be that smart in these matters, to this day I have no idea what made me add an extra belt to the cleaning supplies which I lined up for the cleaners. As a matter of fact, he knows me better than anybody else; therefore I also do not understand why he found it to be perfectly natural to find that belt, where no man, who knew me, would look.

Somehow we survived Friday. It was still raining, which meant indoor recess, an occurrence nobody appreciated, except the neighbors, who live around the school. The lights went out during lunchtime, which caused hundreds of overwrought children to scream with mock panic in the murky darkness of the basement lunchroom. Everything turned out just as badly as the three of us feared. The children were climbing the walls and the teachers weren't far behind them. At one time, during the day, between disciplining children, listening to irate parents, who were already upset at the thought of having to deal with their children for the next ten days, and while soothing teachers, who had maybe one single nerve left that had to last until the buses pulled out, it occurred to me that there must be an easier way to earn a living. For the first time I was able to visualize a life after teaching or supervising. It did not look bad at all.

"How was your day?" I asked my husband when we met at seven in the evening in my stuffy and very shabby apartment.

"Best be forgotten," he shrugged. "I wonder if we'll ever feel any other way, except dead tired and frustrated."

"As far as I'm concerned, I wish to elope somewhere, and start life all over again."

"But don't you see? That is exactly what we are doing now! Our new life will start tomorrow at noon. But in the meanwhile, let's go and eat somewhere."

We drove to Seligenstadt, a lovely little town, quaint and tranquil, dreaming a never-ending dream on the River Main, wondering why it is never on anybody's itinerary.

We chose a restaurant near the river, and sat at one of the big windows facing the water. Children fed ducks and seagulls and under our window the first spring flowers colored the beds with pastel hues. Our dinner, starting with snails in garlic and parsley flavored butter, was followed by veal steaks cooked to perfection, almond covered potato puffs, and tender new vegetables. The feather-light finale of Salzburger Nockerln and Rüdesheimer coffee, enriched with cognac, whipping cream and mysterious flavorings was superb. For a little while we forgot about our troubles.

"We almost made it," he told me after our meal, as he lifted his cognac snifter. "We made the right decision, and peace is only months away. The little time we have to endure until then is short, and we can survive it, even if we'd have to spend the time until then on our knees and in straitjackets."

"I still can't believe that we made this decision. It is so enormous."

"All true life decisions are enormous. And sometimes you cannot make them any other way except being shoved into a situation. Or else, you must close your eyes and jump into it, like you would into an extremely cold pool of water."

"I hate the idea of your going back. I hate being without you. This week, despite all the mishaps and exhaustion that went with it, was great, because you were here," I said.

"This will be the last time in our life that we'll be separated," he promised. "As soon as you finish working, I'll be back to pick you up. We'll have the kind of life we always wanted. And from now on nobody is telling us what to do and what not to do."

I smiled at this. My husband was still chafing from the constant "Verboten" and "Darf man nicht"—forbidden and not allowed. At one time we wanted to put a nail on the outside wall to anchor a trellis for the climbing rose (planted by our landlord). The rose was not only determined to enter through the front door and live with us, but also caused serious injuries with its vicious thorns, when we were not watching it. The landlord's unequivocal answer was "Verboten". When we asked permission to install a peephole into our front door, that too was forbidden. It was the age of terrorism and we were briefed non-stop by the military how to protect ourselves from attacks. One of the recurrent warnings was not to open the door without knowing who is on the other side. Get a peephole, the military said. Verboten, responded the landlord. The other carbon-copy houses did not have a peephole, and

for heaven's sake (*um Himmels Willen!*) we should not destroy the uniform-
ity so dear to the Teutonic heart. On top of it, we always lived under the
constant threat of having to move. Landlords played strange and un-
ethical games with tenants, especially if said tenants were foreigners,
hence inferior and conveniently uninformed about the murky laws regu-
lating housing. Even the frazzled agents in the military housing department could not always protect our rights.

We drank our cognac as darkness was spreading over the river. Soon
he stopped talking and reached for my hands across the table. I was
emotionally torn, very scared, and he knew it. I still had vile memories
of visits to Communist Hungary, nasty customs officials, long waits and
rudeness at the border that was very close to humiliation. I still recalled
the vast electrical fences at the Austro-Hungarian border, the mined
fields, the angry fighting dogs, and the lookout towers, manned by armed
soldiers. It was not a place where I enjoyed staying. Now the Berlin
Wall was down, the fences cut, dogs retired, lookout towels crumbling,
and Communism swept out, but like so many others, I too worried. Could
this frail democracy prevail, or would Communism return? Could the
people, trained, raised and brainwashed in Communism and not knowing anything else, comprehend the concepts of freedom and self-gov-
ernment? And if not, then what? Would everything end in shambles
again, and would we have to leave the country, although nowhere to go,
and lose everything we own in the process? Aren't we a bit old to risk all
we have?

I knew that if I had put up enough resistance to the move, he would
have backed down. But I could not think of a better solution either. The
responsibility for accepting the move was totally mine.

While we watched the lights from the houses and from the slowly
moving barges spill over the water, I longed to tell him that even though
I was very much afraid and even unhappy, my home would always and
ever be where he was. But somehow the statement sounded a trifle too
corny and I chose to remain silent. We are such perfect slaves to propri-
ety and are so mortally afraid to appear sentimental and kitchy that we
often clam down when we should talk. Unblushingly we can undress
the body, but exhibit the shame of the virgin, when our soul is bared.
We can discuss our orgasm, or the lack of it, either scientifically or hu-
morously, (like the often repeated and probably never uttered statement

of a pilot's wife, who supposedly exploded in exasperation. "That man can find, with eyes closed, all the major airports in the world. He can fly with self-confidence even with his communication system gone, and can land in the thickest fog of the century. He can, on a snow-covered tarmac, drop his damned 747 on a dime. But after ten years of marriage, he hasn't got a clue how to find my erogenous zones. And he thinks he is a gift of God to women!") So we are outspoken about the body; (what would our grandmothers say to this?), but we hesitate to tell the Significant Other that life would be unbearable without his smile. Better not take any chances. We hate to make fools of ourselves and our fragile sophistication would not permit any sentimentality to cheapen us, or our relationships. Instead of talking, I just smiled at him.

"You are a hell of a woman," he said in a husky voice and with the smile I so love. "It takes a special kind to do what you have done during the last few months. Life is unthinkable without you. I love you and will always love you to the end of our days. And long after that, if at all possible." So, there it was. He dared to say what I couldn't. And it was good. I guess, men have less hang-ups than we women have.

Next morning, while the cleaning crew scrubbed, brushed and steam-cleaned, we embarked on our romantic trip to the city dump. This took much longer than anticipated, because we did not sort our rubbish according to the prevailing rules. It was the age of carefully differentiated garbage, and heaven could not help the moron, who accidentally mixed a high gloss magazine between the pages of the common newspaper. As far as I knew, there were no rules or regulations for the proper disposal of our weekly garbage at the house. The only stipulation was not to dump hot ashes into the garbage cans. This was easily observed, since we had no fireplace. Otherwise, our two containers were regularly and noisily emptied once a week and the sanitation crew disposed of it somewhere over the hills. Once a year they got their bottles and the envelopes of money, and everybody was happy. As far as I know, nobody investigated or cared about the unsavory contents of our dumpsters.

It was a different story at the city dump, where the amazing ritual of separating glass bottles by color, and the sorting of various refuse were refined to an art. By the way, the Germans call the dump by the elegant name of *Mülldeponie*. Even though I speak German, and know exactly what the compound word means, I always associated the word with ponies, horses and green pastures and perhaps water mills. The dump, of course, was nothing like that, but more like a futuristic landscape frozen into cement platforms and cubicles, elevators, look-out towers and centrally operated gates.

Not being familiar with the newest procedures, and thinking that garbage was garbage, we assumed that as long as we separated glass, plastic, paper, wood, metal and toxic substances, it would do. This naivete was our mistake, and a big one too. After being sternly advised, we spent the next two hours rearranging our trash. The problems were overwhelming. For example, into which category does a barstool belong that has wrought iron legs, but the seat (over a sturdy wood frame and matting, probably made of some plastic fiber) is cloth covered? The cognoscenti and the regular habitues of the dump regarded us with disdain. Tsk, tsk.

Of course, we were quite conspicuous with our mountains of refuse, which was spread out in random piles on the spotless and paved "depository platform". I am sure we were categorized as one of those totally irresponsible foreigners, who doesn't even know his own garbage. The uniformed personnel, who looked more like nuclear scientists and not ministers of sanitation, had *Verboten* tattooed on their foreheads and had no mercy. They inspected every item separately and quizzed us about the origin of every piece of trash, its past uses and wanted to see the official document of its half-life, before they permitted us to deposit it into its eternal resting place.

Having accomplished this task we returned the hired van, then rushed home to meet the landlord. He was as solemn as a funeral director at a Mafia internment, and inspected every square inch of the house with a magnifying glass for hidden scratches or dirt. He stayed for a record time and checked out every nook and cranny, discussing every tiny bowel movement left behind by an irresponsible fly on the patio pavement. I am sure that even a nuclear plant could be inspected by the team of opposite players during this time frame, let alone a totally empty townhouse by a finicky landlord. He expected to find his house, after ten years of skyrocketing rental fees, in the same condition he first let us have it. I winced when I saw a crack in the patio's stone, because I could not remember seeing it before. And my heart practically stopped, when I saw a thin line on the windowpane of the library, until I realized, it was merely a smudge line made with the window cleaner. I could have re-marked that during the ten years we practically paid the entire purchase price of the house, but kept my thoughts to myself, and dutifully trailed him up and down while I was sure he could hear the lub-dub of my agitated heart. But eventually satisfied that we did not destroy his house, he signed the paper stating that he received the house in the exact con-dition he rented it to us a decade ago, and with that our departure was accepted by him. We were on our own.

"I repeat," my husband whispered as we were leaving the house that was our home for so long, "this is the very last time we have to feel like guilty kids and play mind-games to survive. This is a promise."

"I'm sticking by you for the same reason I married you: your positive outlook and your bull-headed convictions."

"Same here," he assured me.

After all this, our ordeal was over. We loaded our car at the apart-ment and although it was much later than we planned, we started our twelve-hour drive toward Hungary.

The rain stopped and the freshly washed sky was the brilliant blue of morning glories in first bloom. We passed Frankfurt, Würzburg, Nürnberg, which all had American military bases, and these were beam-ing the music and the news to our car radio from the American Forces Networks. The news had less impact on me now. I was moving out of the world where these happenings were of any real concern to me. The weatherman predicted more rain for the coming week, and that still touched my life. As did the music, following the news. "Five hundred miles..." somebody sang and I could not help it; tears were rolling down my cheeks. Five hundred miles from home? More like five thousand. I turned my head to hide my tears and gazed at the sun-speckled after-noon. I think my husband knew that I was crying.

We were too exhausted to drive more than four hours in the heavy weekend traffic, so we stopped somewhere in Austria to spend the night. It was late Sunday afternoon when we arrived in Zalaszabar.

CHAPTER TWO

I have seen the house we inherited only twice before and my most tolerable memory of it was as I saw it in the summer. Somehow when it sat among flowering bushes and climbing grapevines, despite its plain features, it managed to have some bucolic charm. In the lazy warmth of a pleasant summer day, it conveyed a faint echo of Walden, of Earth Day, and at least temporarily, I could identify with it. For a fleeting moment that summer, I had a mellow yearning to leave our complicated civilization behind and live close to Nature. For a brief moment I felt that Zalaszabar might be the very place where a new life style could be created.

But the fleeting moment passed quickly enough, because above all I really prefer civilization that includes an honorable government, paved roads, snow clearing, indoor plumbing, garbage pick-up, canalization, telephones, decent transportation, a library, medical services, personal and property safety, gas for heating, some entertainment, stores with a reasonable selection of goods, and a few other things I always took for granted.

Zalaszabar had none of these. Instead it did (and does) have a mayor, who does not seem interested in any of the above. Like Guareschi's Peppone, minus the basic humanity and charm, he too is a product of the last fifty years of wicked politics, and seems dead set against any sort of progress. With a leap of admirable imagination he created a new definition for democracy, and seems to suffer from the delusion that through divine grace he alone is blessed to make all decision for the village, without ever considering what people really want. He elevated himself into the role of the guardian angel over the inhabitants, who are, according to him, imbeciles, not capable of making decisions. He knows how to twist the wires of his puppets, and with the loyal assistance of the notary public, is quick to dole out punishments for those who oppose him. Ironically, or infuriatingly, he considers this to be democracy.

Twisting and mocking an ideal I honor is bad enough; keeping people in line with fear is immoral; and being manipulated by anyone is humiliating. This can eventually destroy the dignity of the individual. These attitudes and behaviors, practiced openly during a period of time most everyone would like to forget, were some of the reasons that scared me from settling here in the first place. In the USA, we have no patience for such attitudes and behaviors. Of course, Man, second cousin to the Fallen Angel, often attempts to undermine the structure of society, in the US, and everywhere else on the globe. But these individuals have reduced chances in a civilized society, because people just won't put up with it. .But in Szabar the population has not yet discovered its rights and its power, and so the village keeps limping into the twenty-first century burdened with a ballast left over from the last soul-destroying decades. The village has little to show in the way of progress.

At any rate, during this first week of April when we arrived, the world was still rather gray and gloomy in this part of the world. Only the hills around the village bore a light green veil of new leaves, promising spring to arrive any day soon. And of course, the almond trees were already in full flower. But the charming bushes and grapevines around the house were hacked away to make place for the addition. The house, minus its bucolic requisites, sat unadorned and gloomy among the unmentionable mess of building materials. Mountains of brick, sand and gravel, cement sacks and general rubbish of a magnitude that would make a city dump look like a child's playground, were all over. In addition we had the refuse of the good people of Zalaszabar too. Not taking the hint that we had the place cleaned up the summer before, the villagers once again used our property as their rightful dumping place.

Zalaszabar never even heard, let alone practiced, garbage disposal in its nine hundred years of history. Environmental protection was definitely not part of their vocabulary or philosophy. Animals ate part of the trash, the rest was burned, or dumped somewhere. In every yard there was a smoking dung heap and an outhouse. A few years later my husband became a devoted activist for the public good (hence an enemy of the mayor and the notary). As a result, eventually we did get garbage pick-up, telephone lines, and as his ultimate achievement, the gas-line. But when we arrived, there was none of that, and people heated with coal, wood, and every type of garbage that would burn. During an atmospheric low pressure one could suffocate from the various smells and gases. Of course, one can't blame the people. Refuse happens, and it has to be disposed somehow. Our future mansion was a logical and convenient place for all the things that could not burn. The village fathers looked the other way and sighed with relief. Out of sight, out of mind. One less problem for them to solve.

"They don't even separate the trash before dumping it on us, " I complained as I regarded an old, broken stove and several slashed car tires.

"Because they have divined that you wouldn't be happy, even if they separated it before dumping, so they didn't bother."

I regarded my future home with silent despair. The windows were small and in a state of hopeless decay. The stucco walls were crumbling morosely and the ground around the house was so wild and uneven that the most talented garden designer wouldn't know what to do with it, unless he could think in terms of bulldozers. The house sits high, but after each rainfall the elevated area erodes gradually right into the roads around it, causing a Sea of Mud on the streets separating it from the rest of the houses. Even Moses couldn't cross this one. I said silent prayers for the drivers of cars who had to negotiate the slick mess.

The property is actually a double lot, half belongs to my husband and half to his widowed sister. Its best feature is its location, right in the middle of the village, on a large, and high triangular island, completely surrounded by roads. The shortest side of the scalene triangle is our front, and across the road there is only an abandoned school building, occasionally used for meetings. The somewhat longer side of the triangle faces a stone wall that was the boundary to the holdings of a landowner. His palace was razed after the war, but the ancient trees left in the park give us constant pleasure. The third, and longest side of the triangle is the front of my sister-in-law's property, right on the main road.. In other words, we would have no close neighbors, except her. We would not bother anyone, and in turn I would not be bothered by early-rising farmers, or the smell of their dung heaps. Never having had any in-laws before, my husband's sister at this time was still an unknown factor in the equation.

Our house sits higher than any of the other houses (including my sister-in-law's on the same property) and was separated from the public road by a sparse planting of inferior bushes. I planned to stop the grave erosion of the steep incline to the road with groundcovers, and planned to replace the existing shrubs with evergreens, flowering shrubs and trees for privacy's sake.

My husband also counted as an advantage the wine cellar on the property. To my amazement I eventually discovered a vegetable cellar as well. What can be more chic than having his and her cellars on the property? However, since my cellar was half caved in, I soon gave up panting with enthusiasm.

After we unfolded our limbs, and crawled out of the car and reassembled our aching parts, my husband opened the rickety front door of the house with the flourish of a prince inviting his beloved into a pleasure palace. Facing the front door and opening from the wide hallway was the big bedroom, made more than a hundred and fifty years ago. The aged beams shone with a soft glow in the late afternoon sun and I surprised myself by falling in love with it. How is it possible, I wondered, that I did not appreciate this on my two previous visits?

To the right of it was the room, which I remembered most vividly with its decaying, northern wall. Decades of heavy rain that had nowhere to go, because the gutter was long gone, had soaked it all the way to the foundation and it had but one wish left: to collapse on itself for a well-deserved eternal rest. This used to be the kitchen. The floor was covered with a hideous gray slate, speckled with red, as if sometimes in the long past a huge bottle of ketchup had exploded over it. There was a walk-in shed directly from this kitchen. Depending on the changing needs of time, it was at times used to store food, or wood, or items no longer used. I recalled it from the summer before as dark and unapproachable. Its earthen floor and the rickety ladder leading up into the attic could barely be seen because of the monumental pile of unidentified objects that was stored there. Somewhere behind this wall of rubbish was a theoretical door serving no purpose, since it had holes large enough to admit a dog and, as my husband was to find out later, several minks and a huge tribe of dormice as well.

To the left of the bedroom was a smaller, sunny room facing the street. And this was the extent of the "ass-kicking, drop-dead house" he promised.

However, during the months while I was packing, my husband had the electricity rewired, the water connected, a water heater installed, the foundation dug out and a septic tank built. He bought almost all the material we would need for the construction. We were on our way to civilization.

The house was clean; thanks to the efforts of two women my husband hired to sweep and scrub and to whitewash the walls. But a quick glance told me that the floors, made of once beautiful chestnut planks, were beyond repair and the windows would have to be exchanged. Something was desperately wrong with the ceiling in the front room and the hallway. The old kitchen was totally useless, and according to our plans, would have to eventually metamorphose into a master bath. A new kitchen must be built. St. Rita, undoubtedly this is a job for you!

"Watch this," my husband said, beaming like a child on Christmas morning. "I have a surprise for you!" He led me through the ketchup sprayed kitchen and opened the door to the shed. Behold, I was facing a glorious, gleaming toilet bowl! My eyes grew misty; I was getting emotional. Nobody knows the aversion I have to outhouses ever since I met up with slugs, snakes and frogs and legions of insects. This was too good to be true. I stepped with holy rapture into this gleaming wonder of a bathroom, almost impersonal in its perfection, and touched the shimmering tiles on the wall to make sure I was not dreaming. Gone were the ladder, the attic hatch, the broken door, and all the garbage. Emptied of everything, the room was surprisingly large and wonderfully light with two new windows. The area was divided into three compartments, separated by tiled walls. One area was a double-size, step-down shower, the other contained the toilet, and the third area was a dressing room with the sink, cabinets and a large mirror.

"The kitchen will eventually turn into the master bath as we planned," he told me. "But it is a long way off, and we can't live without a bathroom, so I decided to start with this. Anyhow, we need two baths in the future. It isn't quite ready," he added hastily, when he saw my rapture. "The plumber should have connected the water, but I guess he did not show up while I was gone. I'll get him first thing tomorrow morning. Meanwhile you can shower at my sister's house. She is really good about it; that is what I did since I came here."

Well, no big deal. I can stand one more night visiting the outhouse.

Besides I don't think snakes and snails are out this early in the year. I turned back to the marvelous spectacle of gleaming tiles, but suddenly I had a sick feeling. I stared and did not quite understand what was wrong with the picture. Then suddenly it dawned on me.

"Where are the faucets, or at least the holes for the faucets?"

"They will be installed as soon as I get the pipes up," came the cheerful answer from behind me. The plumber, noticing our arrival, made an unexpected visit to greet us. (Later I found that nothing could be done in the village without everybody noticing it.) János is a short little man with a nervous twitch in his eyes, a strange raspy voice, and an overcoat like the doctors wear, except his is brown. I never saw him without it. He calls me "my lady". Not milady, but my lady.

"Excuse me, but I don't understand," I told him after introductions.

"It is quite simple. I'll put the water pipes up around here over the tile." He pointed vaguely in the general direction of the beautifully tiled wall.

"You can't do that! Nobody makes plumbing like that," I gasped, but already knew that his mind, or whatever he used instead of it, was made up. "The pipes ought to be inside the wall, not outside of it, and especially not on top of the tiles!" I insisted stubbornly.

"But my lady, this is the only practical way, and it makes excellent sense," he rasped cheerfully. "Look, one pipe will come here from the water main carrying cold water. I'll install another pipe into the hot water tank and the two will meet right here at the bottom of the shower stall. I'll take both pipes up to the showerhead. Then with an elbow pipe out of the shower stall I'll guide the pipes over these walls and down again to the wash bowl. A separate pipe, laid flush on the floor, will go directly to the toilet. It takes some time to guide all these pipes up and down, but my lady, I guarantee that tomorrow evening you can have your first shower in your new house."

I stared at him stupidly.

"You mean you are going to attach ugly water pipes on top of the tiled wall, then take these awful things across the floor and up the wall and down again…"

"You got it, my lady," he smiled in obvious appreciation because I finally understood his grand scheme. "But these are not ugly things, as you are pleased to call them, but practical implements, hence beautiful.

Pipes are the essence of plumbing and you need not be ashamed of them, my lady. And it is the very best solution. Think of it, what would you do, if your pipes busted? Never thought of that, have you? Well my lady, if you had the pipes in the wall, you would have to rip off the tiles in order to get to the pipes. This way everything is open and handy."

"It is hideous and unsanitary. It is the ugliest thing I ever saw and how am I supposed to clean under and between them? It is Stone Age. Neolithic. No. Make that Paleolithic."

"Don't swear at me, my lady. I have been polite with you."

"So sorry, and I apologize. But in all honesty, how often do you suppose my pipes would burst?"

"Numbers don't count. Once would be too many. You'll learn to appreciate my design," he assured me, then added with some concern, "The real problem is not with the pipes, but with the water tank of the toilet."

I was afraid to ask what the problem was, but he offered the explanation quick enough.

"You people cut a window above the toilet seat. So where do I put the tank if there is a window up there?"

"But the tank does not go up there, János! It goes right behind the seat."

"Is not possible. How would you flush then, my lady?" It was bad enough to discuss how I would flush, but in addition I had the feeling we were not even speaking the same language with this raspy little man. Finally my husband was the one, who first understood the problem. Apparently the plumber has only seen old type toilets with the tanks high up at the ceiling level. The water is released by yanking on a chain, and the gravitational force takes care of the rest.

"Well, that should not be a problem at all," I said much relieved. "You see, this tank is different from the ones you know. I assure you that it will flush from this height too. Just mount it behind the seat."

"Can't, my lady," came the laconic answer. "I already cut the hole in the floor to connect the bowl with the sewage line, and now the hole is too close to the wall. Nothing would fit behind it. There is no way I could move the seat forward, my lady. It will just have to go up, like all water tanks should."

And of course, once the hole was cut and his mind set, I could see that the tank could not be installed behind the seat. But the plumber was a kind-hearted man, and when he saw my unhappiness he was willing to compromise. He wanted it high above; I wanted it low. He suggested a solution in-between. After many hours of twisting and turning the pipes up and down the corners, he mounted the tank halfway up between the seat and the window, using an extension pipe of a different color, because none could be bought anymore to match the original. He was touchingly pleased that he could solve the problem at least to his satisfaction, and could not comprehend that his handiwork looked hugely ridiculous. With its resemblance to a slightly retarded ostrich with a swollen head, our toilet is quite a conversation piece now. Even with this noble compromise the seat is still too close to the back wall, causing the seat-cover to play unexpected and nasty mousetrap games with anyone who wishes to use the toilet with the seat up. Our male guests, after some fancy quick-stepping, make many an inappropriate, but doubtlessly witty remark about the twisted mind of the designer. There are some remarkable philosophical and wine-mellowed after dinner conversations dealing with the real purpose of the automatic down-snapping of the lid.

Later the stone mason, bless his soul, corrected as much as he could, by installing a step-like, tiled ledge to hide most of the pipes, but it entailed a lot of backtracking and superfluous work. All this reminded me of the long-distance race the animals once organized. One after the other, the rabbits, the gazelles, the leopards and the rest passed the two snails, who also participated in the race. Round about the fifth day one snail said to the other,

"A good thing we are moving so slowly."

"How is that good?" asked the other.

"Well you see, we are all heading in the wrong direction and everybody will have to turn back anyhow. It is a good thing we did not get all that far."

There was a frightening similarity between our building project and that race. Even when things moved, it was very slow and far too often seemed to be going in the wrong direction. Once, on an exploratory excursion on the Rio Orinoco in Venezuela, I saw a funeral in a godforsaken Indian village. The pallbearers made the point of not wanting to let go of the person who just died, so they made three steps forward and one back, to delay having to bury the loved one. I had no idea that the Indian culture reached all the way to Zalaszabar

Anyhow, despite my husband's and the plumber's optimistic promises, it took more than one day to complete the plumbing.

After we ate supper with his sister, I showered in her bathroom, then walked back up to our new home to leave the two alone to talk about family and friends. I placed my half-wilted roses in fresh water and walked through the tiny domain that was to be our home for the rest of our life. Five hundred miles…what a haunting melody. I opened the small window in the bedroom and stretched out on the huge bed, which we found on the property during our summer trip. It was more than a hundred years old, a carved, roomy, serious piece of furniture. I thought of all the babies that were born in it and the people who died in it. I thought of the many people before me, who sank into it, weary beyond words from the heavy toil, which was their unrelenting destiny. They were simple, poor people, who worked until they dropped, and their nightly rest must have been the closest thing to death. Somebody once told me about his parents. His mother was extremely religious and his father worked very, very hard. One day he found his mother sobbing in the kitchen.

"He won't say his evening prayers," she wept bitterly. "All he says when he goes to bed, 'Lord, your beast of burden now drops down to sleep…' and he is already snoring. He'll go to hell for not praying properly." The son, who used to be a choirboy in the local church and picked up some Latin from the parish priest, consoled her.

"*Ora et labora!* In translation it means 'pray and work'. You pray and Pa works, and it'll work out fine." But she did not buy into this modern concept of division of labor, and remained unhappy.

The spirits of these long gone people entered the room. I was not afraid of them, but they made me feel out of place. I was an intruder in a place that was made sacred by labor and by suffering. My life appeared very pampered in comparison to the lot of these, and I felt I was usurping their place. I have not earned with sweat and blood the right to be there.

But then a bird called, then another and suddenly the night was filled with the sweetest sound I ever heard from a bird's throat. Only later did I learn that it was the nightingale courting his bride. I snuggled into the huge bed, designed for an entire family, in which the king-size spring and mattress I mailed to may husband earlier, almost disappeared. Feeling the fragrant, soft sheets on my skin, I finally reached complete peace. It was a good house with a kind spirit hovering over it, and it loved me. I could feel that. I soon fell asleep, drunk from the fragrance of spring streaming in through the window in the magnificent silence, broken only by the exquisite song of the nightingales and the occasional bark of a dog.

Monday morning came, and it rained as predicted. It must have started up again sometimes during the night, and showed no inclination of ever stopping. The heavenly downpour converted the surrounding area into an area of mud, which was absolutely catastrophic for a moving day.

The name of Zalaszabar is made up of two words. "Zala" is the name of the small river that flows through it, or near it, on its way to Lake Balaton. Every village located on its banks, from practically the Austrian border to the lake, carries the name of this river in front of its true name, like an exalted title of nobility. So we have Zalakaros, Zalakomár, Zalaapáti and so on. Thus, if we were snobbish, Zalaszabar could be ennobled by calling it *Szabar de Zala*. I could print calling cards with a small coronet, and impress the jet set, which would instantly admit me into its exalted circle, believing that I am a member of European nobility.

Unfortunately some linguists and Sumerologists are convinced that the word Szabar means mud in the Sumerian language. I can't argue with this assumption, because I know very little about that extinct civilization, but I can see the logical connection. Several villages in the neighborhood contain the Hungarian word *"sár"* (mud) in their name, such as Sármellék, (near the mudflats), Sárvár, (mud fort) Sárhida (bridge over the mud) and so on.

Our area is a large territory west of the River Danube, and the most outstanding geographical feature of it is the beautiful Lake Balaton, which the Hungarians like to call their very own sea. Zala, the main river that feeds it, is usually a well-behaved little stream of little consequence; however, during spring thawing it used to spread peacefully over a very large stretch of land. This inundated area never quite dried out and was always a marshy, boggy, mysterious world, a natural reservation and a haven for thousands of birds and other living things. But at one time, the practical Communists found this to be a total waste, and decided to drain it and create agricultural fields in the area. In a few years it was obvious that this wouldn't work; there are instances when Nature does not permit itself to be forced into a new role. The lake suffered, the fish didn't have a good place to spawn, from the agricultural lands large quantities of chemicals and fertilizers were washed into the lake and made it sick. The birds were threatened with extinction, and the agricultural dream newly gained, also proved to be a total failure. The Zala was used to its own ways, such as stepping out of its bed each spring, and it was not about to give up an old habit. When this singular joy was taken from her, she knew how to revenge herself. The comrades then had to hatch a new plan and flooded the area, thus creating the Lesser Lake Balaton, now a reservation and bird sanctuary. Everybody was happier, but the memory of lots of mud did not dry out, as the names still show.

But on a second thought, I won't have those cards printed after all. While there is definite charm in such titles as *Madame de Rochefoucauld*, *Madame Turenne de la Tour*, or *Madame de Savinien-Hercule de Bergerac*; the elegance is totally missing in such a title as *Madame de Mud*, (or *de Szabar*, or *de Sár*), which is a most ordinary and dirty name in any language.

The second thing I noticed that morning was a note on the pillow from my husband. "The moving van will be here at eight. I am driving to Nagykanizsa to get the customs people to open the seal on the van. Love you."

Dutifully I eased my aching body out of that wonderful bed, and looked at the oozing mud around my pleasure palace. My sister-in-law's chickens, ducks and geese huddled in the rain, and glared with obvious ill-humor at the soggy world. I had to decide whether a shower, brushing my teeth and a cup of coffee were worth crossing this Sea of Mud, while doubtlessly be attacked by her ill-mannered flock of feathered folk.

The desire for the coffee triumphed, but a few minutes later I started to regret it. My sister-in-law, who tells very often, and with a properly tragic emphasis, that she is over seventy and very frail, is the most high-strung and energetic person I have ever known. She has a keen intellect, plenty of energy to drive the turbines of a major power plant, possesses the curiosity to keep generations of cats going, has a great love for talking, and an unrelenting urge to tell everybody what to do, how, when, and how many times. In addition she has the talent of worrying about everything, and in case there is nothing to worry about, her vivid imagination will, without any apparent effort, fabricate a problem. She also has a heart of gold, as big as it comes.

An early riser, she already had plenty of time to get herself into a state of extreme agitation. Even while I was drying myself after the shower, she was hollering through the bathroom door.

"I'm so terribly nervous," she repeated, as if I could not see that. "If only I can manage to live through this day without getting a heart attack! Why didn't the van come yet? I can hardly stand it…you know, my heart at my age…I just know something went wrong. What will you do if the van does not come?"

"Probably go down on my knees in gratitude, " I hollered back foaming at the mouth from the toothpaste. "I am not yet over the trauma of loading, and am not looking forward to unloading it."

"Shouldn't you call somebody?"

"Relax, Darling," I soothed her through the closed door. "First, it is not yet eight. Second, I wouldn't know whom to call. Third there is no telephone on which to call. Let's you and I have a cup of coffee, and not think about the van."

I was finishing my make-up when she was at the door again, her white hair in disarray from excitement and her blue eyes dancing in delight because of the titillating bad news she was about to deliver.

"Well my dear, I just knew it." She took a deep breath and paused for a second to achieve the maximum effect for her scoop. "It was just on the news. There is an extremely chaotic situation at the border. Some trucks have been waiting for two days and are still not allowed to pass into Hungary. Jesus, Maria, Joseph and all the saints, whatever will we do? I'm totally wiped out. My nerves cannot take any more of this. This stress is too much for me. You should have moved a week earlier. This was extremely bad planning on your part."

We too worried about the habitual delays at the borders. The very real possibility of delays was the reason our drivers were so anxious to start as soon as they could. But she was so agitated that I was afraid to upset her further by agreeing with her fears.

We just poured our coffee, when my husband arrived from the county seat, minus the officials.

"At the customs house they don't believe the van would arrive on time," he told us. "Although the real delay is at the eastern borders and not where our van is to come through, but the situation is not too promising anywhere. The guys refused to come with me before the van is actually here." My poor man did not know that he was just pouring gasoline on fire.

"I knew it! I told you so!" she screamed, grabbing at her chest to indicate that a coronary attack was imminent. However, there was no time to faint, because just then the frightful bulk of the *Hungarocamion* pulled up in front, taking up the length of the house and some. My husband gulped his coffee and was back in the car.

My sister-in-law was in her element. She asked the drivers into her kitchen and inquired breathlessly what breakfast I planned for them. Shamefacedly I admitted that none. All my kitchen things were sealed in the van, and of course, arriving on Sunday evening, I could not buy anything to satisfy two men with huge appetites. I was caught without a breakfast to my name. This pleased her enormously, and immediately started to bustle between the kitchen and her larder, while muttering remarks about my inadequacy. She fried bacon strips, broke eggs into a bowl, cut huge slices of country bread. On a restaurant-sized platter she arranged sausages, ham and other things recommended for people, who wish to increase their cholesterol level.

Whenever she found a spare second, she lectured me on the duties of the wife, whose husband is building. She referred to my husband as the "master of the construction"; I was to be, apparently, the mistress of cooking.

The drivers ate silently, oblivious of everything but the food, and I listened just as silently while she listed my duties. She was rapidly displaying traits that were sure to bring about a very strained relationship.

"I have plenty," she assured me of the obvious, "I'll feed the customs officials too." Since it is all of a twenty-minute drive from Nagykanizsa, I was not convinced that they would arrive near starvation at nine in the morning, but did not argue.

"It is our custom, dear, to feed everybody. Food is the sign of friendship and good will. People who come in good faith, expect this. You will have to cook for every person who works at your house."

If this were a movie, after the ominous words died away, a dramatic piece of music would be played in. A close-up of the star (me) would flash on the screen as she is staring meaningfully into the distance at a point off camera. Her eyes would be wide open (don't forget Visine to get the red out!) and this would indicate that she understood the divine revelation and is duly shaken up. The light would be slanting from the back to increase the drama of the moment; it would also permit a slight quivering of the lips to be seen. The audience would then know that something very significant has been revealed, which would have a real effect on the development of the plot.

But this was not a movie. There was no music, no close-ups, no significant look, and I was too busy with the problems of the moment to grasp that my future, in which I would be a perpetual cook, was just being revealed. I ignored my grandmother's advice to always watch for destiny at every turn. So much for my sensitivity. And this is how it came about that my husband often refers to our home as "the house that Judith cooked for us." Perhaps that would have been a more appropriate title for this book.

Meanwhile a large crowd gathered around the van. There are few, if any, entertaining happenings in this village and the arrival of this large vehicle was a world event. My sister-in-law ran out at predictable intervals, giving up-dated information to the rain-soaked spectators. She was fully aware of the power position she now had, as she was the only one who knew what was happening.

"Yes, they are moving home...my brother has gone to get the customs people...they'll be here any minute...the drivers are eating breakfast, and I must feed the customs guys as well...if only I'll have the strength to live through this day...this huge van and the trailer is full of their things...they even have a machine that washes their dishes...my heart...". Her excitement rose to such a pitch that I was soon worried that she would indeed suffer a stroke or something equally dramatic.

In the midst of all this, my husband returned with the customs officials, one of whom turned out to be a beautiful young woman. Her very presence gave my sister-in-law a fresh reason to indulge in renewed hysterics.

"That is all we needed! A woman! Women are terrible when they get some power. I hate her looks. She'll fuss, you'll see that she'll turn everything inside out! And in this rain too! What bad luck to get this prissy princess! You should have come last week!"

The young lady seemed to be in charge, and ignoring the curious audience, stepped up to the van and broke the seal. She glanced at the paperwork, checked off something in her book, then extended her hand first to my husband, then to me.

"Welcome in Hungary and I hope you'll be very happy here." Smilingly she shook the rain off her smart uniform, then added, "In our part of the country they say, when it rains during the first day of a new venture, it will bring you luck. I hope this will be true in your case." With that she disappeared into the kitchen of my sister-in-law and endured her endless stream of questions and remarks, without letting it disturb her appetite. We started off-loading with the drivers and the ten men my husband lined up for the job.

In spite of the steady rain and the mud, the work went smoothly and rapidly. I blessed my husband for making me mark the boxes; it was easy enough now to direct which should go to the house, which to the barn or garage and which to Esther's (my sister-in-law) spare room. The things that would go to the rented house we packed with foresight into the back of the truck, and did not have to be touched just yet. Because there were so many helpers, I had to be quick giving orders, and soon could not help feeling tense and tired. The rain fell steadily, ten people wanted ten answers every minute, while the audience watched us with rapture. I half expected an applause after an especially well executed down-lift. My body still ached from the long drive of the day before, and windmills were turning in my head.

At this point the lavish breakfast was finished, the officials departed and my sister-in-law appeared on the scene, ready to take over. She was everywhere, telling people what to do. It did not bother her in the least that she had no idea about the contents of the boxes, or my intentions with them. This insignificant detail did not deter her from giving orders in a voice that carried to the next village and beyond. Even my husband could not help me here, because it was I who packed, and I alone knew what should go where.

But Esther, with the self-confidence of a field marshal, ordered the rain-soaked troops around, until everybody was ready to wring her neck. The rhythm of the off-loading came to a screeching halt, when the men got contradictory orders and were made to race back and forth in the pouring rain with their awkward loads, slipping and sliding in the mud. It was pure slapstick, straight out of the Three Stooges, except there were ten of them. There was a moment when I thought they would all leave us to our own devices.

Meanwhile she wanted to know everything about the items being off-loaded, and of course, she had plenty of opinions about everything.

"Dear Lord, what on earth is that? Take it to the barn. No, better take it into the garage. Why did you bring that thing? What is it anyhow? Where do you plan to store all that? This isn't Paris; this is a muddy little village, you won't need those things. But it is your life, your house, do as you please. I'm only warning you. Heaven help us," she interrupted herself in her own tirade of warnings, "They even packed planks of wood! Don't you know that you can buy lumber in Hungary? Just dump those stupid planks in the corner of the garden, you guys." I shrieked over the noise of the crowd and just prevented in the nick of time the certain ruination of those planks. I explained to her that those were the pieces of our dismantled sauna cabin. She did not know what a sauna was, so I told her in two words or less, and she was dumb-struck for ten seconds. As soon as she came to herself after her half-swoon, she explained to the crowd that her crazy sister-in-law even brought an entire room along, where she can sweat if she wishes to. Heads were bobbing in disbelief. She displayed that unique talent which could drive a saint to commit homicide.

I was standing high on the van counting to ten and wishing she would take a short vacation on the moon, or at least contact laryngitis, when my husband sauntered by, carrying a large package and wearing his customary "the-world-is-a-great-place-I-love-you-how-about-you?"

"I love you too, but I am not a saint," I told him, then added rather louder than I intended, "But do something to your sister, before I kill her." I was being unfair in a big way. She was good to us. We tracked mud into her house, used her bathroom, ate her food and piled numberless items into her spare room, including a piano, making a total mess of her house. I wondered if in a reversed situation I too would have been this generous. And now, instead of thanking her, here I was, contemplating ways to end her unselfish life.

He grinned at me, without a trace of hard feelings after I so unfairly attacked his sister. Had he done that to *my* sister, I would have exploded in a royal rage, and our marriage would have suffered a temporary state of deep freeze with all smiles cancelled. Thanks to the Lord, he is made of better stuff than I am, which is probably why our marriage turned out so well.

"I knew this would happen and I already arranged to be rid of her," he said lifting his large package. I hoped he did not plan to gag and bind her, or worse.

As it turned out, while he was in town that morning, he bought half a lamb and now asked her to make a stew for the crowd. There are few things she loves to do more than to cook and she is very good at it. It was also of prime importance that while she cooks, she refuses to leave her pots and pans even for a minute. "It is the mistress's watchful eyes that give the food the extra taste," she explained to me about a hundred times. Immediately she grabbed the meat, and inspected it with knowing eyes, turning it this way and that.

"Mighty good piece; you chose well," she admitted grudgingly. Because she is convinced that she can do everything better than anybody else, she usually does not find a reason to praise, so this was quite an event. She marched off toward her house and soon the comforting aroma wafting from her kitchen assured us that we'll be having a scrumptious meal and also that we could complete off-loading without involving the homicide squad.

During the next days I unpacked the essentials and tried to arrange our living quarters as much as it was possible. The new bathroom was wonderfully usable; I did not even see its ridiculous shortcoming any more. The ketchup speckled kitchen, still a long way from becoming a master bath, was used for what it was originally destined. Balázs, the cabinet maker, nailed together a makeshift counter with open shelves below and above, to hold some of the essentials for cooking simple meals, and János connected the kitchen sink to the water main and the sewage line. The microwave and a hot plate with two burners were placed on the countertop and there was even a small table with two chairs, where we could take our meals sitting down. There was no place for the drier or my huge upright refrigerator-freezer, but we did install the tiny refrigerator that used to be in the party room.

The most awkward arrangement was the washing machine. Summer was coming with big time construction, and that spelled dirt. I knew I would have to wash almost constantly. There was but one way to solve the space and drainage problem: we placed the washer in front of the countertop, smack in the middle, so the water could flow into it from the faucet, and it could then drain into the makeshift sink. It was unbelievably awkward, because as I cooked, I had to keep walking around it from the work area to the other side where the hot plate and the microwave were. When I used the sink, (right behind the washer) I had to stretch either over the washer or reach it sideways. I could advise Jane Fonda on some good exercises. By the end of the summer I could have qualified for advanced ballet lessons or acrobatics, because I was that limber from stretching for hours while preparing the meals. I recommend this kitchen arrangement for all weight-watchers. Monika L. too could try it, free of charge, as I have not patented it yet. But actually this inconvenience was a small price to pay for letting a machine do my washing.

Every square inch of the house was piled high with furniture, crates and boxes. At times we thought we were buried alive under the collection of our material things. We needed a snow shovel, a compass and a week's supply of food and water to find our way from one corner of the house to the next. We could have used a walkie-talkie too, but that would have been too extravagant. It was already pointed out to us that this was not Paris. On account of the place packed beyond capacity, we could only commute sideways in the tunnels we built under and around our belongings.

The only oasis in this warehouse was the huge bed, which became the calm center in our chaotic universe. It was the only place that was neat, clean, cozy and inviting; the only place where we could retreat for a short while during the hectic days. Miraculously I found the chest I sent to my husband, and in it the bed canopy and drapery I once bought in a state of momentary insanity, but then never used. Now it became imperative that I attach them to the beams over our bed. Everything around us was so totally awful, so unbelievably ugly and foreign that I had a passionate need for something frivolous and enchanted, where we could hide. Our enormous bed, fitted with silk sheets and piled with lacey pillows and cashmere throws, partially hidden by the softly cascading drapery from the canopy, became our lovely, incongruous island, a place totally detached from problems, dirt, dust and construction. Here we were in our own safe world and felt protected and invulnerable.

"Beds are mostly for sleeping and for sex, or a place to be sick in or die," my husband laughed. "But this bed has become our entire world. I'm not complaining," he added.

We often took our drawing boards and ideas there, together with a pot of tea, which we placed on the bed-table, as we worked on the details of our house.

"I want a fireplace, several verandahs and patios and fig trees, a winter-garden and a dipping pool near the patio to use after the sauna," I told him. "I also want a house with many rooms, so that every mood and every season, and every job should have a place which is just right for that moment, that time, that purpose. I have a recurring dream, which I love," I continued, as I poured us some tea. "I dream that we are moving into a house and as I walk through it, I keep discovering hidden, delightful rooms, which I did not notice at the beginning. It is such a wonderful dream, so much fun and so exciting that I don't want it to end; therefore, this is how I want this house..."

"Would you also like walls and a roof? Perhaps doors and windows?"

"I knew that you would come to that. I guess we'll need those things too," I acquiesced, "but mostly I just want many different rooms and corners."

We were both working very hard and each evening I fell into our bed so exhausted that I found new meaning to the words, "My Lord, Thy beast of burden drops herself down..." I was on my way earning with the sweat of my brow the right to live in this house. The ghosts of those peasants long gone surely were looking down at me now with new respect and acceptance.

Meanwhile my sister-in-law developed the nasty habit of running in and out of our house, without invitation, or even knocking on the door first, as if our modest home were public domain. What is more, she often brought visitors, who were all interested in our "heavenly bridal bed". They wanted to see the wonder of a canopy and lace on the pillowcases, the decadence of silk sheets, which Madame de Mud seemed to prefer in this god-forsaken place. I was reminded of a TV sitcom series played several decades ago, starring Eva Gabor. If my memory is correct, it was called Green Pastures, or something like it. The story was about a spoiled city woman moving into an old farm house. Not being able to adapt very well, she found herself in absolutely hilarious situations every week. I felt that I was suddenly cast in that role. It was a very unfair casting, because all I got were the misadventures, while Miss Gabor had all the glamour and beauty, not to speak of her lush salary, when she played the airhead from the city.

But this was no TV series, and I was furious at Esther for bringing these strangers unbidden into our house, which was really not in any shape to receive company. It did not help to hiss at her; she was totally insensitive to my warnings. Her friends wanted to see live what they only saw a few times in the movies. During the years of Communism, western entertainment was not allowed to filter into the Eastern Block countries for fear that the carefully molded Communist attitudes would be polluted, and heaven have mercy, people might start yearning for those decadent things, which ran contrary to the approved ideal. The movies, which Big Brother approved, were drab, insultingly righteous and shamelessly used as a vehicle for brainwashing people to accept the delights of Communism. No canopies or silk sheets there. In those movies people slept in unadorned rooms and ugly beds, but their faces shone with otherworldly happiness, because they were serving the true ideals to the smiling approval of Big Brother.

I do not know if these old ladies swallowed any of it at the time, but they sure were curious about how the other half of the world lived and slept, especially since many of them were familiar only with the straw mattresses they used. To them, the abundance of silk, brocade and lace whispered of sensual distractions, bordering on delightful sins and poetic depths. It was all made piquant for them by imaginary flirtatious revels, and a sensuality, which in its luxurious abandon was absolutely unknown and titillating to them. They could always have sex in the past if their husbands wanted it; but luxury was out of bounds, almost unimaginable. Sensual luxury was strange and thrilling, and they wanted to see it, touch it, inhale it. They did not envy it, had no desire to experience it, wouldn't even know how, but enjoyed their chaste shudders, provoked by just being allowed to look at these wondrous things. Just letting their imaginations fly satisfied them. Many touched the sheets and the drapery with hesitating fingers, in the same manner their mothers would have touched a holy icon.

Esther and her ladies (all well over seventy, and pillars of the village society) giggled a great deal in our sanctuary, but should have had their thoughts on prayers and other saintly things, as befits dignified ladies. Instead, they made inappropriate remarks, verging on the bawdy, the kinds one hears toward the end of those raucous wedding receptions, where too much booze is imbibed and good taste (if there ever was any) goes to sleep under the table.

It so happened that at the time when we cleaned up the bed for our use, we neglected to check the condition of the frame that holds the innerspring and the mattress in place. Nor did I hear of woodworms before. Anyhow, these hungry worms did their nasty and secret deed and gobbled up part of the frame. Then one night the inevitable happened, and the bed collapsed under us. It was unbelievable, but there we were, covered with silk sheets, frilly pillows, tied up in the drapery of the canopy and it was pitch dark. It did not help the situation that we laughed until our tears came, and so for a while were unable to climb out of the wreckage.

Next day we had to call the cabinetmaker to fix it. Naturally, my sister-in-law, who does not miss a thing, knew it long before the man arrived with his toolbox. She was laughing so hard that her tears were rolling down her face, and although not usually incontinent, she probably peed in her pants. Within minutes the entire village knew about it. I cannot figure out how she manages to send messages so fast. NASA and the Pentagon could learn a thing or two from her.

Of course, from the manner in which she related the event, everybody understood that we were the last of the hot lovers. The men openly admired and commented about my husband's "manly condition", and the woman could not hide their envy. They just knew that those sheets would do it in the end. There was a lot of crude teasing about our sexual virtuosity and it was pointless to talk about woodworms, because these good souls did not want to believe a word of it. The fact that our midnight crash was the topic of conversation for days, shows how very little happens in this village.

Would we be able to live in this kind of peaceful languor, so deprived of intellectual and amusing stimulation that it is but one step away from stagnation? In a few years, would we too be cackling helplessly at the hilarity of somebody's collapsed bed?

Before we moved, a friend told me, "Moving to a village? Good luck and *mucho* patience, so you can stand it. You'll find that the people there might have a pulse rate, blood pressure maybe, but very little else to show that they are alive. Most of all, don't expect intelligence. I know all about it. I'm a backwoods girl myself." I shuddered then, but did not quite believe her.

During the following days we could not find any of our things. Fortunately for our mental health, at the time we had no idea that this would be more or less how we would live for many, many months. We spent a large part of each day searching for things necessary or valuable. At times I thought that the simple words, "Do you know where we put…" could trigger instant madness and violent behavior. My husband was not yet aware how delicate my psychological state was, so he did not hesitate to ask one day, "Do you know where we put the refills for the ballpoint pen?" Surely this was a sign of severe dementia on his part, but my reaction was not terribly rational or normal either.

"It is in one of these 280 boxes, dispersed at five different locations. Don't let me stop you from looking for it," I blurted. He was actually hurt, because I snapped at him "for no good reason". Men are so different from us that it is a miracle we can love them and live with them.

He made his peace by bringing me a glass of wine. It was a sunny day, but still cold. April promised a new life, but May did not yet explode with its riotous joy. We sat on the old stone steps in front of the house, wrapped in heavy sweaters. He told me that we'd soon have a phone. I did not believe him, but he was convinced. Remembering a cousin, who worked at the central telephone office, he made extensive inquiries through her and wonderful promises were made, but they cautioned us that the installation would be carried out in very small steps. Initially they would install a switchboard into the village post office and ten lines would be attached to it.

But we should not lose heart, because the long-term goal is to extend the telephone network, so that in a short while we would have 24-hour phone service, and could even dream about connecting to the Internet. This was not very likely, but it was nice to nurse these dreams. In just a week I already learned that in order to live here and not lose one's mind in a short while, it is important to have patience. Even God needed seven days to create the world, an old man told me, so why would I want things instantly? Things happen at their own good speed, he added. I don't know about that. Seeing how things are run in this village, perhaps God should have taken a bit more time before He created His people in this neighborhood. Two weeks, maybe.

I received my first mail in my new home from my daughter Andrea.

"Dear Mom, how is moving? Sucks, huh? It won't get better until the end of the decade. By that time you'll have given up, and it won't matter that you can't find your car keys, your jewels or your car...Your sister-in-law sounds just like what she is: an in-law. Anybody who tells you her in-laws are great is either lying, or living five thousand miles from them. Most people can't even stand their own relatives, why should they love the various misfits of their spouses? You were lucky so far, because you had none, but I did, so believe me when I'm telling you, there is nothing you can do to improve an in-law. They never get any better. Yours sounds like a classic case. Maybe you'll get lucky and she'll self-destroy her vocal cords. But there are other ways of coping. Next time she comes over, pretend that she is naked. Not a pretty picture, huh? It should be good for a laugh and that should help you through her visit. You can play this game indefinitely. Displace her body parts, or move her stretch marks where she would want them least. This won't soften her stupidity, but it gives you something to do, while she drones on. I dealt with your husband's second wife like this for years. Also my father-in-law's second. Now that took some imagination!... Winter may be over, but it is too soon to tell. It hasn't snowed for two days, so I am optimistic. It doesn't take much...My house is falling down around us. The plumbing is seventy years old and we have replaced most of it. The two pieces we did not replace, blew out this week. One on Monday, the other on Tuesday. On Monday the kitchen pipe to the dishwasher blew out and a damned tsunami wave roared down the hall. White caps and all. Thank God, Mike was still home, because I just stood there and screamed. He shut off the water and we started mopping. The floor has never been this clean. I used every towel I had to mop up. Water does terrible things to oak floors. I hung up all the towels in the backyard, and they weren't even dry when the second floor bathroom shower blew out. Water, water everywhere. As far as I am concerned, *this* is the year of Aquarius. It is maddening, because exchanging these pipes was next year's project. This year the garage roof has to be redone, but instead, Mike is up on the second floor, making big holes in the wall and exchanging pipes. Of course, the holes are here to stay, until we get around redoing the ceiling. The bathroom is totaled, and it was the only room that had wallpaper, rugs, curtains and accessories to match. Now it looks like Sarajewo. I quit. I want to live in a grass hut on an island off the coast of anything. With no woodwork. No plumbing. No magic-flush toilets…"

"My poor baby, my poor baby," I sobbed that night in our bed. "This is awful!"

"No, it is not. You have to look at it rationally. She is young and funny, is living in a gorgeous Shaker Heights century home with a wonderful husband, and two super kids. Sure, there are mishaps in her life, and just like all the young people, they too are struggling. But her lot is half as hard as yours," said the man. "She is strong like a bulwark. Can't you sense the underlying marvelous humor? Her entire life is ahead of her. She'll come out of her troubles smiling and unscathed. I only hope, so will you."

I reached for the tissues and couldn't really explain to him that it is this false optimism, which makes me so upset. When I was young and had to struggle through a very difficult life, this is the kind of speech I always heard. I was told then that I was young and strong, and things would work out later. But they never did, and my youth was gone down the drain and all I have left from it is the memory of never-ending troubles. And now I am old and what did it bring me? I'm huddling in a wood-worm-chewed, second-hand bed in the middle of a nightmarish storage area. I am dealing with my lost career, the painful distance from my family, and a bleak future. Are these the good things everybody promised me? A difficult youth, capped by a difficult old age? There must be more to life, at least for my daughter. Even the nightingales could not soothe me that night. I was spiraling down a dangerous black hole, and even forgot that my old age is neither difficult nor hopeless, because I have a wonderful and loving man at my side. Dear God, forgive your errant daughter's ingratitude.

During the week, visitors, other than the curious ladies, stopped in to wish us well, and to give us gifts of welcome, to offer their help. One of the first visitors was Pista bácsi. (Bácsi means 'uncle' in Hungarian. Formerly children used this term to address older male relatives; now everybody is addressed thus, instead of the honorific "Mr.", which the

Communist considered too bourgeois, and banished from common usage. Sometimes it is downright funny the way these old gentlemen call each other uncle, as if they never grew up.)

Pista bácsi was a tall, well-built, powerful man, unbroken by his eighty years. His inquisitive, clear blue eyes did not miss much; he was nobody's fool. A no-nonsense man, he would have appeared almost stern, but there was a general kindness about him that softened the raw edges. He came bearing gifts: a bottle of excellent wine from his own cellar, a smoked ham, tomato and pepper seedlings.

Although my husband knew him from the times before he left Hungary as an exile, I first met Pista bácsi during the off-loading on Monday; he was one of the spectators. After the van was emptied, I stood there in the rain looking at a pile of very cheap blankets, which we purchased from the moving company. They were used as padding between the furniture, and were useless for anything else. Pista bácsi stepped out of the crowd and asked in his unhurried way if he could have them for his horses. I gladly gave them to him, but warned that in twenty-four hours they would self-destruct, and only fuzz would be left. He did not seem to mind. Now he came to express his gratitude for the rubbish that I was only too glad to be rid of.

This was our first inclination that it is not possible to give anything, or do the slightest favor in Szabar, without immediate and lavish reciprocation. The village motto is, "I can't owe a thing to anyone". Their prompt "return favor" is usually quite out of proportion to the original gift, or favor.

We ushered him through our tunnels into the front room. This was the area where I put in the most work during the week. It was still a long way from looking civilized, but was better organized than the rest of the house, except of course, our bed. But I could not scandalize an entire village by inviting him there. This room was to be our study. Fearing mold and mice, my first job in Szabar was to unpack the hundreds of books, and to place them on the shelves. The room was still piled high with crates, but the books gave it a respectable look. We gained a small clear area where the cartons of books used to stand, and I placed a few chairs and a small table on this spot to serve as our living room. He looked at the books with appreciation, almost awe.

"Like a library," he whispered. "Did you read all them books? It must be wonderful to be that well-read." He could not take his eyes off this bounty.

"Almost all of them are in German, or English, or some other language and not in Hungarian," I apologized, "so I can't lend you any."

"Wouldn't have the time anyhow to read. I work all day and go to bed while the sun is still up. Thanks anyway." For a while, we talked about common things, but then his gaze went back to the books.

"I guess you read a great deal, but I bet I could tell you a story or two, which you wouldn't find in any of your books, " he said. "For a start, did you know that this village is more than eight hundred years old?"

Well, yes and no. Some ideas and concepts held sacred by the inhabitants here could qualify as twelfth century superstition, and the social norms are no less advanced. On the other hand, because many of the houses were built from the local clay and mud in adobe-fashion, the structures do not last long. Unlike in Italy and other places, we have not seen here any architectural proof of great antiquity. Pista bácsi leaned back triumphantly. He did not have a study in his house, let alone hundreds of books, but knew things about which we were totally uniformed. By the smile on his face we knew that he was about to share some of it with us. My husband poured wine into the goblets and we were ready to listen to his tale.

"Good wine," he announced after he sniffed it, inspected the color and turned it on his tongue as if he were rinsing his mouth. He was a good storyteller and instead of rushing into it, he played a little with our patience to increase our interest. "This wine is not from your sister's cellar. Hers is a more robust wine and a bit on the dry side. This bouquet...and this deceptive lightness... this is real quality. Let me guess...am I right that it is from Imre bácsi?" He did not even try to hide his pride when we told him his guess was correct.

"I know wine, all the best and the worst in the village. I can even tell the condition of the barrel in which it was fermented and stored...Oh, yes; I was about to tell you the story of the village. I can't tell you exactly how old Szabar is, but documents written in the eleventh century already mention the village as a strong settlement with a fort. But the interesting part starts a little later, perhaps at the beginning of the thirteenth century, with the history of a nobleman called Buzád II, a gifted son of the powerful Hahot family. He inherited, or bought these lands around here and established his residence. Buzád was an educated and cultured man, a rare thing in that dark age. He was quickly recognized for his talents and was appreciated for his loyalty. As a result, he rose steadily from position to position, collecting vast amounts of wealth on the way up his career ladder. By the time he was appointed *bán* (palatine or viceroy) he was a man of power and influence. Once, when he was involved in a recurring squabble of royal succession and was branded as traitor by the king-to-be, because Buzád opposed him, the pope himself intervened to save the palatine's head and position. He married and had four sons, everyone of them destined for great glories and important positions." At this point, Pista bácsi contemplated his empty glass with great interest. My husband understood the gesture and quickly refilled it.

"A noble wine," he clicked his tongue appreciatively. "When you drink mine, you must compare it to this, and tell me what you think…Well, our Buzád was on top of the world. He could not go any higher, unless he wanted to be king, which he did not. And then his wife died. We don't know anything about her, not even her name. In the old times the names of wives were seldom noted, unless they were queens, saints, or famous courtesans. She must have been quite a woman though, because after her death he became a changed man, a mere hollow shell. After the funeral he divided his estates among his sons. One of the boys was an archbishop by this time, and in my opinion he hardly needed the inheritance, but fair is fair, and Buzád divided evenly among the four of them. Then, shocking everybody, he renounced the world and entered a Dominican monastery. With his great influence and excellent education, he must have been a welcome addition to the order, but nothing much is known about his monastic life, except the end. And it was not good. When the Tartars were invading Hungary, the prior of the monastery placed all the monks in safety, hundreds of kilometers to the west. However, Buzád begged to be left behind to give support to the population, which had to face the oncoming hordes. His wish was reluctantly granted and so he remained with the people, giving them encouragement, then burying them. But it did not last long. Just as the prior feared, Buzád died a martyr's death at the hands of the Tartars. On December 8, 1243 it was. The Tartars hated the clergy, and their cruelty and blind fury was let loose without any restraint. The Catholic Church registers him since as Buzád the Blessed.

One of his sons, Buzád III. inherited the property in and around Szabar and he too established his residence here, just like his father. He founded a monastery nearby and founded our church…"

"You mean that pink abomination? Come on, you are pulling our legs. It hardly looks seven hundred years old!" I protested.

"Of course, not," he laughed. "The pink box is an addition. Buzád built the northern part with the lopsided windows that don't seem to match. It is used now as the sacristy. Don't be surprised, village churches used to be very small in those times."

The power of tradition! Seven hundred years later Béla, our stone-mason, still has a hard time using a level, or making straight walls and his windows do look like authentic twelfth century constructions.

"Buzád III. was just as good as his father was, only luckier, because he did not die a martyr's death," our storyteller continued. "The family grew and branched out. They were the ancestors of the Bánffy family, as well as of László Csányi, whom the Austrians executed after the War of Independence (1848-1849). So history repeated itself, and many centuries later this late offspring became a martyr and a hero, just like his ancestor, Buzád."

Pista bácsi knew his favorite story well. He sounded like a talking encyclopedia. Later I checked it out at the county library, and found that he was right about both Buzád and the sacristy, and I also discovered a statue of László Csányi in the next town.

We sat silently for a while; I was ready to believe that the ghost of Buzád had joined us for a while. In the gathering dusk I looked out toward the hills and imagined these powerful men riding on their horses over the ridge, or heading toward the same thermal lake, where I go to soothe my aching joints. Perhaps, if one would look real hard, traces of the ancient residence could be found. After all, the sacristy still stands, why not part of the castle, where he lived? I looked at Pista bácsi's beautifully chiseled noble face, and wondered how many in the village carried those exceptional genes of the palatine.

And what about that woman, who in the so-called Dark Ages, when women were no more than chattel of little consequence, meant so much to her husband that after her death he no longer wanted any part of the glittering world, or his considerable wealth? How did she do it? What were her secrets that tamed a medieval powerhouse of a man? What was her hold on him? Without her he felt an emptiness, and a loss so great that in order to survive, he had to fundamentally rearrange his life. He chose a new path, where nothing and no one reminded him of the past, and of her.

I could just see the mighty man as he stood at her bier, unable to comprehend that she was no more. The thick candles flickered fitfully in the four heavy silver holders at the corners of the draped catafalque. The moving, soft lights tricked the grieving eyes, and for a moment he thought she moved; he even detected a hint of sweet color in that fright-fully pale face. For a moment he believed that the heavy lashes moved and presently she would open her eyes in sleepy amazement at all the pomp surrounding her. Then she would quickly slide off her resting-place, and rush into the kitchen in order to have food prepared for all the people she suddenly found in her home. But soon he saw that it was just an illusion. He roared then, like a mortally wounded animal, and chased out the bewildered guards, the four sons, the weeping ladies, the praying bishops, the knights and the gentlemen from the Court, who came to pay their last respects. He wanted to be alone with his lady, and he knelt at her side, in measureless pain, saying his farewell. And after he was done telling her the things that were meant only for her, he gave up his wealth, his position, his power, and his influence. He wanted nothing more of this awful world. A monk's rough garb and sandals were good enough for him; a simple cell, void of beauty and comfort, was all he wanted. Nor did he run away from certain and terrible death.

"You liked my story, eh?" asked Pista bácsi with obvious satisfaction. "It is all true, therefore, beautiful. But young people are no longer inter-ested in the ancestors. They move too fast and have no time for the past. Noble things bore them. They need the excitement of crime and violence, which the television offers aplenty. My grandchildren think that good people are dull. Buzád? A sentimental fool. 'Oh, Gramps, don't come again with your ancient hero! You know what he was? A wet rag, who could not handle the one grief fate handed him. He nursed a death wish ever since his wife died, but had no guts to commit suicide. He let the barbarians finish him off,' my grandson tells me. He thinks it smacks of a Sunday school parable. I no longer understand the world and the world does not understand me. The world and I don't even appeal to each other any more."

Obviously, he was in a black mood, and of course, he was wrong. We met his children and grandchildren long before I knew him. They are intelligent, upright citizens, full of healthy common sense. Any parent or grandparent would be rightly proud of them. Pista bácsi knew this quite well, but from time to time he has the need to complain about the world in general and his family in particular.

He finished his wine and we walked with him to the gate.

"It is good that you moved to Szabar," he said as his final farewell. "People, who read, can think better than those, who don't. You got to be informed if you want to step forward; otherwise you might fall into a hole. Maybe this is why they call educated people 'enlightened'. They can see better by the light of information, and so won't fall on their faces. This village used to be a place of some standing. People from the neighboring villages looked up at the Szabarians. But the light went out a long time ago, and stupidity lurks in the darkness here. We have sunk so low that we could stand comfortably, with a top hat on our head, under a frog's ass. And there would be space to spare. And believe me, that is very low indeed. A promise, a man's word of honor is not what it used to be. People are scared to stand up for their rights, and can't be bothered with principles. Most of these people can be bought or black-mailed into submission; it does not even take much. I don't want to discourage you; you'll find out on your own. Buzád, no doubt, is turning in his grave. But maybe people, such as you, could bring back the light. The Lord and Buzád know, how much we need it."

We stood at the gate and watched him walk away in the deepening dusk. His back was straight, his walk purposeful, and even after his form blurred in the evening shadows, his rich silver hair gathered the fading light, and was visible for a while in the distance.

"Buzád's noble descendant," my husband said quietly. "Strong, wise, thoughtful, and not afraid to lash out at something that seems wrong to him. A handful of such men could make, or change history."

"Dramatic too. And beautiful. Even at eighty, he has an infinite mas-culine appeal. Most men don't manage to look that good at the height of their manhood; present company excepted, of course. I really like him."

"Don't, please, don't repeat this to anyone, if you want to stay out of harm's way," he whispered in mock horror. "His wife suffers from a terminal case of jealousy and when she gets going, Xantippe appears as a pussycat in comparison to her. "

"How old is she?"

"That's just it. She is pushing, — but denying — eighty-one, so she is older than he is. By almost a year, so she worries about her young husband, and never lets him out of sight for long. I suspect his present black mood has something to do with his domestic bliss, or the lack of it."

Well, that explained that.

The welcome parade of the people in Szabar was touching. They came shyly, gave us their present, stayed a short while, then left just as quietly and suddenly. Advice was given. Friendships were established. We also learned a great deal about our new home from our visitors. Many were openly shocked that we chose to move to Hungary.

"You are moving here from the West? Why? What I wouldn't give to live in Germany, or in the United States!" was often repeated. We tried to understand their political views, which were far from uniform. The first free election and the dismantling of the Iron Curtain opened the door to democracy, freedom and progress. But people were fragile, inexperienced, and spoke timidly of the possibilities. Many had only vague ideas what democracy or capitalism are all about.

"The election brought us what we wanted and needed. But it came too late. We were sick before, but now we are dying," our new family physician told us. "During the last forty years something snapped in us and we are not ourselves any more."

"But things will surely be different from now on, and the initial inertia will evaporate, won't it?" I asked with the naivete of those, who know too little, but fervently hope the best for everybody. My attitude was honest, pure sterling, and very American.

"Perhaps. Now that the light finally reached us, we can see in the sudden illumination, how bad things are, and how much there is to be done. The Iron Curtain insulated us, and only now do we realize the staggering distance between us and the rest of the world. Grave damage was done to this country psychologically, physically, economically and culturally; I wonder if we'll ever find the energy, the endurance, and the money to fix it. Communism did not collapse because somebody destroyed it. It simply could not hold itself up any longer. Like an old building, full of holes, it collapsed upon itself, but in the process, it managed to half bury us too. There are no victors, only victims left. We bank our hopes on the generation following us, which was born into Communism, and was thoroughly brainwashed. These younger people can't shed overnight what was beaten into them for as long as they can remember. Communism was their religion, and although they let it go, they cannot yet trust an other god which could replace it. The very strength of the system was the skill with which they could convince people that black is white. They trained the people not to think, purged them of opinions, individuality, or any aspiration that was divergent from the central idea."

"But the parents, where were they? Why did they not interfere and counterbalance the brainwashing?"

"They were afraid," his wife said quietly. "Children were taught to inform on their parents to the teachers, who passed on what they heard to the authorities. It did not take much to clap down on parents, so they were very careful what they said to their children."

"The current life goal in this country is to be rich. Agreed, this is superficial as far as goals go, but people missed out on too much. I can't blame them. As they are heading toward late middle age, they know there is not much time left to grab some of what their western counterparts always took for granted," he continued. "They are not clear about the concept of government. In their politically immature mind, the leader of the nation is a sort of Santa Claus, but with vastly more expensive gifts than that which the Socialist Father Winter brought them. They dream of a socialistic state, where they are well taken care of, but quite incongruously they also want the life of the super rich western, capitalistic upper crust, and do not see the contradiction. For them nothing is fast enough, and if this present government can't deliver the good life in the shortest time, they'll turn from it in a heartbeat. They want luxurious vacations, fast cars, big apartments, good steady jobs. They dream of shiny shopping centers, elegantly renovated towns, and the latest and best in public services. They want to run first class, even before they learn to crawl, or walk. And they think the government should provide all this, and do it within a two-year time-frame."

"But don't you think that things should improve now by leaps and bounds, and that some of the reasonable things most people want would soon be available?"

"Yes. A nation would loose its collective sanity if it could not hope anymore. But our economy at this stage is such that no matter how the people exert themselves, it is not possible for them to achieve even the simplest of goals. Our people are industrious, talented, smart, eager and learn quickly. The quality of the population at large has never been a problem. But much as they try, they don't succeed. Somebody, government, luck, God, or just about anybody needs to step in, they feel, and help solve the problems. Progress will reach us, to be sure; but I am afraid that people are too worn down, too pessimistic, too poor, too disappointed to hold on, until it gets here."

"It won't take long," Eva, his optimistic wife insisted. "Already it is so much better. The constant terror, the fear from our government, from the police, and the secret service is gone. There were times when we were never safe, not even if we lived like deaf, dumb and blind saints. A careless word, a misunderstanding, somebody's envy, an absence from a brainwashing session, an informer's report, and God knows they were everywhere, was enough."

"And then?" I asked as quietly as she was talking.

"Then you were hauled in for interrogation. It was acceptable to incriminate yourself, and you can be sure that they beat out of you the confession they needed. And it was not possible to defend yourself, because by definition you were guilty. The only reason for the interrogation was to make it look legal in the end, and to give an opportunity for sadistic individuals to live out their depraved dreams. They would get you when your turn came up; it was just a question of time. Usually in the middle of the night. Everyone knew what would follow. They took my father this way and we never saw him again, never found out what happened to him, or even why it happened to him. They took my brother and when he returned, he was not the same man."

We fell silent, because words of condolence would not have been appropriate. We were, after all, not discussing dignified death due to illness.

"For as long as I can remember," she added, "the ringing of the doorbell at an unusual hour was enough to make people physically sick, because of fear. We even had a name for it, "bell-jitters", or "doorbell-shakes". It was the age of universal Angst. People feared each other.

They feared the mayor, the parish priest, the notary, their very own children and relatives. Anybody could be an informer. The victims, who survived, find it difficult to talk about the things they had to endure. One needs to forget those things, and it is best accomplished by not talking about them." Again there was a space of silence. The sun streamed in through the window and glanced off the yellow and blue dishes on her shelves. There was a small bunch of snowdrops in a glass vase on her kitchen table. It was lovely and peaceful, and the words we just spoke did not belong into this setting. She must have felt the incongruity too, because after a while she spoke again, but now her voice had a little smile hidden in it. "But we must hope for a good future; I'm sure it is written in the books for us. This country had so many tragedies in its one thousand years of history and it was always able to rise, like a phoenix from the ashes, and start all over again. And we have so many talented, clever people! They are our hope and our future," she concluded, then added an afterthought. "One day somebody needs to write a book, 'What Hungary Gave to the World'. It would be compulsory reading in our schools, so that kids once again learn how to be proud of their country, and how to continue on the incredibly rich cultural path laid down before them. Up to now, this was denied them. Forgive me for preaching."

We sat in the cozy kitchen sipping our tea, and the future was suddenly not quite so hopeless. And this woman was raising two superior children. That too is a start.

"There were and still are, problems of mismanagement . The sheer lack of know-how is mind-boggling," somebody pointed out to us later that day. Of course, we knew about that. During the forty years of Communistic rule everything belonged to the state. Agricultural land, forests, factories, restaurants, hospitals, beauty shops, apartment buildings, hotels, business concerns were all owned by the state, and everybody was a state employee drawing almost uniform, small salaries, and uniform social benefits. There was no real sense of ownership; therefore, nobody really cared how these concerns were run. "Profit" was a dirty, capitalistic word. There was no creativity, no growth, no self-actualization, no challenge, no risk-taking. Einstein's theory of relativity was better understood than the basic principles of how to run a snack bar successfully. Out of long habit, customers were ignored, and nobody cared about their wishes, or needs. Moldy bread, uneatable cheese, and vegetables in a state of terminal decay sat on shelves. Store managers did not seem to care which items moved quickly and had to be replenished. Sales clerks were habitually rude and uncaring; the customer was never right. It was not unusual to wait in line for an hour on a regular weekday at the bank or the post office.

'To every thing there is a season', but not in this country. Stores never attempted to stock seasonal items; it was impossible to buy a snow shovel in November, a tree ornament in December, or a dozen matching champagne glasses before New Year's Eve. Good salesmanship was not yet discovered. Few people knew how to run an establishment on profit, nor could they see any sense in it. When timidly I tried to make suggestions to owners of shops and restaurant, the answer was a frosty withdrawal and the standard statement, "This is not the USA. What works there would never work here." But I can't see why, because selling moldy, outdated and unsafe food does not work anywhere, as far as I know. Offering a lighter or a vegetarian choice to tourists in restaurants (who were used to it and demanded it) never hurt an establishment.

"We went to the workplace to sleep and to steal," an old careworn man told me. He was skin and bones, his teeth were beyond repair, his hands deformed by hard work and accidents. He inhaled the smoke of his cheap cigarette, then tossed his head defiantly. "They paid us so little and bothered us so much that they had no right to expect from us anything more than the physical presence of our bodies. It was illegal to be unemployed, so we made sure that we showed up each day at work. But that was the extent of our usefulness. It was a shared code of honor to steal as much from the damned state as we could, may all, who ran it, be sent to the hottest corner of hell. And the way I see it, things haven't improved a great deal since the elections. The only difference is that now we know all about the dirty deals that go on. Get the drift? Communism was supposed to be sacred. It was so clean, and so noble that crime just did not happen in this hallowed, man-made heaven. Crimes happened in America only, or maybe in some other democratic country. In this sanitized world nobody ever heard of corruption. Of course not, because nobody would dare mention it. Bullshit. Did you ever see a society without crime, without a little bribery, a little illegality? It is the nature of Man to be rotten. The comrades told us day and night that we live in Paradise, and that integrity and intelligence could only be found behind the Iron Curtain. For you see, this here was the true Nirvana. Everything was perfumed, cleaned up, drenched in antiseptics and society was just dandy, thank you. Our politicians were all saints. At least this was the official image. We ended up almost believing it. The big-time crimes in government, thefts on the grand scale, the torturing of prisoners, the awful conditions in the 'dislocation camps' which were really concentration camps by another name, the general unease of the population, the total lack of freedom, the medieval state of health care, the officials getting filthy rich behind closed doors, these things were all kept top secret. During forty years everyone glowed in white-hot virtue and no crimes were ever reported. Now in contrast, the newspapers make a big deal of all the shit that happens, and people believe that democracy caused all the bad problems. The crimes were imported from America, of course. Does this surprise you? You have no idea about the anti-American propaganda that was our daily fare. While Communism is crime-free and noble; democracy, (always equated with capitalism), corrupts the soul. The belief of a deeply criminal and ignorant America is bolstered by the huge influx of incredibly stupid and violent crime flicks, made in the USA. Simple people believe that these inexcusable creations on celluloid represent the true face of America. It is easy enough to learn to despise a nation through these flicks, if one believes them to be true. " He fell silent just long enough to search for another of his abominable cigarettes, and then went on with his list of complaints. " Open your damned TV set, and you get an hour long program, depicting all the crimes committed daily in this country. None of the gory details spared, mind you. People are horrified, and say that this never happened before. They are stupid or naive, and don't understand that once again they are manipulated. You can't talk sense to these blokes; their judgment is totally paralyzed. Like a broken record they keep saying that things were run better when the Communists ruled. Don't ever underestimate the power of brainwashing, and the effect on people by a manipulated media."

"We have democratic dreams, but a socialistic mind-set," the dentist told us. "We want to be like the rest of the western world, and everybody talks about democracy without understanding what it means. We scream for free enterprise, but expect the government to finance book publishing, film making, theaters, health care, universities and so on. Not that I blame the people for wanting government help, because nobody earns enough to pay for the needed services. We wanted to get rid of the autocratic state and were able, more or less, to achieve that. But instantly we found out that the money we earn is not enough to pay for the things we need, or to finance the kind of state that we dream of having. A monthly income of about 150 dollars is about average. But the prices of goods are steadily rising and we find that we can barely make ends meet any more. There is nothing, or very little, left over for things beyond the bare essentials. Funny, isn't it, how in the end everything boils down to money?"

Almost immediately after the election a new word was added to the common, household vocabulary. "Decentralization", alternately called "privatization", meant that licenses for private enterprises could be obtained, and that the formerly state-owned concerns could be bought by private individual; in theory, by anyone. The idea was a necessary step toward democracy and free enterprise. However, the noble plan was complicated by several factors. The first was that since almost everything the state owned during the last forty years, was at one time confiscated from individuals, many of whom are still alive and want their property back. Thus the question of legal ownership is shaky at best. What the Communist government confiscated from the citizens, is now being sold by a different, new government that claims it has nothing to do with Communism. Of course, a process of compensation for those who lost property in this manner was initiated, but it was not nearly adequate, and many a shady deal went along with it.

The second problem with privatization is that very few people had the faintest idea how to run a business with profit, and it was feared that the country would sink into total financial disaster as a result.

Third, there was no capital to speak of. It was simply not possible to save or to inherit any money during Communism, where everyone, regardless of position or education, earned about the same small salary. The only people who could stash away a fortune during those times were (and are) the real enemies of the people, the comrades in high positions, who could stash away tidy fortunes. "Once rat, always rat," Pista bácsi said about them. They were the ones, who benefited from the Communist regime, and they were now the ones, who had the means to acquire all the real estate and business ventures, which they formerly confiscated. They got it coming and going.

After privatization became a fact, such enterprises that did not need a large investment flourished. Small shops, tiny restaurants, beauty shops, roadside stands, souvenir shops mushroomed, proudly displaying signs that it was "private". Foreign tourists were quiet confused, because they did not understand that this simply meant the establishment was no longer state-owned. Once a vexed Austrian visitor asked us where one could eat in this country, since every other restaurant is "private". She thought these "private" places belonged to clubs, and were open for members only.

Because of personal interests and involvement, these places were run better than state-owned concerns, and business was brisk. However, the big concerns that could really make a difference in the nation's economy, were beyond the reach of almost everyone, except the has-been political bigwigs and foreign business concerns. "You cannot build an empire on wreaths of garlic, hot peppers, painted pots, seasonal fruits, and wicker furniture," mumbled Pista bácsi. "The ventures that can make a difference in the economy, or in personal lives, is still in the hands of the comrades."

And opportunists did not lose time grabbing what was offered. First a great many shady individuals, fly-by-night foreign investors, appeared and acquired property and business for next to nothing. After they got out of them whatever they were after, often nothing more than money laundering, the projects were abandoned, or passed on to somebody else, until they expired due to mismanagement and disinterest. The foreigners evaporated with the morning mist.

Those concerns that did not pass into foreign hands were picked up by the former comrades. They discarded their cheaply made garbs, sported tailor-made three-piece suits, and learned to wear a tie. With the swiftness of professional actors, they changed their costumes and social pose, and bingo! the former Communists turned out to be the new millionaires, and created for themselves a life patterned on American wealth. They now move about with infinitely refined snobbery, and would like to give the impression that they built their fortune on hard work and creative ingenuity. I suppose, in the end they'll believe it themselves.

The smooth and bloodless transition in Hungary, so often praised by foreign news correspondents, also meant that the former Communist leaders did not have to give account of their doings, (many of which were blood-soaked), but through incredible luck, or an even more incredible blindness on the part of the new government, they were permitted to become the new upper class. And the difference between the lifestyles and the incomes between the small circle of these new barons, and the rest of the population is tremendous and potentially dangerous. These bloodsuckers always lived well, but during Communism out of fear and a sense of self-preservation, they kept their wealth well hidden. After all, their basic political tenet and state religion was that everybody is equal, everybody shares and shares alike, and nobody may have more of the common goods than any other citizen in the country. It made excellent sense to hide the fact that they lived better than many a western millionaire.

The comrades understood psychology quite well (in and out of the interrogation cells) they knew quite well that Man has three powerful traits which even the long process of civilization could not wipe out. During the long evolution the three traits were tamed, disguised, or sublimated, but not eradicated.

One is laziness of mind and spirit, the next is deception in all its sophisticated and barely recognizable forms (including cosmetics) and the third is envy.

The comrades were not much bothered by the first weakness. They loudly sang the praises about the ennobling power of labor, but were careful not to do much of it themselves. The second trait, deception, was their very nature, so they did not have to learn that skill. But they knew that envy could topple them, so they were very careful not to provoke the patience of people, who still struggled in impossibly cramped apartments and yearned for the simple things that most western societies take for granted. The comrades enjoyed their wealth and good fortune behind closed doors and draped windows.

However, after the Iron Curtain was torn down and the old religion was swept out, the age of conspicuous consumption dawned. The time of secrecy was gone. Their cars, their houses, the shops and the restaurants they frequent, the vacations they take are obvious to everyone. Never before was there such a stark and provocative difference between the handful of wealthy people and the rest of the population, who are hopeless have-nots. And the newly rich are unable to see that they are sitting on top of a volcano that could erupt any minute.

And the new barons not only continue to control the wealth of the nation, they are also occupying far too many key positions in law and the government. A person, who does not belong to their network, has very little chance of being protected, or judged fairly in case of a lawsuit. And this is not merely based on personal experience.

"I have a very old joke for you," said the gardener where we bought the evergreens for the hedge. "It shows how the top comrades lived in this Communist Paradise, while an entire family struggled in a single room, shared kitchen and bath with several families, and learned to live without the simplest luxuries. By way of an example, my wife turned sixty-five years old last March and this was the first time I could ever buy her a bottle of fine cologne. The junk sold in the stores up to now did not count as luxury. It was only good as an insect repellant.

Anyhow, this story could be just about any one of them Communists, but let's say it is about Stalin… One day he decided to bring his mother to the Kremlin, because he was eager to show her how far he made it, how powerful he was. He waited for the little old woman at the airport, then drove her to his palace in the Kremlin in a chauffeur-driven stretch limousine. He took her into the luxurious suit, prepared just for her. Although it was in the middle of a harsh winter, she barely glanced at the masses of white roses and lilacs, her favorite flowers. She ignored the blazing fires in every gilded fireplace, the iced champagne, the Beluga caviar prepared for her snack. She had no comment about the swimming-pool sized marble tub in the gleaming bathroom, and sat quietly through the fancy dinner of lobster, roasted pheasants and out of season vegetables and fruits. Stalin was getting upset. Can't he impress her at all? He took her to the theater and they sat in his private loge. In the intermission imported French goose-liver pate with truffles was served, followed by chilled champagne and strawberries. Not a word from her. In the morning he sent to her suit a hairdresser, a masseur, a manicurist and a sable coat. She accepted it all with timid silence. In frustration he took her to his dacha, showed her his fine horses and hunting dogs, took her for a sleigh ride and covered her with a huge fur blanket of the softest mink. When that did not make an impression, he took her on his sailing yacht down to the Crimea. The food was exquisite on the ship, and he engaged a balalaika group to entertain her. After dinner they relaxed in the lounge with cups of imported coffee from Costa Rica, and cognac from France. Priceless paintings hung on the wall and the white leather upholstery was soft as silk. She still made no comment. Finally, in absolute frustration he practically sobbed, 'Mamushka, aren't you at all impressed? Don't you like all of this? Aren't you proud of me? Did you ever think in old Georgia that your son would get this high?' The old lady wiped the tears from her eyes with the back of her care-worn hands, then whispered sotto voce to him, 'Jusuf, my dear boy, I am speechless at so much wealth, But I worry terribly. Son, what will you do when the Communists come back and take it all away?'" He waited until our laughter subsided, then as he helped to load the trailer with the evergreens, he added, "You see, they all preached Communism, but not one of them lived by the word. Just like the Catholic Church. They too preach poverty, but then look at the pomp and circumstances in Rome or in the palace of any archbishop."

"I'll tell you what it was like," said Elemér bácsi quietly. We were sitting in his enclosed porch and were enjoying the solar heat radiating through the glass panes. His wife placed a plate of sweets on the table and offered home-made loganberry juice. "It must have been around 1952, in the spring. The Communists decided to collect the animals in the villages to put them into cooperatives. They were all over this place, like vultures that got a whiff of death. As soon as one of us returned from the field, the Comrades simply made us unhitch, then hand over the animal. I had the wife and eight kids. We had one cow, Riska, and one horse, named Vihar. When I saw what was going on, I left the house while it was still dark and took the cow and the horse with me to the woods. And then I just did not return. I slept out there and lived like a wild man. Days and days passed, I don't even know how many. I figured these brigands must have gotten all they wanted and certainly they must have moved on to the next village by now. It was a mistaken calculation. They were waiting for me, and didn't even give me time to water the horse or to milk the cow. I pleaded with them. I told them I can't do the work without the horse. 'Hitch up your damned wife to the plough; she has a wide enough rump. Shut up and do as you are told if you know what is good for you.' The loss of the two animals was catastrophic for us. But what got me were the eyes of those two beasts. Because I loved them so much, and we were so dependent on each other, I thought I understood them. There was something endlessly sad in those dark, liquid eyes. They sensed that something strange and terrible is going to happen to them, and they seemed to plead, and wanted some reassurance. But I could not help them. I did not even know how I would help ourselves without their help. They might as well have cut off both my arms. What good is a man, who can't help those who depend on him?" He looked away.

"My husband did not say a word for three days," the wife said softly.

"We are up to our eyes in you-know-what, and see no way of climbing out of it," Árpád bácsi, an octogenarian neighbor, told us later over his fence. "This nation is badly ruined, Jesus Christ himself couldn't fix it. They were all crooks up there in the government and with a few exceptions, they remained there, because nobody kicked them out. Did you ever see a wolf change into a sheep? Well, these brigands never change either. They sold our country. Sold it? They damned well gave it away. Tied a red ribbon over it and smiled when the bastards grabbed it. Probably pocketed a share of it too. The rest they divvied up among themselves. Damned traitors. Criminals. They deserve the rope, all of them. The comrades begrudge our children the skim milk, while they wallow in cream. Look at our incomes, look at our hospitals, look at all our aches and pains. No money is dripping down to us, but the ex-comrades are living like pigs in heaven while they are selling out our country's assets for chicken shit. The same goes on in the villages. There is plenty of money flowing down to the councils, but where does it all go? Who gives account of it? How much goes to the people? This entire nation is dressing from the thrift shops and the food they eat is not adequate. How come these crooks are not declared war criminals? Or peace criminals, if you please. Some of them have very bloody hands, others are such seasoned crooks that even their questions are lies. They are so corrupt that a decent man would not shake hands with them. Sure we elected them, because you have to put your X somewhere, but that is the end of the democracy as far as the citizens are concerned in this country. We are never asked what we want, and almost never vote on an important issue. " He spat bitterly in a wide arc, then lit his pipe and sank into morose contemplation.

"I saw you talk to Árpád bácsi over the fence," Etelka, the pharmacist laughed when we stopped to refill our medications. "He is a sour old cuss, all right. Any time you feel too happy and need to dampen your spirits a bit, just stop at his place. He'll take care of your happy mood."

"He made some points which probably are not totally unfounded," my husband said.

"Of course not…could you stop in tomorrow for the rest of this pre-scription? I don't have enough on hand to fill it…"she said after rum-maging in her drawers. "But I'll tell you what is wrong with this nation. It ails from the same malady that Árpád bácsi has, and I haven't got a medication for it. It is an all-pervasive sense of pessimism. I do not know why it is so. In some nations the majority of the people are habitually happy, in another country the people are mostly arrogant. Some coun-tries are known to have produced melancholy, or slovenly people. Who knows why? Their climates or their food, or their history, or something in their past formed them this way.. It is their national trait. Hungarians are pessimistic. During the sunniest time of the day they like to dwell on the shadows. It is such a contradiction, because they can be wildly happy and the fact that they got themselves out of a multitude of na-tional tragedies during the past thousand years proves that hope is al-ways prevalent, otherwise they could not have done it. But when you talk to them, you sense what the end of the world might be like." She slipped the medications into a bag and rang up the purchase on the register. "Don't forget to stop in for the rest of the medication, I already charged you for it."

"Your black thoughts are etched on your face," my husband com-mented as we were returning home. "Forget the gloom and the doom. Things are not as bad as you heard it today. I too was lectured about these things when I first came here, but then they quit haranguing. You are the new kid on the block, and everybody has to tell you all the bad things they can think of. As soon as they have exhausted their supply of bad news, they'll get back to normal and to happy. Maybe Etelka is right; what we see now is the secret pessimistic trait that surfaces from time to time. Or they simply need to talk about the bad times in order to exorcise them from their memories. Let's forget about these dark ghosts tonight."

He had tickets to a concert of chamber music to be held in the beautiful Festetics palace in Keszthely, and knew that it would make me happy. "Just to show you that Hungary has a refined population with a pronounced need for culture. We'll meet friends with a refreshingly positive outlook, and you will see one of the reasons why we chose Hungary for our final home. We'll go to a place tonight where you can wear a fancy frock, provided you can find one. Then we'll have a wonderfully satisfying evening for the price you used to pay in Frankfurt for parking when you had your hair done. Oh yes, and I want to show you that there are places around here that are not covered with mud."

The Festetics family, in whose palace the concert was taking place, has been long admired by Hungarians for their many talents and good works. In 1739 Count George Festetics acquired at the western tip of Lake Balaton a small and insignificant community, named Keszthely. The community's history goes back to prehistoric times, but other than the distinction of its age, it had little else to show. The Count was an officer in the Austro-Hungarian army, but by the age of thirty-six he was intensely disappointed with his career, and decided to retire to his new acquisition at Keszthely. He built a fabulous palace and dedicated his talents and wealth to improve life on his latifundia, and to put Europe's largest thermal lake, Héviz, on the map.

This enlightened aristocrat of exceptional intelligence and cultural horizons, founded the Georgikon, the first agricultural academy in Europe; established a library famed all over Hungary; built a church and a high school; donated property and money for the establishment of the Lake Balaton Museum. He also instituted and financially supported the so-called Helikon Days, where progressive Hungarian writers of the day could meet, discuss and present their works. He offered room and board for poor university students in his palace at Budapest and was instrumental in developing Keszthely into an elegant town, a flourishing summer resort, which became a center for intellectual and artistic interests. Thanks to him, Héviz, just a few miles from Keszthely, became a famed international spa of excellent reputation.

The family was also unique in that not only Count George, but all his descendants carried the outstanding genes and they were all philanthropically inclined. In turn, each family member added something to the arts, the politics or to the sciences. What Count George started, the rest of his family brought to full blossom. By 1911 the family head was raised to the rank of prince, and their palace, perhaps one of the most beautiful residences in Hungary, became the meeting place of European nobility, including King Edward of Great Britain, King Albrecht and the later assassinated heir to the Habsburg Empire, Grand Duke Franz Ferdinand.

Princess Festetics, a young widow by the end of World War II. refused to flee from the oncoming Russian army. The cannons could already be heard, but proudly she still had the princely flag flown from her tower. Almost in the last moments the chaplain, Dr. Sándor Károly Klempa, finally persuaded her to leave, if for no other reason, then to save her young son.

Her Lancia was barely through the glorious wrought iron gates, when the chaplain moved in with a crew of packers and stonemasons. He moved the most valuable objects of the palace into the spectacular library, and then had the door ripped out. The mason built a wall in its place. The paint barely dried when the Russians arrived, occupied the city, took possession of the palace and turned it into a military hospital.

Dr. Klempa approached the Russian commanding officer and explained to him what he had done in order to save the treasures. The Russian happened to be a cultured and understanding person, and fully approved of the plan. What is more, he had signs made with warnings of highly infectious diseases, which indicated that the sick were housed in the wing where the library was. He declared the entire area off limits. The fear of germs proved to be a most effective guard, and this almost unbelievable gambit saved the irreplaceable treasures from plunder and destruction. The Festetics library, which beside a large collection of antique books and codices, is the proud owner of a complete set of the books and graphics done for Napoleon during his military campaigns. It is the only library in the country that was saved in its entirety from the ravages of the war.

In the years following, the palace was used for just about everything that could ensure its total decay. However, at one point somebody with rare insight recognized the cultural significance, and its potential tourist attraction and the palace was gradually restored to its original splendor. Now it is open for tours and the gilded, mirrored ballroom can be rented for weddings, used for state receptions, or as in this case, as a concert hall.

As we walked up the wide, ornate staircase and then took our seats in the magnificent hall, I wondered how Prince Festetics, now living mostly abroad and only returning here for short visits, must feel about this place. He certainly must remember when it was his home, when he was living in these same rooms, when he walked with his beautiful mother on these same walkways in the park. Personally, if I were in his place, this would break my heart. It is not a question of being sad or upset, or disappointed about lost wealth and social standing. It has nothing to do with pride in material objects; it is something more personal and harder to define. A home, be it in a palace, or a hut, is very much part of us. Our dreams and our childhood, our first experiences, and the awakening sense of self, are all interwoven with it. Our very personalities are shaped by the home in which we grew up, and ultimately it defines who we are. Losing a home is like losing a part of our very self, of our soul. When strangers invade it, it is a deep violation of our inner self. I was thrilled to see this beautiful place, but felt like an intruder in the home of the Prince.

The concert was marvelous and the friends we met there agreed that the evening couldn't yet be finished, so we voted for a restaurant by the lake. We were practically the only guests at this late hour, and chose a table next to a large window. The waiter dimmed the lights and lit the candles on our table; a gypsy band played discreetly in the back of the room. There was a full moon outside and its pale light reflected softly on the edges of the tattered clouds and shimmered on the mirror-smooth surface of the lake.

The main attraction of our meal was *fogas*, a perch-pike fish indigenous to Lake Balaton, with white, flaky, and very light meat. It was breaded, fried, then placed on a bed of buttered spinach with a sprinkle of nutmeg and ground black pepper, then covered with sautéed wild mushrooms, doused with Mornay sauce, sprinkled with grated fresh Parmesan and broiled for a few minutes. It was absolutely decadent. The total silence around the table was the highest praise for this unusual and seemingly incompatible mixture of flavors and textures. The dish was created around the turn of the century by the famous Hungarian cook Károly Gundel, whose restaurant at the zoo in Budapest was, and still is, justly famous. We had bottles of Riesling from Badacsony to go with the fish and we felt pampered and mellow.

"Good food is like good music," sighed Katalin. "Everything must harmonize, everything must carry its own melody without the slightest dissonant interference, but all must happily support the main theme."

"Don't take her seriously," her husband warned. "She is always embarrassingly poetic when she has good food on her plate."

"Food is not only sacred to all cultures, but it is the great sensual pleasure of our younger years, before we were introduced to sex. And it lasts a great deal longer too," she argued. "It is the divine gift that keeps us alive."

"So does bread and water," someone said, but was ignored.

I was waxing poetic myself as I considered the grand finale. It was a dish concocted of a feather light pastry, brandied fruit, almond paste, whipping cream and other sinful ingredients. Man does not live by bread and water alone, and I gave in to the temptation.

A few days later I left Hungary, tired and emotional. I had a taste of the good and the bad, but the van was unloaded and all further ruminations were superfluous.

Naturally things went wrong once more for me, when it turned out that because of a mix-up I had no confirmed seat on the plane. The weekend flight was packed and the stand-by line long. I could not take a chance, so took the night train instead. As the train pulled away from the station, my husband appeared so very small and vulnerable standing there at the rails alone, waving after me. I pressed my head against the cool glass of the window in my sleeping compartment, and since nobody saw it, I cried freely. It was insane to leave him behind with the terrible workload, the endless frustrations of trying to build a home in a country that was definitely not at the cutting edge with service jobs or retail sales. Or of anything. What was I doing, leaving him in this mess, where he can't find his socks or the refills for his ballpoint pen?

The train whistled and picked up speed. We raced between tall trees, and I could see him no longer. The emptiness and fear was almost unbearable. Just then the steward knocked on my door and offered refreshments. As I reached into my purse for money to pay for the tea, I found the folded piece of paper between the bills.

"I know you'll bawl when the train pulls out. Don't. Everything will be all right and the first day of our separation is almost over. Only ninety-five are left. I love you," he wrote. I dried my eyes and settled down with my tea. Suddenly I knew that indeed it would be all right in the end. How else could it be otherwise, when I am fortunate enough to have such a man by my side?

CHAPTER THREE

The weeks dragged on toward the end of the school year. I missed my husband, hated the dump I now called home, missed my things, my personal world. In my loneliness I drove 200 miles to visit my husband's daughter, and once, just to make the weekend pass faster, I signed up for a short trip to Prague. We were to leave the base around ten at night.

Only after I was on the bus did I realize that it was filled with women, and that the goal was not sightseeing, but to shop until you drop. It was too late to get off.

"Whatcha gonna buy?" my seatmate wanted to know. "I'm in for chandeliers and decanters this time." She pulled out her pillow and comforter, placed her thermos handy and put on her slippers for the night ride. She was, obviously, a seasoned traveler and a discriminating shopper.

"I don't like crystal,' I confessed. "And I hate shopping."

"Then why the hell are you going to Prague?"

"I have never been there, and would like to see the city. I like buildings."

"Honey, in that case you need a drink," she declared and with some stretching and heaving she pulled a second glass from her bottomless satchel, and poured an amber liquid from her thermos. "Good stuff. You like Wild Turkey? Drink it up and you'll feel better. If you change your mind about shopping, I'll tell you about the best stores and the best places to change money."

After traveling all night the women looked worn and wrinkled, but the sight of the first store rejuvenated and energized them. The bus barely halted when they were already elbowing their way out and charged into the first store with such vehemence that the line of security guards, apparently used to such onslaughts, could barely slow them down in order to prevent death by stampede. Their vulgarity would have been funny, had I not been ashamed what the natives must be thinking of Americans. With admirable abandon they bought immense quantities of mostly useless knick-knacks, most of what looked suspiciously like cheap glass. They were under the delusion that just because they were in Prague, everything made of glass must by definition be lead crystal. Totally oblivious of the charm of that lovely city they rushed fast-forward fashion in and out of stores, lugging ever-larger boxes to the parked bus. I figured that they could not possibly use, nor give away the piles of goods they bought, even if they lived to be a hundred. No matter how stormy their marriages would turn out to be, they could not smash that many vases to make a point during a conjugal disagreement. The greed and fervor were astounding On that one morning they gave a kick-start to the economy of Czechoslovakia.

I was exhausted, and my lonesome wandering in the town became dull. It was no fun to see things by myself. Here I missed him even more than in my dreary apartment. Tired and cranky I promised myself to return one day. With him. And on a day when the shops are closed.

Toward the end of May there was another public meeting about our situation, and again the Regional Director explained that some of us were "excess". Well, he said that before, so why waste time after a hard day's work? While he droned on, I tried to picture my future, which no longer seemed so hopeless. In truth, during the last months I started to make the adjustment for retirement. Step by step I was separating myself from the present circumstances, and Szabar was becoming more desirable with every day I spent away from it. Although this would have been unthinkable even a year ago, now I discovered with some astonishment that I no longer belonged to the school. I could hardly wait to leave it. I was getting too old for the daily stress, and was ready for the slower pace, the contemplative life. There were books to read, letters to write, flowers to plant and a man to love.

Now, instead of jotting down on the yellow pad what the Director said, I found myself calculating how much I would receive in severance pay. Our finances were starting to be as lifeless as a poinsettia in May, and we needed a bit of infusion. The Director was still talking to his captive audience and I glanced at my wristwatch. His projections bored me. He still hoped that by August some of the people could be placed. (Did he expect that between May and August some more of us would erode? Maybe so. I sure was heading in that direction.) "I examined every available data and studied the situation carefully," he told us, "and am still confident that in the end every educator would be in a teaching position next school year, including the excess ones." Blah, blah, blah. God knows, we heard all that before. I guess a larger than expected number of "military dependent teachers" left with their husbands, and stateside teachers, seeing what was done to the overseas schools, were not rushing with applications. It looked that the projections were somewhat skewed, and after all a slight and totally unexpected shortage of teachers ensued. That was his problem, not mine. Let him drone on. "We care for our educators; therefore, the placement of everyone is important. It was decided not to initiate RIF (Reduction In Forces) procedure for civilians, hence there will be no severance pay..."

Almighty God! Did he say no RIF? No severance pay? No early retirement? He repeated the verdict into the stunned silence. There was no longer any doubt about it. For the handful of jobless administrators and teachers it would not be necessary to initiate the procedure that would help us over the worst problems while trying to adjust to a new life, find a new job, or as in most cases, tie us over until retirement funds would be forthcoming.

But why? In most countries the private sector is known to be generous in such cases, and the governments are not all that stingy either. Even in a poor country and with a staggering number of unemployed, like Hungary, the government finds enough money at the bottom of the piggy bank to compensate government workers if they lose their jobs due to no fault of their own. The young woman, who cleaned up our house before we moved in, worked for the village council for five years as a general cleaning help in the office and in the school building. When the work-force was downsized and she lost her job, she was given a two months written notice, a lump sum equaling three months of salary, and in addition she received her regular pay for six months after her employment was terminated, regardless whether she stayed home or went to work elsewhere. I would have been very happy to get the same treatment from my vastly richer country. My last hope was gone as the possibilities for early retirement and for severance pay were wiped out. Come to think of it, I did not even get a formal notice of my termination.

I needed some air. My ribcage felt tight as if my heart suddenly needed twice the space. I walked slowly to the car, dead tired and lost. During the last year, one by one, my hopes and dreams were dashed, and now, even this very last one, a settlement on which we could build our fragile life, was taken. I gave as much as a human being can give to a job, and in the end I was merely an excess, without a shred of hope or even the slight financial compensation most people receive in such a situation. Thank you, we enjoyed working together, Ma'am, but the door is thataway, if you please.

I should have used my time and our money to loaf on the beaches of the world, or should have built a house somewhere on a hill, or spent it on anything else, except invest it in my education, only to find myself jobless and an excess by age sixty-one. And in a strange way, I was ashamed of the treatment. I did not want my husband to see how my country dealt with me in the end. I was always a proud American, and told him wonderful things about my country, but this was not very wonderful, and I knew he would have his non-too flattering opinion about the situation. My balloon was pierced and I plummeted to earth.

To add to the general unpleasantness of life, a sudden and most unusual heat wave threatened to grill us alive, and especially me, in my attic apartment. It was unbearable up there, and I tried to spend my evenings elsewhere. But there was a limit how long I could stay on the streets and other public places. It was Saturday and the German stores were already closed for the weekend. I rushed to the PX on base to buy a fan.

"Ma'am, we haven't seen one since the Christmas before last," the salesclerk told me. That should teach me not to ask stupid questions. But on my way out of the store, while digging desperately for my car keys, two soldiers passed me.

"It just came in, I'm telling you. Saw the truck in the back with my own two eyes," one said.

"No shitting," commented his pal.

We were well enough taken care by the buyers of the commissary and the PX, but often the shipments would reach us fitfully. We would be missing some items for a while, then suddenly they would appear in rich abundance. It was our habit to inform each other about new shipments, in order not to miss them. This was no time to be shy, so I butted in.

"What came in? Hummels? Lladros?"

I have seen women, like those in Prague, with shopping carts at full speed, running over the hapless, and leveling the aisles to grab as many cutesy-cute Hummel figurines as they could, the minute when a new shipment came in. Ladies, who were observed wearing white gloves at the tea party given by the base commander's wife, were capable to fist-fight to secure an elongated, pale, giraffe-necked Lladro girl.

"Hell, no Ma'am, none of that. A truckload of gorgeous blue and white fans just came in. If you want one, better step on it, before people fucking total the place. 'Scuse me Ma'am for the word. In a second the back area will be designated as combat zone."

I followed them, pushed onward by the crowd. Who knows by what means news travel; by now everybody in a hundred-yard circumference knew about the shipment. Although I was pushed away several times just before reaching my goal, I still ended up getting one before the truck emptied completely. Actually the fan was not all that big, nor especially gorgeous, but it did have three speeds with which it could move the hot air from one end of the room to the other. One should not expect air-conditioning for a mere forty-five dollar. When it comes right down to it, the fact remains, that hot air moving around is better than hot air standing still. I took my sweet burden to the cashier to pay for it, when a hollow-eyed Lt. Colonel accosted me. In a polished, black-market whisper he offered one hundred dollars for my fan.

"My wife sent me to get one. It is either a fan, divorce, or death," he added in a dark tone. Well, we all have our problems and he'll have to solve his without my help. My life was difficult enough, and life in his roomy government quarters could not be half as bad as mine in the airless attic. No deal. He was not on the evening news, so I guess he finally found a kinder (or greedier) soul, who was willing to sell.

There were only three weeks left until the end of the school year and I had to face the inevitable. I had to sell my car, the only luxury car I ever owned. My children were grown and long gone from the nest, I no longer needed a wagon, vinyl seats, or a luggage rack. It was the first car I ever bought without having to first look at the price tag or evaluate its practicality from the standpoint of growing, gum-chewing children and hair-shedding dogs. Its style, understated elegance, youthful vitality and shameless luxury were the reward for graduating from another passage in my life. When I bought it my children nodded knowingly, "Mother finally reached her mid-life crisis". My husband smiled with indulgence. He knew about the crisis women go through and felt that a snazzy car was mild in comparison to mini skirts, hair dyed green or purple, and all sorts of hysterics for which Prozac was invented. But I had to part with my baby, because we could only take one car to Hungary duty-free and the duty on this number was more than its original price.

I advertised everywhere, without results. Due to the massive withdrawal of American troops, the market was absolutely clogged with used cars of every make and year. Many came to have a peek at my car, perhaps take a ride in it, but not one had the money or the honorable intention, and nobody made a proposal. In addition, to tell the truth, I was not overly comfortable when these fellows appeared at my door, wearing one earring, black leathers, lots of brass, and extraordinary tattoos and wanted to take "the little baby" for a spin. They were probably quite harmless, but they did not look that way.

Finally I decided to visit a showroom, which specialized in luxury used cars. It was probably not the smartest thing to do, but the alternative was not very clever or even safe. Time was running out, and I was quite happy to be cheated in exchange for peace of mind while somebody else took these jokers for a test drive.

When I entered the salesroom, the word went out through telepathic message, "Hey fellows, here comes a born-again blonde, an old bitty. She is asking for it..." And instantly they came out of the woodwork, uniformly dressed in medium cheap suits, flashy ties and flashing the same synchronized fake smiles, while in unison and perfect harmony they belittled my beautiful car. It was sporty and luxurious, loaded with all the impossible conveniences that carmakers could dream up, and was in excellent condition, practically brand new. And these sharks knew it as well as I did.

"What is it," they jeered. "A pimpmobile? Who do you think would buy a car with all that crap in it?"

"I did," I answered meekly in the futile hope of damming up their insults. "It has eight cylinders..." I don't exactly know what cylinders do, but I heard my son and his friends discuss enough cars to guess that the more cylinders there are, the more respect is given that car. Somebody once mentioned in our recreation room a limousine that had twelve cylinders. After a moment of awed silence, the blue-jeans-crowd stopped masticating their sandwiches and put their bottles of coke on the wall-to-wall carpeting. I fully expected them to genuflect. Rather naively I prepared for the same reaction in this glittering showroom. But the sales team was unimpressed. I guess, religion was not their thing.

"So what? It's a gasoline guzzler; that's what eight cylinders do. The Japs have shown how to make good cars with smaller appetites. Everybody wants economic ones."

"Excuse me, I must have missed the address. I thought I was at a place that deals in luxury cars, and not in pedestrian vehicles that run on a prayer and three drops of gasoline." I was angry by then.

"Hey, don't get sore, lady. We meant no harm. What else can you bring up as an excuse for this shiny heap of status symbol, this toy for rich kids?"

"It is practically brand new. I just got it, having ordered it before the draw-down started. Now I am...giving up my job and just can't keep it. It is new and barely used."

"New?" They laughed in concentrated derision, slapping each other on the backs in the way males do when they have just agreed in harmony on a rotten scheme. "Lady, that car was obsolete the day it left the showroom. Here is the offer. You take it, or else the deal is off." I gasped at the price, and knew I was being badly cheated, and so did they. But I accepted the offer, because I had no other choice.

One of the salesmen drove me home. As I got out of the car, I tossed him the second set of remote-control keys. He looked at it for a moment, then had the decency to slip off the key ring my husband gave me.

"You might want to keep this," he said and I wanted to believe that he felt something akin to shame, or remorse for having done it to me.

I walked into my dreary, hot apartment, clutching the silver key ring that simply said, "You are #1". Was I? Would somebody who deserves to be called Number One lose a job the way I did? Would she be as meek as I just was while I was practically robbed, getting less than half the purchase price? I was far from being the terrific woman the key ring indicated, and I did not deserve to be called that. Unless the statement would be qualified with the word "failure". I was Number One Failure.

I made a cup of tea and sitting in the dark room found that I could not even cry any more. Even the thought that without a car I would be a prisoner between the attic and the school, failed to upset me. I was so drained that I thought I would never be able to get up from the chair on which I sat.

But the three weeks passed somehow. Time was as totally insensible as DoDDS was about my feelings. Neither cared what was left behind on the battlefield. Friday was the last day of school and we survived it, but just barely. It was past two o'clock and I was just getting ready to go down to supervise the departing buses, when Christine buzzed me to come to her office. She handed me a letter, written by the Director of Education. It was sent from a city some sixty miles away by special messenger. I took the envelope and felt the same kind of sick tension I usually felt when I had to take a test in school.

Usually I am not terribly fussy about such things, but now, glancing at the envelope and seeing my name misspelled on it, made me "so angry that I was mad", as one of my children used to say. On the inside my name was again misspelled, only the letters were scrambled in a different order from the one on the envelope. My misspelled name underlined my own insignificance. I was a zero, an excess, a non-person. My name was merely approximated on the letter that informed me that my future had been decided behind closed door by people, who could care less about my concerns, aspirations, goals, wishes, or even my name. Unbidden, an incident came to mind. I was severely reprimanded once when during a supervisor's observation in my enrichment class for the gifted I had a slip of the tongue. I called one of the students Ronald, instead of Roland. This was the first month of school, and I used to see approximately 120 different students every week for only a few hours. I was giving them the time of their lives, but I guess I was not a fit teacher, because it was beyond me to learn all their names in that short period of time. No doubt, we were operating with double standards.

The letter was as harsh as our superintendent's style earlier, and it was clearly to the point. It was decided (the letter informed me) that in order to save me from joblessness, I have been placed in a fourth-grade, self-contained classroom in the same school where I was working as an administrator at this time. I would retain my current, administrative salary for two years, after which I would be back into the pay scale of the teachers.

I was choking by this time. How dare they arrange my life without even consulting me to find out if I am able, or willing, to do what they have decided for me? I sacrificed a great deal to reach the position I acquired. Whatever made them think that I would be thrilled to be back at square one? And what about this clause about pay scale retention for two years only? I could barely think of anything more underhanded. At retirement the average salary of the last three years is calculated and the retirement benefit based on that. It did not take a mathematical genius to figure out that if I would retire at sixty-five, I would draw a teacher's retirement and not that of an administrator. They get you coming and going. And why let it be known so late? After our lease on the house was given up, the furniture shipped out of the country and the car sold at a grave loss?

The letter also stated that DoDDS retains the right to place me back into an administrative position if the need should arise, even during the middle of the year. The new position could be anywhere in the world where American schools are maintained. Should I refuse this option, I have the right to retain my teaching position at the current school, but then immediately I would be put back into the teacher's pay scale. If this was not a threat, I don't know what else is, barring physical abuse. Sure, send me to Cuba in October, while my husband lives in Hungary. It is the common dream of every happily married woman to be a continent away from her husband. In case I should refuse this offer, they are ready to accept my resignation, he concluded this remarkable letter, but then immediately I would lose all privileges, continuity, seniority and the chance to get unemployment compensation. In other words, I would be without any income, until I turn sixty-five.

I had to respond to this offer until Monday. Since it was Friday, I was given two weekend days to make my decision. During this time, natu-rally, it would be impossible to contact any legal advisor, or even my husband, to help me make a rational decision, which would involve our life and our future. I was given no time to find out whether I had any rights, or other options. On the very rare occasion when we had to put a teacher on probation for poor teaching skills, or some outstanding failure, we spent months of documented effort to help resolve the diffi-culty. If this help from us failed, and we had to make the decision for suspension or termination, we had to give weeks of notice in order for the teacher to seek help from the Union and to get legal counseling. I was not given a similar courtesy, although I was an innocent party in this sorry play, and not a person, who failed in her duties.

After I picked up the broken pieces that was me, I left Christine's office and started to act, racing against time. In order to survive, I had to sustain my own awareness of self , and had to maintain that inner order which would help me surmount the wrong that was about to bury me. I also had to repeat my mantra that it was not my fault, that I was innocent, and a victim. If self-doubt would wash over me, I would surely be crushed and not be able to act rationally. The only way I knew how to achieve this state was fighting actively for what I thought were my rights.

I called the Regional Office and I explained why I did not wish to teach in a regular classroom any more. I said that I was willing to wait for an opening in administration, or would be willing to accept early retirement at sixty-two with a cut in benefits, but I was not willing to teach, because of certain limitations. I quoted my age, and the fact that I have been absent from a regular classroom for more than a decade, and going back to it would almost be like being a new teacher. The classroom material was familiar to me, since part of my job was to supervise teachers in the classrooms, but I had no teaching aids, no established routines. Paradoxically, I considered the job, for which I was overqualified, overwhelming.

I must say in defense of the Regional Office that I was not cut off mid-sentence. But the man listening sixty miles away, whom I have never seen, and who certainly never observed my teaching, did not hear what I was saying. In a honey-coated voice he assured me that I was a master-teacher, one of a kind, and that it would not be difficult for me to go back into the classroom with my awesome talents. He assured me that I would enjoy the change tremendously. This is what all former principals, who are now in classrooms, are telling him. It is fun, fun, fun. Blah, blah, blah.

While he paused to catch his breath, I tried to explain that it was not a question of "hard", "difficult", "enjoyable", or even "fun", but a question of what I was capable and willing to do. Changing strategies, he whispered a new version of "Uncle Sam Wants You". He said in a tone rich with melodrama how the little children are all waiting for my arrival in the classroom because only I could offer the intellectual stimulation to these eager little souls. At this point, out of curiosity, I almost accepted the offer. I was dying to see those fourth graders, who were supposedly panting for intellectual stimulation, because I have not yet encountered that species. Up to now I spent countless hours to dream up things to stimulate and motivate them, and getting them interested was perhaps the hardest part of every lesson I ever created. Once in March, when interests seem at their lowest and we had to start a new unit on the Middle Ages with a group of fifth and sixth graders, I actually dressed up to represent the Black Death. On my black robe (in which I received one of my master's degrees) I pinned the date 1350 A.D. cut out in white paper and did not say a word for about twenty minutes. It took some time until my students got over the shock and got the idea that they have to run to reference books and figure out some things on their own before I would talk to them. I spent the time praying to all the saints I could think of, to keep my supervisor from entering the classroom. I did not want him to question my sanity or methods, or both. I must say that seldom did I see students motivated more to learn something than on that gloomy March day. But the interest was not born in them; I had to implant it. Now I was aching to see the kids, who without any gimmicks whatsoever, would pant with enthusiasm on their own.

But my curiosity passed quickly. The disembodied voice over the telephone was by now telling me that he is offering the means to my own self-actualization. At this point interest and curiosity were totally gone. It took a lot of nerve on the part of this faceless man on the other end of the crackling military phone, to say this, since he did not know me from Montessori, never saw me teach, and probably did not know how to spell my name either. Nor did he ever see the hills of Szabar, or a sunset over the Lesser Lake Balaton, or felt the thrill of creating a dream out of a pile of rubbish. That is where my self-actualization was right now.

He concluded our conversation warmly and with more compliments about my astounding qualities, then added one more lie. "Please, understand that it is not cost-effective to pay you an administrator's salary while you are doing a teacher's job. We are going through a very difficult time, but believe me, we are doing our level best until we find a position for you for which you are so well qualified. Until then, believe me, teaching is better than retirement. Blah, blah, blah." I'm glad he knew me so well, but was sorry to say that the time when I believed anything that came out of the Regional Office has long passed. He hung up knowing that I was not a very nice person.

I was not ready to give up yet. It was Friday and getting late, but I took a chance and called an American lawyer in Frankfurt, well-known for fighting discrimination cases, and successfully representing DoDDS employees in the past. I wanted to know whether indeed I could be forced by gentle blackmail into taking a job that I did not want, and for which I was overqualified. I wanted to know if I had the right to hold out for a better position, or if I could insist on early retirement under these circumstances, or at least for some sort of a compensation.

I was lucky, because the lawyer was still at his office. He listened patiently to my miseries and I felt that unlike the Spokesperson at the Regional, he understood completely what I was talking about. He expressed sympathy and promised to call back after he consulted with his associates.

In less than an hour I had his return call. He was very understanding and assured me that if I wish, they would take on my case, because it does smack of discrimination, and there are some labor questions that hover on the edge of legality. However, he advised me not to start proceedings.

"If you have money to waste, and if it gives you a deep personal satisfaction to cause them a great deal of annoyance and grief, go ahead and sue and we'll do all we can. And we can make it pretty hot for them. I understand how you feel and if I were in your shoes, I too would feel that I needed to hit someone square in the jaw. But as a person, I advise you against the lawsuit. Even a class action has a hard time winning against such a formidable institution, and as an individual your chances are less than nothing. I would hate to take your money and then not win the case, unless you have piles of it to burn. Consider buying a punch-bag instead."

I thanked him then hung up. I was tired to the bone, and knew I was getting old. I no longer had the fire in me to fight this to some sort of a conclusion. And I did not have the money to do it. I suppose this is the big factor in lawsuits. They are so expensive, so time-consuming and the outcomes are so unpredictable, that people get tired and hopeless before the first deposition. Therefore, they would rather drop the lawsuit, and choose peace instead, while the perpetrators get away with a belly laugh.

This lawyer, whom I have never seen, told me as it was. He was right when he advised me against the lawsuit and against banging my head against the wall. He was a decent fellow, and did not even charge for the consultation. He behaved honorably toward me. Although, I must admit that it did cross my mind that he could, in some way, be serving DoDDS on the sly, which is why he advised me against the lawsuit. But instantly I was ashamed of my wicked thoughts. This is what this year has done to me: I could no longer trust anyone and I hated myself for it. I sat there staring at the telephone for a while. Just like with my car sale, I was again forced into a corner, and had no real choices left. And already I knew that after a very difficult weekend I would call Regional Office first thing on Monday morning and accept the unacceptable. I would have to take the job. There was no other way to face the future. We used up too much of our savings, were in the middle of a major construction project, our lease was up, the furniture gone, my car sold and I lost the hope for getting severance pay. Either I accepted the offer to teach again, or be without an income for the next five years. I did not need to think about the choice for too long. Number One capitulated again. I think it is written all over me, "Please, kick me and knock me down, then watch me get up again."

Joyce stuck her head into my office and interrupted my destructive thoughts.

"Chris told me all about it. I just came to tell you that I have some absolutely important work to do for ten more minutes. Then I will be back to pick you up for cocktails at the Club, then have dinner anywhere you feel like eating. We'll compare opinions, throw darts, engage in Wicca and send witchery curses. And then I won't let you go home to that unrelenting prison of yours, where you would just continue to brood. You'll spend the weekend at our house; my girls are looking forward to your visit."

And because she is who she is, her big, expressive, Junoesque eyes swam in tears.

Joyce and I had to work three more weeks after the children and teachers left. During this time we rewrote the teachers' standards and the job descriptions for the entire staff, the handbooks for parents and children and we planned the enrichment program for the coming school year.

When we started our projects, it all seemed futile, since we would not be in a position to use them, or to see how it all worked in practice. However, as soon as we started working, our involvement and excitement grew and it was a very good, creative period for both of us. Ideas seemed to explode as we planned, discussed and evaluated the material. We could not write fast enough to keep our ideas from escaping us. Even after she left in the late afternoons to take care of her children, I stayed on in the school building to continue our work. The only other lighted window in the huge complex was that of Christine, who worked just as hard on her projects as I did, only a floor below my own office. Neither of us had a family and work was an opiate against loneliness for both of us.

But it was a happy time. Our profession finally had more content than when our days were filled with just lunch, playground and bus duties, disciplining the same children day after day, or diffusing the anger of the same handful of malcontent parents. It is true, that there was a great deal of job satisfaction or "fulfillment" in the obligatory visits to the classrooms to observe teachers doing their job. I found it stimulating to see so many different styles, approaches and outstanding ideas. When I met the next teacher, I loved passing on a particularly successful method I just saw. The exchange of ideas, of observing others doing the same job, and learning from it, is sorely missing from the educator's professional life. The teacher, after receiving a university degree, is banished to a classroom to practice his/her craft behind closed doors in total isolation, without outside stimulation, and only limited help in the process of growing. In addition to passing on what I have seen, if my schedule permitted, I would sometimes "substitute" a teacher in class, while she/he slipped into another classroom to observe a fellow teacher at work.

It was also exciting to discuss educational philosophy during the post-observation conferences with teachers. This was the time when new ideas, new approaches were born, when a cohesion of the staff was built and our visions confirmed.

But all the fun was dampened by the fact that no matter how seriously we insisted on the contrary, we all knew that one of the purposes of our visits was to evaluate their work. Teaching is as personal as writing, an extension of the self. Even the most sophisticated teacher, just like an author, cannot completely believe that the judgment of his/her work does not touch on personal values. Who does not remember the agony when in school one of our compositions was read aloud to the class? When my generation was young it would not have occurred to a teacher to ask permission to read our work to a mostly uninterested class. We felt naked, violated, vulnerable and ashamed beyond words. Our very soul was bared for everybody to see its imperfections. No other experience in school was quite as devastating as that.

Trained in psychology, the supervisor is carefully discussing the teaching process that was just observed, but the teacher always has a hidden suspicion that the real issue might be his/her personality. While no supervisor worth his/her training and salary would ever do that, the concern is not all that farfetched and certainly not a sign of a paranoid persecution complex on the part of the teacher. Because teaching is basically "doing", we are not merely looking at a lifeless material product with which the producer does not personally identify. When observing teaching, we are actually looking at the behavior of the educator, which is very much part of the individual's personality. Too much is at risk here. This is why a lower rating in evaluation or a rejection letter from a publisher can hurt so intensely on the personal level.

Like in all other professions, there are only three categories in teaching: excellent, mediocre and marginal, although when we wrote the evaluation reports, for the sake of peace, we worked with a much wider scale, and included several steps and refined modulations in each category.

DoDDS is very selective when hiring educators and we were blessed with a large staff that would be rated above average by any school system, anywhere. We always considered our staff as a special gift to the children at our school, so supervising, and rating teachers was always relatively easy and painless.

The most gifted teachers were so good and secure in their profession that they did not even notice when we entered their rooms for observations; evaluating their teaching was a joy. They were terrific, and supervising had nothing to do with their excellence. We praised them and thanked the education god that we were blessed with such highly talented people.

Those, who in comparison to these stars would be rated as merely satisfactory, also did an excellent job and very likely many other school systems would consider them above average. When we popped into their classrooms, some of the less gifted teachers put on a show for our benefit, although we knew that their teaching was usually not up to that level. But since they were good by any standard, and since their results were excellent, the show did not make much difference.

In either case I don't think that our observations and evaluations made much difference in their teaching styles. They did a good job, because they were born talented, or trained well, or both.

Only very rarely could marginal teachers slip into the ranks of DoDDS. Trying to convince them that a change was necessary, then showing them how it could be done and then if all failed, attempting to remove them, took up most of our administrative time. This was hard on everybody and caused a lot of frustration and wasted time, but the complicated steps were carefully prescribed, and closely supervised by both the teachers' union, the superintendent's office and the lawyers on both sides. The process of removal, if ever accomplished, could last a year; in some cases longer than that. This was unfair and sad, because such a teacher's rights were always strictly upheld, while thirty children in that particular classroom lost a year of their lives. Life would have been beautiful without these awful hassles, but it was all part of the agreement. And I was getting tired and weary from it.

But in the silent, deserted building, we were finally doing something for which we were trained and which would surely make a difference in the quality of teaching and in student behavior in the coming year. Not a bad way to say good-bye to a profession I loved.

Time flew during those three weeks and before I realized, my husband came to pick me up for the summer. He bought a covered trailer, because there were still a lot of things in the attic apartment that were just crowding the place, but were needed in Hungary. Of course, we spent many hours discussing our altered situation.

"I can't believe they did that to you" he fumed. "I wish I could offer a way out, but every option I have sucks. There are some things though that we must consider. First, I do not believe that your job will last. Up to the last day of school they had not the palest idea whether they should or could find a position for you. I bet you that by the end of this school year once again you'll be without a job. Therefore, we can't afford to abort our plans in Hungary, especially since we already moved, at our own cost too. Second the house there is nowhere near ready and I could not leave it in this half-built, half-open state, with our stuff spread all over and asking to be plundered. There are still no doors or windows I can't leave, until we can put everything behind locked doors. I had to hire a man as a guard to sleep at our place even while I came to pick you up. I wonder if those bastards know what they did with our lives?" He poured drinks and continued.

"For the time being, we'll drive to Hungary for the summer. Much as I hate to say it, in September you'll have to come back." I winced, but he put his hands reassuringly over mine. "As soon as it is feasible, surely before Christmas, the house in Hungary would be completed to the point where I could lock it up and leave it. I'll come back to Germany then and we'll look for a decent, albeit smaller, furnished apartment, and live the best we can until your retirement, or until they'll can you again. Since I no longer work, we can get away with having just one car. We'll spend the summers in Hungary and step by step we'll complete the remodeling. There is something good in every calamity: the summer break for teachers is much longer than that for administrators, and we'll be able to spend more time doing the things we have to do. Nothing has changed in our plans, only our time schedule is somewhat off. Retirement won't happen next week as we planned, but if you can just hold on until the house is somewhere near completion, we are home, free."

It was an awful situation, but there was nothing we could do about it, so we tried to cross out all the bad thoughts. At least there was a plan, a time schedule, which could be checked off, day by day, month by month. We granted us a few days rest before returning to Hungary for the summer, but as it turned out, much of our time was spent in stores to buy the seven hundred things he had on his shopping list.

"It is difficult, if not impossible to get these things in Hungary," he explained. "Without a telephone (we still did not get it!) to let my fingers do the shopping, I have to spend hours in the car searching for the needed items. It is very frustrating, especially since I usually don't find them anyhow."

The list, in its crazy diversity was amusing enough. It would have been a hit on some sort of a game show. "Ladies and gentlemen, take out your shopping list, if you have one. If the following items are listed, you will win the grand prize of ..." And surely we would have won it and the grand prize could have eliminated some of my fears. Who else in the audience would have had on the list a mailbox, light switches, typewriter ribbon, computer paper, furniture polish and band aid, a pump for a well, shower curtain rings, two transformers, detergent for the automatic dishwasher, Christmas lights, paper towels, celery, Taco chips, replacement for the garage opener, fresh ginger, soy sauce, rust-proof padlocks, cream of tartar, maple syrup and cold tablets. And this was only the first half of the first page. Some of these things simply were not available in Hungary; some were, but we did not yet discover where. In all probability, some of the things could be substituted with other things. I suspect that life is possible without maple syrup or Estee Lauder, but during those first, difficult, transitional times, it seemed so important to have the things to which we were used. We needed them not so much for the things themselves, but more in the way a kid needs his security blanket.

More than anything else, I hate shopping. However, I was so grateful for his presence that I tagged along happily to a number of plumbing and electrical stores to select strange things. My husband belongs to the class of men who get emotional in a hardware store. Whenever he can put his hands into little boxes with nails and washers and rivets, he is happier than any woman at a shoe store or at the cosmetics counter trying out outrageous things. My husband held long and loving monologues about various plastic or metal objects of absolutely no consequence to me. I felt richly rewarded when he considered me smart enough to ask my opinion about the whatchamacallit in his hand.

"Do you think I should take the 3mm or the 3.5 mm one?"

I tried to look intelligent and concerned and he looked at me with a beatific smile often seen on holy pictures. With the clarified happiness of saints he announced, "I'll take both. And the 4mm too. I might need them for something, don't you agree?" I definitely did. Whatever turns him on.

Before we left, we visited his daughter and her husband. When it came to say farewell, she was very quiet. A singularly self-possessed young woman, not given to emotional outbursts and sentimentality, she hugged me and said in a very little voice, "Now you are leaving us. I will miss you so. I can't even talk about it right now, but hope that you won't regret it."

"I'll miss you too," I answered, "But you do realize, don't you, that we are far from leaving you. As a matter of fact, the way it looks, we might never leave at all."

"No Judith, I feel that this is really good-bye," she sad sadly. "You are leaving us." I shuddered. There were occasions when I was almost scared of her insights. She would somehow delve into mysterious depths, look at landscapes not familiar to the rest of us, and come up quietly with statements that seemed tame, almost inconsequential. But we were always stunned when it came to pass exactly as she predicted. "How lonely the years ahead," she added.

Strange words from an extremely successful, independent, professional woman; happily married to a professional; swimming in money and surrounded by caring friends. And these words were addressed to her father's second wife, who entered the scene after the daughter was already gone from her father's house. For all practical purposes, I was a stranger to her. If she felt that sadly about thinking of the distance of a mere 1000 kilometers on the same continent, how must my own children feel on the other side of the globe? But I could not dwell on that topic, because I needed all my inner strength to say good-bye to her without making a fool of myself.

Two days later, at the crack of dawn we started the long trek to Hungary. The early start had two reasons. First, we wanted to make the trip in one day, because we did not want to park the trailer at night, packed like a well stocked general store. We did not want to lead anyone into temptation while we slept. Second, our speed was seriously restricted on account of the trailer; therefore, we wanted to avoid the heavy morning traffic in the Frankfurt area, where our slow moving vehicle would cause several brain hemorrhages as well as intemperate language from the irritable morning drivers.

Germans must be the world's most aggressive drivers. According to their technocratic religion, anything that does not move with the speed of sound and does not carry the price tag of at least a Mercedes or a BMW, should not be permitted on their expressways. Our four-cylinder put-put with an outmoded, bright-orange trailer did not belong to the Dallas category. Our poor-relative appearance would give them indigestion and bring out the worst in their characters.

They are addicted to speed. I had a good laugh in Ohio once, when I saw a young guy sporting a T-shirt that said "I survived the Autobahns of Germany." No wonder. These speed demons consider all express-ways to be racecourses and get royally vexed at slow-moving cars. Through very animated sign language they would surely show us our approximate and shatteringly low IQ levels. Or maybe the gestures mean something else, equally uncomplimentary.

As much as we both hate to get up in the morning, we made the supreme sacrifice in order to avoid the insults on the road. Being signed for hundreds of kilometers as total idiots is not the way we like to start the day. So we staggered out of bed and half-comatose rolled out into the highway at the dawn's earliest light.

But as a matter of fact, the dawn's early light was nowhere, and the road was much busier than we anticipated. Sleepily we congratulated ourselves for the early start, because at least these early birds were not as nervous as the later group, which was breaking its neck to get to the workplace. Still, between the time I uncapped the thermos for a cup of coffee and the time it took me to find my mouth, three drivers let us know in case we missed it, that something was seriously wrong with our intellects.

At one point we absolutely had to pass a truck moving even slower than we did. Its load of logs seemed to wobble dangerously, and we felt intimidated behind it. As we were passing it, the driver, obviously ticked off that such a lowly vehicle as ours dared to pass him, rolled down his window and spotting me in the passenger seat yelled the insult at me, "*Alte Hexe*". I was spitting fire. I could (maybe) forgive the word *Hexe* but old??? Old witch? Who does he think he is to call me that? What did I ever do to him?

"I'll hex you, you old warlock," I fumed, but of course, he couldn't hear me.

"Relax," spoke the Man at the Wheel calmly. "He is in some sort of a rage, and until he fixes himself, there is no helping him. It has nothing to do with you; it is entirely his problem. Maybe he is constipated, or had a row with his wife before he left. Your trouble is that you under-stand the language; therefore, the words have the power to injure you. But say *alte Hexe* in another, more poetic language, which is less familiar to you than German is, such as the Italian, or French, and you'll sense the difference. Doesn't *vieille sorciere* sound enchanting, like the name of an expensive perfume? Or take the robust *vecchia strega* and you can see the Tuscan hills and smell the exciting fragrance of thyme and garlic. I get hungry just thinking it. Both mean approximately the same, *alte Hexe*. But what a difference! If you know the language, words have associations attached to them; if you don't, you only react to the melody of the strange words. You know what I mean? It is a sort of a cultural literacy. You share with that driver a lot of nasty memories attached to the word *Hexe*, as in Hansel and Gretel; therefore, by applying the word to you, he has the power to insult you. But *sorciere* is virginal, void of any connotations as far as you are concerned. It could be anything you want it to be, even a compliment. Look at it that way and it will stop bothering you what these yokels are blubbering."

While I finished my coffee, he was warming to his subject.

"Of course, you could always yell back to get even. There are really wonderful insults to use. For example, *pachiderma insensibile* that in his own language would translate as *dickfelliges Nilpferd*, meaning thick-skinned hippopotamus, which is not exactly complimentary in English either. Or you could resort to words that have similar root words in many languages and are easily understood even by those who can hardly speak their own correctly. *Idiota, deficiente,* or *cretino* really mean the very same thing they keep signing to us. Unless, of course, you'd rather not sink to their level. In that case ignore them and give me a slug of your coffee."

We laughed and my anger evaporated, although it is still a mystery, why the driver of a vehicle, who is pulling a trailer and is observing the speed limit imposed on him for the safety of other drivers, is necessarily retarded. And why would his wife turn automatically into an old witch? To amuse myself, I imagined a party or a reception, where dressed in evening attire, with a glass of imported champagne in our hands, we would be mingling with cultured guests in polite company. Suddenly, one of these drivers would appear, also dressed in his best. Then I imagined the hostess, a most gracious lady, glide up to us in her evening gown and pearls to make the introductions. Would the said driver then say to my husband, "Hello, you congenital idiot; glad to meet your stupid face," then turn to me smilingly and say in his best company voice, "How do you do old hag? Do you still ride your damned broom, or have you finally learned to handle a car?" Maybe he would say that, but I never had that kind of experience yet. Thank goodness. Why would he say that while riding on the expressway? Does his car empower him to be insulting?

When something goes wrong, such as a strange noise from the engine or an insult on the road, I like to turn on the car radio. It wipes out the sick sound from the engine and drowns out the insults from the passing cars. We were just in time for the five-thirty news. After the familiar clarion sound, the date and the time were announced, after which the designated driver almost drove into the median strip, trailer and all, he was that shocked.

"It is not five-thirty! It is midnight!" His voice faltered with disbelief and pain. He sounded like the man, who just discovered that after all, he did not inherit the ten million dollars he expected. "It's not morning yet! It isn't even night yet!"

I must have messed up the alarm clock when I set it. We were more than fifty miles from my apartment, and it was midnight, definitely not five in the morning. For the next five minutes my husband was serious about turning back for the sake of a few more hours of sleep. Fortunately, there was no exit for the next thirty miles and by that time he calmed down and common sense prevailed. We drove on. According to my recollections, this was the only time we were on the road at the time we planned to be there. As a matter of fact, we were several hours early. Anyhow, it worked out quite well, because by noon the longer part of our journey was behind us. This was fortunate, because by then the heat was melting the roof of our car.

Half of our team in this marriage is rational; therefore, he bought the hardtop version as opposed to the canvas-top, convertible model of this car, for reasons of longevity. Not ours, but that of the roof. Maybe the roof would indeed last the life of the car, but with that inhuman temperature I seriously doubted whether we would. Oh, what I wouldn't have given for that happily flapping roof of the other model that could be peeled back, while passengers and belongings would all be blown out of it. But the Man, in his maddeningly rational manner, explained that with an open roof, we would probably have to make six trips to haul home all my junk. (Note the possessive pronoun!) We had to use a shoehorn to fit everything in, as it is, he added darkly.

Actually the car had an air-conditioner, but since we pulled such a heavy load, the above gentleman, a real stickler for such things, did not permit me to turn it on. He felt that the AC would take off too much power and, if we drove any slower than our present speed, we would be going backward. I was the captive audience of a very boring lecture, the main points of which had to do with the weight we were pulling, the capacity of the engine and such. The enlightening information was closed with the dismal reminder that we must pamper the car, because who knows when we could afford to replace it, if ever.

So, we melted away by degrees, while the car was laughing at us through its tailpipe. I was keeping myself alive by recalling the snow-blown winters of 1976 and 1977 in Cleveland, when schools closed, traffic came to a sliding halt and the snow was so immense that it had to be carted away in trucks from the parking lots and the roads. The big heroes of that year were not the Cleveland Browns, but the snow-clearing crew.

We took turns driving, and there were times, when my husband snoozed while I drove. My eyes were smarting from the perspiration dripping into them from my forehead, so very quietly, gently and with the cautious, precise movement of one, who is getting ready to defuse a bomb, I reached for the knob and turned on the AC. But this man, who will not waken for an earthquake (not a figure of speech either, since we did have one and he *did* sleep through it), immediately opened his eyes when the cool air started to flow.

"Dearest," he said. As I said before, it is no good when he calls me 'dearest'. It is a sure sign that he is vexed. "We agreed not to use that damned thing." And with that, the subject was closed for further discussion. I was slowly frying behind the wheel and did not wish well for the car that was pampered more than I was.

I passed the time thinking of ways to improve the car. Could a can-opener be used to make the Tracker into a convertible? We had an opener in our lunch kit. Would Detroit consider a plan for building a mini-pool into the car seat? The idea was irresistible. I could see myself splashing down the highway in perfect, cool comfort, waving insulting signs and shouting in Hungarian 'izzadt bivaly' –sweaty buffalo—to the sweating German drivers. If there are bucket seats, why not tub seats? Detroit has no imagination when it comes to practical things.

During the long drive we also had time for talks. He was filling me in with the work that was happening, or not happening in Hungary on our house.

"It is so difficult to get the craftsmen and their helpers to show up at the promised time," he complained. "I visit them daily and we make up the schedule for the following day. Nobody shows up. I'm baffled. People want to work; they need the jobs, the money, yet I cannot count on them. They accept more jobs than they can handle, so as not to lose an order, and then they juggle things. They would work here a half day, there a day, so that nobody is satisfied, but nobody is totally frustrated either, because when it comes to the breaking point, unexpectedly they would turn up and work furiously for a day. Things do get done eventually, but you never know when. Whoever said that Canaan was the Promised Land? The real land of promises is Hungary. I spend my time running after people who promise and promise and promise, but never deliver."

"But things do get accomplished, don't they?" I asked, because I was worried about the promise that he would join me before Christmas.

"In a manner of speaking. Sooner or later. More like later. And you know, they have no plans how they would proceed with a job on any given day in the unlikely event that they would actually show up, when promised. They don't know, or don't tell, what materials they need to accomplish a task. When their complicated schedule permits it, they would show up at six in the morning, or even earlier, without tools and in need of all sorts of material they never mentioned before. So I jump into the car trying to buy a truckload of sand before the sun is up, then go in search for a truck that would deliver it. After barely three hours (while said workers sit and smoke and watch the clouds float by) I get back from my seven-town excursion and count myself lucky for having been able to secure sand and truck in record time. Are they ready to work now? Hell, no. Now they want six sacks of cement...By the time the cement arrives, their time is up. But they promise to get back soon."

This did not sound like the house would ever be finished. And my personal glue was holding me together only as long as I could hope that he would join me in Germany before Christmas.

"But amazingly, we are still making progress," he continued. "The brick walls are up, the roof was removed and rebuilt to make the old house with the addition into a coherent unit."

"And?"

"And nothing more. It is a miracle that we are as far as this. The world wasn't created in a day either." Where did I hear that before? "There are still no windows, doors, floors, electricity or plumbing in the new wing."

"And the old part?" I wanted to know. "Will those rooms be livable at least?"

"I don't want to upset you and it is not as bad as it sounds. And it will be fixed in no time, don't worry."

"Don't worry about what?" I knew that he would tell me news I didn't want to hear.

"The roofers, after removing all the shingles from the old house, were not showing up for two weeks," he explained. "The roofless house was totally exposed during the downpour that lasted on and off for a week. I tried to pitch a huge sheet of plastic where the roof used to be, but it did not work well and within hours it was torn to shreds. Water did get into the house."

"I see." And I could. Waterlogged books and clothing, smelling forever of mold. The pale brocades of chairs and couches displaying crazy, map-like watermarks, my exquisite oriental dining room furniture warping its ebony finish. I briefly considered the state of televisions, video, and computer that are not recommended to have extensive baths or moisture treatments. I recalled the condition of the ceiling in our future study that was ready to fall down when I last saw it, before the deluge.

It was a strange ceiling anyhow. At the start, more than hundred and fifty years ago, the room had open beams, like the other two rooms, but a later owner found it too rustic and not elegant enough. Ingenuously, the long dead craftsman wove and wired sheaves and sheaves of reeds into flat pieces of mat, which he nailed to the beams. He filled the cracks with mud, which he mixed with chopped straw, then applied an uncommonly thick stucco over it. The result was a much lower, flat, white ceiling, the epitome of city elegance, as far as he was concerned.

"Well, the ceiling caved in," he told me. "But you have no idea how beautiful the beams are that are suddenly exposed. They are even better than the ones in the bedroom. We wanted to rip out that ceiling anyhow, so now we do it a little earlier than planned." That is my man. He would see some advantage in the bubonic plague.

"Does it look bad?"

"Naw, although I have seen better scenes. I covered the furniture and the crates with plastic. But you should have seen what everything came down from the ceiling! Entire skeletons of chickens and ducks. Apparently some meat-eating animal was holed up there and it liked to take its meals into its parlor." He was cheerful and probably did not even notice my shock. I was wondering whether the house would be completed by the time my grandchildren graduate from college.

And then to change the subject to something happier, he finally confessed what he did not have the nerve to tell me all week.

"We have a dog!" I was stunned and he took my silence for speechless delight. "It is some kind of a terrier, a male, and very, very smart. He was lost, hungry, full of ticks and so skinny I didn't think it would make it. But he is clean now, has all his shots, eats like a horse and you'll love him."

I had my doubts about that. Indeed, I love animals, but I had years of experience with "strays", that used to follow my son all the way home. As a result, we spent a fortune on veterinary bills and dog food, and became experts in the art of tick removal. While they recuperated from the vicissitudes of their adventurous life, we had ample opportunities to discover all the weaknesses of their character that made them strays to begin with. Unlike our own dogs, which could not be chased away from the house, these guests did not stick around for long. I think the word was out that we are a combination of halfway house, hospital, hotel and gourmet restaurant. Like tramps, they must have left signs behind on the roads for other strays. "Don't miss this house. Food, shelter, medication and a bunch of real suckers."

But as soon as they felt their strength returning, the road with its siren song called, and they were gone, leaving a broken-hearted little boy behind. I hated when they appeared, because it was written all over them that all they wanted was to get well, then get on with their irresponsible lives. If room service was offered, so much the better, and my son's sorrow was none of their business. Incidentally, unlike our own pets, these were all males.

Boys will be boys, and apparently my husband was not much different from my son in this respect. And his new dog was a male, no less. Knowing their straying habits, their preference to pee on prize bushes and flowers, I swore long ago that no male dog would ever enter my house. I happen to be choosy when it comes to pets. I would accept goldfish, a bird perhaps, (but not a chicken) a neutered cat could be negotiated, a bitch any time, but definitely no male dogs.

"How did he follow you home, when you do not consider walking fifty feet if you can avoid it?"

"You are so unfair. I do take long walks. The dog needs the exercise." It did not elude me that he did not answer my question. "He is wonderful. I took him to the vet and he also says that it is a neat dog." Why wouldn't he say that? The terrier is his patient, and my husband is a paying customer and an obvious sucker. Veterinary ethics calls for a praise, even when none is warranted. "You'll love him," he repeated his mantra. I know. Isn't that what the man at the Regional Office told me too? You'll love teaching again. The world sure knows what I would love.

The dog already had a name, Törpi. It is a sweet, diminutive form of the word dwarf, or troll, or leprechaun. Like a ceramic garden dwarf. Come to think of it, I hate them as much as the pink flamingoes, but did not want to make an issue out of what he decided to call his dog.

"Why Törpi?" was all I asked.

"Well, he is sort of vertically challenged. Nice body and all, but sort of short legs."

"A terrier, built like a spaniel?"

"Not really, You'll see. Long, stiff hair and a huge, intelligent head. Of course, if you don't like him, I could give it away. Several people want him real bad. They say it is a great dog for boar hunting. But I'm sure that you'll like him. In the long months while you were not here, the best moments were when he put his paws on my knees and just looked up at me with those wonderful, big, faithful eyes. This is the first dog I have since I was a kid, and it is wonderful. It's all in the eyes, you'll see."

The mesmerizing eyes of Törpi of the short legs and the big head reminded me of a story told by a friend of ours. He had an uncle, who was widely respected for his keen intellect, classical education, cultured taste, wit, and delightful conversation. He was a youthful sixty-year old, tall, elegant, and sought after for social gatherings. People felt honored when he invited them to his magnificent home and to his lavish table, for which he was justly famous. One day, out of the clear blue sky, this discriminating professional bachelor announced at a family gathering that he was getting married. The surprise his words evoked was only topped by the degree of disbelief when he named his betrothed: his corpulent, bossy housekeeper of limited intelligence. She was not pretty when she was young and that was so long ago that even she could no longer remember it. The passing of years did not improve her looks, although she was very kind, cooked superbly and was obviously devoted to her employer.

When the shock subsided enough so that a halfway intelligent conversation could resume, someone gasped, "But why? Why from all the women in the world did you choose Annie?" The gentleman thought about this for a while, as if the question did not occur to him before, then answered in a convincing tone, "She has fabulous eyes."

So perhaps the eyes really have it. If she could get married to a most desirable bachelor on the strength of her fabulous eyes, why should Törpi find it difficult to get adopted with a similar feature?

I did have a fear all along that this enforced loneliness of my Significant Other would prove too much for him. I wasn't really worried that he would cheat on me, but I was not prepared to face a four-legged rival with beautiful eyes. The question is: am I sexy enough at sixty-one to compete with this intruder? I will need to practice putting my hands on his knees and looking up at him faithfully blinking my fabulous eyes.

"Your sister-in-law used to think that he was beautiful," my husband reported. "But then one day he snatched several of her chickens and took off with the loot. Now she hates him."

Aha. There are some shady areas in his character after all. On the other hand, I too hate those chickens. They are noisy, smelly and not very picky eaters. I have seen them gobble up such awful things that as a result I don't even want to see them roasted and served on a bed of watercress and arugula. Maybe, after all, I'll learn to get along with Törpi. We might need each other yet.

We arrived at the Hungarian border in the early afternoon. The heavy traffic slowed somewhat at the border check, but mercifully it never came to a standstill. In that heat it could have had sinister consequences. It was hard to tell who was more exhausted from the inhuman temperatures: the passengers in their overheated cars (at that time many of the

European cars did not have air conditioning,), or the officials in their smart uniforms, designed for another climate.

I was nervous, as I always am, when I see uniforms. I don't know the reason for this phobia, and although working for over a decade on military bases, it diminished some, but never quite left me. I get uptight when I see a policeman, or these agents at the borders. I understand dogs that go ballistic when they see the uniforms of the postal deliveryman or the UPS man. Only a sense of dignity holds me back from howling along with the canines.

This blurred sense of anguish, induced by the sight of uniforms, was quite focused this time. After all, we had about hundreds of pounds of strange items stashed away in our car and in the trailer. In addition to the household items that we hauled with an official permit, all the cracks, nooks and crannies were padded with stuff I bought 'to tie us over'. For someone who hates to shop as much as I do, I managed to collect an amazing amount of supplies. I was like the ant in John Ciardi's poem, a delightfully lop-sided version of the old fable. (John J. Plenty and Fiddler Dan, 1963). I was the industrious but very materialistic ant. While the artistically inclined cricket sang about the beauties of the world, and so added to the delight of anyone who heard him, I was blind and deaf to it all and concentrated on rushing about collecting things for the lean times. An imperative voice, like the one Ciardi's ant heard, commanded me relentlessly, "More! Get more! Get more!" Soon my good intentions and responsible foresight were demoralized into common greed. At the very thought that henceforth I would have to do without what in my opinion were life's essentials, I was totally immersed in a state of panic, verging on the pathological.

This fear did not tolerate common sense, and I never considered the reaction of the custom agent when the boxes of potato flakes and bottles of nail polish removers would be revealed. The car was packed, and the trailer was limping from its shameless weight. Too late I was worried sick that I had too much of everything. Deeply contrite and fully aware of my guilt, I remembered the six boxes of dishwasher detergent. Also, there were twenty boxes of Jell-O, all lime, lemon and orange for the summer salads we both love. What is the amount of sun-dried tomatoes that is still within the legal limit?

And what if the agent would ask me to list what I have to declare, like they do on an airplane? My mind went totally blank and I could not remember more than five items that we packed. Even as I write this, I cannot recall what was it that we pulled across three countries on that hot summer day. But there we were with the loot and I prayed for heavenly intervention. I also swore that this would be the first and last time when I would let myself be carried away with shopping, or with attempts to smuggle. I would never have more than one item of anything, if that much.

There was only one thing I wanted to do at that point. I wanted to turn back and throw the contents of both the car and trailer into the nearest city dump, then return to the border crossing, all clean and innocent. And with the air-conditioning going full blast. But this was an idle dream. Behind us, in triple file, were about six hundred cars in each lane. We couldn't have turned back if I were in the last stages of labor pains before delivery. Also, I was sure that Austrian dump guards were no less lenient than the Germans. They too would have us sort the things according to size, color and expiration date. The plan was impractical.

It was our turn at the booth and my hands were dripping with nervous perspiration. I so wished I could be cool about this thing. I admire those sassy, young and beautiful ladies in the movies, who do the most outrageous things, then get away with it by flashing their personal charm. I could just see Barbra Streisand, Goldie Hawn, Whoopi Goldberg, Julia Roberts or Oprah Winfrey in my shoes, and I was seething with envy. They would get away with it and make the audience roar with laughter as they were doing it.

Even when young and better looking, I did not have their spunk or glamour. There was not a chance in a million that I could joke my way out of this now. I knew that when questioned, I would babble and look guiltier than Pinocchio. They would immediately know that a world class smuggler was caught. I suddenly realized that one does not really need all those trivial things that I felt compelled to buy. One can live a meaningful life without Jell-O. And what about those nails my husband bought? My pulse was racing; blood pressure and sugar were probably off the chart by now, and my mouth felt like cotton. I always respected every "thou shall not" warning and never stepped on the grass when the sign said not to. And yet, despite such impeccable past, there I was with maybe two hundred kilos of God knows what. (I switched into thinking in metrics, because it sounded less.) Then it was our turn.

The agent did not even look at our papers, could not care less that we actually had permission to haul at least some of the stuff. He waved to us to move on. Was that all? No questions, no forms to fill out, no duties to pay, no inspecting of every box and bag? No quizzing under a single light bulb, no torture chamber? Am I getting so old that I no longer look capable of criminal behavior? It was quite clear that no drama was to take place. The guard mumbled his greeting, which he repeated thousands of times, "Welcome to Hungary and have a pleasant stay," then he turned his wilting smile to the next car.

It was astonishingly easy and I should never have worried about it at all, as my husband was rude enough to point out before and after the encounter. For heaven's sakes, I should have bought some more of that Jell-O, especially since it was on sale. Five packs for the price of four. And why was I so frugal with the dishwasher detergent? How long will six boxes last? When it is all gone, I might as well throw away my dishwasher, since I won't be able to buy the detergent for it. Contrition, like good intentions, lasts just as long as that.

"I'm sorry to inconvenience you sir," intruded my husband's polite voice into my blissful state of relief, "but we have guns."

The guns! In my worry about the Jell-O, I totally forgot them.

"Oh, god, no!" groaned the officer in extreme pain, then asked hopefully "When did you receive the permission to bring them into the country?" When he heard that it was in March, more than three months ago, he almost wept as he directed us to pull to the side. If the guns are brought in within a certain period of time after permission is granted, a simple stamp on the documents is sufficient. As it was, some serious paperwork was ahead.

My husband tried to find a shady spot to park in order to avoid a car meltdown and a deep-fried wife while he followed the arduous steps of the red-tape dance. All he could find was the slender shadow of a telephone pole, where he left me in melancholy solitude.

He is a hunter, or at least that is what he calls himself, which is why we have the guns. I know this runs against some people's moral beliefs, including mine. I don't like Bambi on a platter, or Bugs Bunny in a stew. I also hate to be left alone for long hours worrying which of the hunters would kill his best friend during this singularly male pastime. Memorable is the farmer, who in order to avoid misunderstandings, painted in large letters "COW " on the side of his animal. As far as I'm concerned, I enjoy target shooting at flying (tossed) clay figures, at circles on a paper, but would never hurt an animal.

I know all the arguments hunters use to defend their practice, the best of which is that of my husband: just like me, he does not shoot at living things either. In his entire life he only shot a single deer and he did that out of compassion. While tramping it the woods under the pretense of "hunting", he came upon the deer. It was caught in a terrible trap and its body was a mangled mass, suffering beyond measure, beyond sound and way past any help. He pulled the trigger then. He knows that this single act will ensure his admittance to heaven. On a red carpet, with Gabriel blowing his trumpet.

But this hunter of mine loves to tramp in the woods. It holds some magic fascination for him. The colder it is, the more he likes it. When snow is crunching under his boots and the world is frozen still, he finds his absolute peace.

He cherishes the long, silent wait in the moonlight, the unforgettable sight of a stag stepping out of the woods, like the apparition from an ancient legend. Holding his breath he would gaze at it in wonder, then let it go unharmed.

He also enjoys the conviviality of his hunting buddies, and that strange male bonding they all seem to need.

He could, of course, do all the tramping and waiting and crunching under the legitimate excuse of taking a walk, and could do all his male bonding in the living room with a few bottles of excellent wine. But I guess one must carry a gun to be taken seriously in the society of real men. Apparently the inconvenience of the added weight one carries and the ritualistic oiling of the guns add something to the macho image. Leaving the forest as they found it, he and his buddies always return from their excursions in high spirits, hungry and thirsty and exuding masculine charm. Come to think of it, this behavior is not so strange. I have a girlfriend who does not know how to swim, but has a marvelous swimming pool. I also have several other friends, who own dream kitchens, but consider cooking an aberration practiced during the past centuries. So, why shouldn't my husband own a gun, but not shoot with it?

So there I was frying, while my husband spread out the papers and stamps to prove that we are licensed hunters with registered guns and we are not smuggling contraband into the country. Let no one think that this process was easy, let alone swift. The minutes sifted down into the impersonal void that was time, while I waited, more or less well done. At long last they emerged from the building, because the agent had to see the guns in order to verify make and model.

Needless to say, it was my privilege to dig out the guns from among Jell-O boxes, bed sheets, Teflon pans, an ironing board and delicately wilting celery leaves. My undignified digging was accompanied by the absolutely wicked glances and cheers of all, who passed the border at the time. Half of our household goods were neatly piled on the sidewalk, while I dug and attempted to look somewhat less embarrassed, but more elegant and dignified than your average bag lady. At that moment a *cretino confusianario* yelled at me from his car, "Hey lady, what are you selling today? Can we have a deal?" He was just lucky that my gun was in the hands of the agent.

CHAPTER FOUR

We pulled up in front of our house at Szabar at the time when the afternoon sun mellowed the colors into muted pastel shades. The blue of the sky lost its midday intensity, and softened into a gentle luminance accented by a light blue haze. Softly sculpted clouds, like dollops of whipped cream, glided lazily, and the air was full of the fragrances of summer. In the strange oblique light, the objects seemed to have dark edges, as if the Supreme Artist had outlined every house and tree, every hill and the steeple of the church with a soft charcoal. It was a perfect and beautiful day. I got out of the car, glanced up at the house on the slight hill, and slowly my tears started to roll down on my cheeks.

The house, our house, was beautiful.

It was still only a skeleton, but what a promise! The solid brick walls, without the stucco as yet, vaguely resembled a medieval castle, at least to my eyes. The spaces where the six large arched windows and the front door would be, were perfect. In Ohio we lived in a ranch type frame house, and I was not used to massive, thick walls, high roofs, or such an elevated foundation. The roof was so tall that we could have easily built an apartment in the attic. There were nine steps from the street level to the garden gate, then five more steps up to the entrance door. We were no longer earthbound. The red tiles on the roof were overpowering.

The windows, or rather the holes, where the windows would be, were my husband's own design and they are absolutely perfect in proportion.

Many hours were spent on our huge bed, while he figured out how large and what shape they ought to be. He remembered that there was a rule for the perfect proportion, which would create the visually most pleasing shape. However, in the prevailing chaos, we could not find the particular reference book we needed. He had to depend on his memory for the formula of the golden section. Unlike his wife, he does not seem to suffer yet from memory loss, and eventually he was able to work it out. He started out with a shape in which the ratio of the width to the length is about the same as the ratio of the length to the sum of the width and length. Keeping in mind this ratio, he calculated the size he wanted, then added to it the arched top and repeated the calculations, just to make sure. Using yet another formula, he divided the wood frame (to be made of Russian red cedar) into segments to hold the glass panes. It was so perfectly worked out that Laci, the carpenter, could hardly wait to start working on it. This eagerness on his part was a miracle by itself, because this man is so slow in completing anything that he was unanimously elected to be the deliveryman of all necessary bad luck. The villagers reasoned that if Laci, known for his legendary snail speed, would be the one to bring it, bad luck would never reach Szabar. But so intrigued was he by this crazy gentleman, (my husband), who used a square root to figure out the shape of a window, that he actually enjoyed making them. In the end, to the immense surprise of everybody, he actually completed them within a year, a rare accomplishment at his speed. He was so delighted by the results that he even asked to be photographed with his finished products.

Even after the house has been finally completed, most people first exclaim about the beauty of the windows. Of course, on that memorable day, when I had my first glance at our home, I did not know (or cared), how he subtracted 1 from the square root of 5 and then divided it by 2 to get an approximate value of the golden section. I did not even think then about the teachers, who taught so well that this man, nearing seventy, could still remember a formula and a rule, which as I suspect, he never had a reason to use in his adult life. All I felt was total awe and bottomless gratitude for the man, who was creating this wonderful home for me, for us. Years later I am quite used to our domain, but the moment of that first glance was so intense that to this day I can clearly recollect every detail, every color, every nuance, every fragrance, every emotion that I experienced at that moment. I even know exactly what he wore and what I wore, although I am not able to remember a good joke told five minutes ago. Names and my own telephone number escape me, but I remember very clearly that moment in time, the same as most people remember what they were doing when they heard that President

Kennedy was assassinated.

Of course at that time, other than the walls and the roof, there was nothing else. But there was a terrace with a recessed portico in front of what one day would be the front door. The red tiles had a warm shine, as if somebody had poured oil over the roof, which hung generously over the walkway on the side of the house between garden gate and front door, spreading shade and as I correctly supposed, protection from rain and snow in bad weather.

"It is gorgeous," I gasped. "I did not think it would be that beautiful."

"I'm glad you like it," he answered simply in that special voice he has when he is fighting emotions. "I think otherwise I would have put a match to it."

And so we entered into the hallway. Or pretended to, since there was no door yet.

The new addition wrapped around the old house like a letter L. The spacious entry through the portico was in the middle of the vertical stem of the L. The entry's partial wall divided the huge space into a new living room to the left and a dining room to the right. The partial wall had two slender gothic window openings (for purely decorative purposes), and it defined the areas visually, without actually closing them off, so that the entire addition was open, airy, light and appeared larger than it really was.

"These are the confessionals," he said pointing at the gothic windows. "You'll sit behind one and listen to the men, and I at the other to absolve the womenfolk. Afterward we'll drink to their sins."

Straight across the new entry was the opening to the old house. The old door was replaced with a new one; the cut glass panes with leaded inserts were already ordered. Behind this door the old house was left intact.

From the dining room, the addition wrapped around the northern wall; this was the horizontal stem of the letter L. This part contained the breakfast area, the new kitchen, and a room that would eventually turn into a butler's pantry, or rather a bar and serving area, when we would be eating outdoors. Unfortunately, we don't belong the privileged class where butlers ask, "you rang, madame?", in which case the nomen "butler's pantry" is stretching it. However, as we were to find out later, it turned into a very convenient and much liked place as the years went by.

A door from here led to the old part of the house, which consisted of the oversized hallway and the original three rooms. These formed a totally private unit of a bedroom, study, one bath, already functioning, and a future master bath, which however, at that time still served as a makeshift kitchen. Thus, we could walk a complete circle in the house, using a smooth and logical traffic pattern. It was absolutely perfect.

There was a back entrance from the butler's pantry behind the kitchen, which would eventually lead into the section of the house that was not yet built. That future area would contain the winter garden, the garage, the guestrooms, the larder, my husband's shop, where he could tinker, and the housekeeper's unit.

But for now this was it. Just the walls and the openings for the future windows. The stucco-like plaster on the inside was still dripping wet. Rubble covered the cement floors to my knees. Piles of bricks, empty sacks, a large assortment of lumber pieces, pails with stucco sticking to them, and above all dozens of empty bottles. But the mess did not bother me. The house would be beautiful, I could see that now, and I was happy and felt compensated for all the ills I had to endure.

It was our first house, and of course, also our last. We planned it ourselves, while alternating between patient care and intelligent exasperation, typical of fairly smart people who are about to do a job they know nothing about, but want absolute perfection. We tailored the house to our own needs and formed it so that its main function would be to make us happy and comfortable. Visual sublimities counted more than practical or economic considerations. I was generating more ideas and wishes then we could use in ten houses, but since I cannot draw a straight line, it was up to my husband to translate my dreams to a graph paper, complete with specifications, if need be with square roots and such. It was amazing how he could grasp what I wanted; he probably missed his vocation and should have been teaching autistic children.

Nobody else seemed to understand what I wanted, and the sentence I most often heard was, "It cannot be done. Nobody does it that way." I remember the inspector who came to see about the electrical wiring. He stared with open curiosity at the window openings in my future kitchen.

"Excuse me, what will be the function of this room and what are those strange openings in the walls? He wanted to know.

"This will be my kitchen and those are very logical windows and not strange openings."

"Windows?" he asked and looked at me with rude suspicion to see if I was all complete in the head. "Near the ceiling? And how do you plan to see out of them? And what about that long low one you people put on the north wall? And that narrow slit there?"

There was nothing mysterious or avant garde about the collection of different shaped windows at different heights in my kitchen. I am not too tall and was sick and tired of never being able to reach the top shelves in my cabinets, of which I have enough to cover two walls, so we placed them lower than most builders would. Not willing to be without the light I love, we planned some of the windows up, above the cabinets, just under the ceiling. But I like to look out when I work, so I wanted a nice long one over one of the countertops, just at eye level. One of the six windows on the eastern facade belongs to the breakfast area, but I wanted even more light there, so we added an identical arched window on the northern wall, but only half as wide as the others. This is what he called "narrow slit". So, it is true that the north wall had an assortment of openings for windows of different sizes and at various heights, but the arrangement was very functional, logical and just right for me.

"Well," he said shaking his head. "I've seen many unusual houses, but this beats them all. Do you have any idea how strange your northern wall looks from the outside?" I didn't, because I never looked at it from my sister-in-law's messy barnyard. I had a need for the cabinets to be placed low, and wanted lots of light. That was that. I really did not care what her chickens were thinking about my wall, or my windows. At least they had something to talk about.

I kept walking through the rooms, delighting in the spacious areas after my cramped attic prison. When I was done looking at every corner a dozen times, we walked outside through the back door and the sight greeting us was truly awful. Aside from the ordinary rubbish generated by any construction, (especially by a crew who would never consider cleaning up after themselves), there was also a small mountain of discarded funeral wreaths from the cemetery. Man to dust, and flowers to compost is the order of the world. But the local people, a frugal lot, do not like to spend money on such transitory things as real flowers, and they embraced enthusiastically the alternative. These wreaths in our yard were made of very cheap plastic flowers, wound into wire frames, now slowly giving up their ghosts to rust. The flowers were made to withstand decay, ice, sleet, snow, rain, extremes of weather, stock market fluctuations and time. I think they would have been able to withstand a nuclear explosion without the slightest change in their basic ugliness.

The creators of these plastic wonders did not even bother to imitate the real thing, but came up with a new brand, mostly in primary colors. The new product was definitely not an improvement over the ones carefully created on the third day and permitted to evolve through eons to become the perfection we recognize today as flowers, and sold at prices one can only negotiate with a platinum credit card.

After many years of sun and rain, the glaring colors of the plastic faded into still uglier shades, but the basic vileness of the concept and execution remained unchanged. One must admit though that these flowers are very practical and cost-effective. There is an initial investment when it is first purchased for the dear departed at the time of the funeral. For the next thirty years a good dusting once in awhile will keep the colors going. However, there are some really caring relatives, who buy a new one every couple of years. Since compost does not happen to plastic, but in time they must be pitched somewhere, we were the unhappy recipients of these slightly used wreaths. I sighed piously as I realized that plastic is indestructible, and unlike the rest of us, enjoys an everlasting life on earth, or more precisely said, in our yard.

"Looks bad, but not any worse than the house did, remember? And look what happened to that in just a few months," my husband reassured me as we surveyed the mess. "Given a little time, the yard and patio will look just as good as the house. What people messed up, people can clean up again." I agreed, and we tried to forget about the extreme difficulty of cleaning up a place when there is no garbage collection, nor a city dump. We stood in the afternoon sun and laughed. And I marveled where all this happiness was coming from, since a few months ago I was still sunk into the deepest depression and ennui.

"We feel this way, because we are still young," he told me. "Life starts at sixty-five. The great advantage is that we have so much experience in living that it is impossible to mess up our life, or our goals. Or the house we are building."

Some people say that two houses must be built, before the right one, the third house, is acceptable. They explain that the first one is usually so bad that it is only fit for our enemies. The second one is better; it is for our friends. The third house is the perfect one, because by that time we have matured to the point where we know ourselves and have discovered what kind of life is good and comfortable for us. This is the house for ourselves, says the folk wisdom. Luckily our house, the one and only we ever built, reflects both the self-awareness and the tranquility we achieved during our lives, and it shows (and serves) the ways in which we like to spend our time and also the things that are really important to us. Apparently we are lucky, because we were allowed to skip building for our enemies or for our friends. Our first house really is for us and us alone.

"Darling," my husband whispered next morning. "I hate to do this to you…"

"Then please, don't, " I mumbled, hoping to sink back into blissful sleep to recuperate from the collection of aches and pains in various parts of my body, a result of the long, uninterrupted drive.

"When in Rome, do as the Romans do; when in Szabar, do feed your workers, if you hope to see them again. They got here at five, expect breakfast at ten, dinner at four. I wish you could rest, but I can't help you. I must be out supervising them," he said. I suspected all along that there was a snake in Paradise.

I stumbled out into the room that was to be my kitchen for a while, and winced. I could reach the makeshift countertop's tiny workspace, provided I moved sideways and watched my step in order to avoid the various traps on the floor. But if I wanted to use the hot plate or the microwave on the other side, I would have to go around the protruding washing machine, as if I was a perpetual pendulum. We did learn in school that a free-swinging pendulum moves through a circular arc, which seemed fairly logical. While the shape of the curve made by this hypothetical pendulum is deducible from the parametric equations (and I have long forgotten how that goes, mostly because I could never see any reason for remembering it) my personal swinging curve was defined by the bulk of the washer. Work on one side, then swing to the other side to cook.

As a child I was fascinated by the rituals of the Catholic Church, and followed with great interest the priest as he walked from one side of the altar to the other. At times he would stop in the middle and turn toward the congregation, spread out his arms and intone, *"Dominus vobiscum"*, or "the Lord is with you". I was very young, and did not yet study Latin (which was the official language of the Church at that time, which proves how old I am!); however, I had a German nanny, and learned to speak that language at a very early age. Misunderstanding the words in the echoing church, I thought the priest was speaking in German, and was asking the people, *"Dominus, wo bist du?"* or "Lord, where are you?" There wasn't anyone there, who would tell the servant of the Church where to look for the hiding Lord. His search puzzled me anyhow; nobody was in a better position to know the Lord's whereabouts than the priest was. But each Sunday the poor man was looking for the Lord all over again, just like my grandfather for his reading glasses. I found it fascinating how he kept walking from one side of the altar to the other, stopping at dead center to sing his question, while all eyes followed him. I decided that when I grow up I'd want to be a priest.

That morning in Szabar, as I tried to start the coffee and moved from left to right and back again, making a slight turn at the center to avoid the washer, I remembered my long-ago misunderstanding. I wondered if it would be appropriate to turn away from the machine and facing an imaginary congregation, with arms spread, sing out a very relevant and pressing question, "wo bist du?" Of course, I knew where the Lord was. He was in His heaven. What I did not know was where my coffee filter was. Or the coffee. Come to think of, I could not find the pot either.

Despite the inconvenience, I was far from being unhappy about the washer or its awkward placement. On the contrary. As far as I was concerned, I was willing to run around the house in circles as long as I had the machine. The memory of the washday during my previous stay in Szabar was still vivid in my mind, and the excuse of "Not tonight, darling... I did the big wash", took on a new meaning. Silently and with contrition I mumbled my apologies to my sisters down the centuries for my cynical laugh at the phrase, and at all the jokes connected with it. I fully understood during the ordeal while doing our laundry, why a normal female could not turn amorous after a day at the tub. This is a foolproof method to practice birth control and I am sure that mothers in the Middle Ages passed it down to their daughters, together with the recipes to make perfect frumenty, mortrews and blank mang.

As soon as my sister-in-law noticed my preparation for the wash on that day (to be done outdoors), she offered me the use of her washing machine. As I said before, she is generous.

"It is an excellent Russian make; the best there is," she assured me as she bustled about setting it up and getting ready to instruct me in its proper usage. "I had it for many years now, and it never disappointed me." She started to sound like a TV commercial.

This wonderful piece of machinery turned out to be a five-gallon plastic drum. The shock came when I realized that it was not made to be attached to a water outlet or to the drainage system. We placed a small chair in the bathtub and placed this excellent state-of-the-art machine on it, then plugged it into an electric outlet. Since her shower hose did not reach it, we filled the drum by pouring buckets of water into it. By hand. I was terribly nervous about this operation, since the drum was practically standing in water at one end, and was plugged into the electric current at the other. Hungary has a 220 voltage and that can quick-fry a washerwoman with no trouble at all. She only laughed at my worries. "Hasn't killed anyone yet," she assured me. After it was half filled, we added the detergent to the water and stirred it vigorously with a paddle to aid in dissolving the soap. At this point she left the bathroom for a moment and I dropped the clothes into the drum. She returned and was aghast while she shut off the machine.

"*Jaj*, my dear, you are doing it all wrong! I told you I'll show you how to do this; this is not the way to wash," she wailed as she was fishing out the pieces of my wet laundry from the drum. "You wash one piece at a time, five minutes each, then stop the agitation. Take out the piece and wring it out (by hand), drop it into this bucket of water to rinse. Put the next piece in the drum and while it washes, wring out the first piece and drop it into the next bucket for the second rinse. Can you remember this?" I tried, although it would have been best to forget the whole affair and go shopping for new underwear. I guess I cannot deny my identity; I come from a throw-away society.

In went a tee shirt, I sat the timer, waited, fished, wrung, rinsed, wrung, rinsed and wrung again. This went on endlessly, piece by piece, one at a time. I was bent down into the bathtub for hours and by the time I washed everything, I was convinced that I'll never be able to straighten out again, and for the rest of my life I would have to walk around with my head permanently stuck in my crotch.

But eventually I was finished and could carry out the load to hang. It was not easy to find a place for the line, away from inquisitive chickens, spraying ducks, and birds that seem to have chronic diarrhea. No wonder women of old washed as seldom as they could get away with it. As a direct consequence, it was only natural that my washer and the drier were the first items that went into our moving van. Walden and Earth Day, and Paradise are OK, but one needs to go either all the way, or forget about it altogether. As early as a year ago I already knew that the villagers here would never accept fig leaves as the proper attire, and considering subzero temperatures in the winter, I wasn't sold on the idea either. We could not go back to Nature all the way, so I had to make some compromises. I apologized to Thoreau for copping out, but as long as I had to live in Szabar and not in the Garden of Eden, I had to have such things as a washing machine. An automatic one.

Although the early morning hour was still a bit cool, I carried out our breakfast into the future living room. The architecture of the place resembled a charming Italianate loggia, but this one was covered with the rubble of two world wars. Discounting the mess, it was lovely. The sunlight entered through the magnificent, arched openings and just as I sat the cups on an improvised table, I saw a stork preening itself on top of the power-line pole in front of the house. What a sight and what a day! But it did occur to me that eating al fresco in January would have some disadvantages.

Dr. Andrew Stangel, the noted art-historian and good friend, often expressed his appreciation for my culinary skills. Once in a rather exalted mood after an especially well turned out dinner he sighed happily. "Your cooking resembles art, and without being blasphemous, I must say that there is something vaguely religious, or sacred about your meals and the way you serve them. Your plates even are octagonal, and that, as you know, carries a deep symbolism." It was easy enough to serve semi-ritualistic, sacred meals, while I could shop for everything I needed, cook in a kitchen equipped like a professional establishment, then serve it in a real dining room that had windows and things. It won't be easy to cook here, religiously or otherwise. A good thing that at least I had the foresight to bring tons of paper plates and cups.

Béla, the happily whistling stonemason and his three helpers were mixing sand and all sort of interesting things, which they were then slapping on the outside walls. This looked like building an extra layer on the house, and not like a preparatory step for painting. But as I said, I was used to frame houses, where undercoating and painting were simple affairs. Even I could do it.

The sky was an unbelievable blue and the sun poured over everything. I felt a wonderful surge of vitality and could not wait to get my hands on things. For the first time in our married life I did not want to linger at the breakfast table.

And there was enough to do before I could start the first meal for our workers. I was being apprenticed to do in Rome as the Romans do. I also learned about things the Romans apparently do not do, such as cleaning up after themselves when a phase of work was completed. They left hills and mountains of trash behind. In addition, during the course of an average day, the team consumed a case of beer and about as much of mineral water, not to speak of the bottles of wine they drank with their meals. But they dropped what they no longer wanted: bottles, caps, paper cups and so on. At home they apparently had a staff of servants, or at least a wife, who cleaned up after them. It was obvious that they expected the same services at our house.

I found a shovel and a broom and started to sweep up the disaster. In a minute Béla sent one of his helpers, a young gypsy, with a wheelbarrow. He took the shovel from me, and between the two of us and with the help of a garden hose, the place was soon cleaned up.

I sent my husband (who was not enthusiastic about it) and the gypsy (who had no choice) to retrieve our garden furniture from the barn. After scrubbing them clean, the chaise lounges and lawn chairs went into the future living room, the picnic table and the benches into the dining room. Tablecloth and bunches of flowers in jars were placed on the tables and the place started to look inviting. My husband rewarded me with a smile and a kiss.

"Without the touch of a woman we would still be living in caves," he said.

"I know. And we women would still be picking up after you. Flintstones and shin bones and yesterday's change of animal skins."

"No arguments from me on that point. I appreciate what you did to this place and for taking me out of the cave. Are you starting breakfast?"

"Of course, but I had to first create a place where the five of them could sit down."

"We used to eat sitting on cement sacks and on piles of bricks. And there are eight of them now, not five." I looked, and indeed, somehow they multiplied since I last counted them. I had plenty of everything for eight, except bread, of which I only had one loaf. Knowing their preference for carbohydrates, I went to buy more, but was told that bread was sold out by eight o'clock. I was given a rather devastating look that clearly said, "You poor slob, get up in time, plan your day and shop when others do. This ain't Paris."

I went back home and surveyed my store of staples, but found most items useless, until I came upon a box of golden grits. It was my treasure, because I feared that after my supply was gone, I could not get any more of it. I would be left with memories only for one of my favorite breakfast foods. (It was much later that I found out what it was called in Hungarian, only to discover that it is more or a less a staple food here too.) But the men had to eat something and with tears in my eyes and with the selfish hope that my good deed would be rewarded in heaven, I cooked a big portion of it. The scrambled eggs and bacon were on a big platter, bread, sausages and lots of green peppers on another, and I poured the grits into a bowl. I was just about ready to plug in the coffee machine.

"They won't drink anything but beer or wine for breakfast," my husband warned. Well, it is their livers not mine, and let's face it, beer is so much easier to serve, especially since they like to drink it straight out of bottle or can. They all trooped into the "dining room" and the gypsies among them looked at their dirty clothing and black fingernails and were visibly confused when they realized I sat the table so that we would all sit together.

"It isn't necessary...we are dirty and would mess up your nice table... we'll just sit here on the steps..." But finally they sat down at the table, stiff with polite discomfort, much like my class of gifted children at the American ambassador's mansion at Bad Godesberg in Germany. His wife, the exquisitely beautiful and refined Gahl Burt had invited them for an afternoon chat. The children left their moon boots with the butler at the entry, and were served hot cocoa and cookies. Balancing their delicate cups, they followed Mrs. Burt into her magnificent living room, where she talked to them, and made lasting impressions that will surely influence their decisions in the future. She, the perfect hostess, seemed relaxed and unaware that instant disaster was only a thin cup away. I aged ten years thinking of spilled cocoa over her priceless rugs. Nothing bad happened, and the children left with an experience and a memory that they'll never forget. But as I found out later, they were about as tense as I was that something inexcusable would happen. Nothing disastrous happened with my gypsies, but they too were as scared as the students at Bad Godesberg. However, they ate with robust appetites, and visibly enjoyed the short rest from their labors.

And the labor was hard indeed, absolutely medieval. There was no cement mixing truck. The delivery truck dumped the sand, gravel and sacks of cement on the street (nine plus five steps below). A small portable mixer that groaned, hiccuped, complained, and was held together by pieces of chains, leather straps and prayers, produced a wheelbarrow's worth of cement at one time. The men pushed this oozing mess in the wheelbarrow up on a ramp from the street. Each brick, each tile, every steel beam, every bucket of mortar was handed up individually, one by one to those working on the walls. The amount of muscle power and sweat that went into building this house was the same as it was hundreds, or even thousands of years ago. There were no whips cracking, but otherwise, this might as well have been a scene in Egypt. I watched their lean, brown bodies, glistening in honest sweat, and looked at their muscles and sinews bulging out like ropes, and was embarrassed in the role of the pharaoh's wife at the construction site of the pyramids.

They ate their eggs and bacon with ravishing appetites. The sausages and the bread were soon gone, but the bowl of grits just sat there, virginal, untouched. The sunlight glanced off the rivulets of golden butter and the pale yellow of the grits contrasted artistically with the verdure charm of fresh parsley and the shadows of ground pepper. I offered the bowl and they eyed it suspiciously. Politely, each took a teaspoonful. After a small pause, not unlike the one a man would take before jumping down to his death, they proceeded to chew it with the same obstinacy and martyred looks my children used to put on while chewing spinach or steamed broccoli. They were polite, but almost gagged on it.

"Don't you care for it?" I asked the obvious. "This is a favorite dish in the United States, especially in the southern states," I explained. One of the boys managed to swallow his mouthful then spoke up for the rest of them.

"That might be so and in all respect, it is all right by me if the Americans like this. But excuse us Ma'am, we aren't Americans. We are Hungarian gypsies and our systems object to pabulum." My husband burst out laughing and the statement stayed with us. Whenever I put something on the table that he does not like (and he is basically a meat and potato man), he tells me that he is a Hungarian gypsy.

As soon as breakfast was cleared away, I had to start thinking about dinner. I had to embrace an entirely new concept in cooking and it was not easy. Everything I knew, or liked, as far as culinary arts go, had to be forgotten, and a very new cuisine provided. Heavy spices, especially very hot peppers, and massive, rib-sticking dishes, prepared with heavy doses of lard, were requested, even during the hottest days. Aside from relearning how to cook in my cramped kitchen with two burners and no oven, I also had the problem of never knowing ahead of time the multiplying rate of the men who came to work. Sometimes at noon I would have double the mouths to feed that I planned for. I was becoming very inventive, although I would not dare to serve those meals to anybody who was not building our house.

Not having a butcher in the village and the fact that my freezers were not yet connected was an additional problem. I operated out of the mini refrigerator, which we used in the party room in Germany to store certain drinks. I needed to make constant runs to the neighboring town to bring home the daily supplies.

After my faux pas with the grits, I learned quickly, and soon provided the meals they liked. One of my greatest successes was a dish, for which I expected to be stoned in public. It was created out of sheer desperation on a day we did not expect any workers, but then suddenly five of them showed up. My husband and the car were gone and my cupboards were bare, as the old woman in the shoe used to say. I had to do a pretty fancy miracle with my leftovers and odds and ends. Praying to St. Rita, and setting potatoes to boil on one of the burners, I sautéed a great quantity of onions on the other, added chopped fiery green and red peppers, cooked it some more, then tossed a lot of chopped tomatoes and garlic into the dish together with two cans of kidney beans and the beef stew, left over from the day before. Then I remembered a length of spicy sausage in the back of the refrigerator, so I sliced that into the pot and cooked the mess for another ten minutes, then served it with the boiled potatoes. I am a good cook and have served memorable lobster thermidors, paellas, chicken Kiev with tarragon butter, braised veal in watercress sauce, rock Cornish hens in a cream sauce of fennel and Pernod, tenderloins in a cream sauce with cognac and truffles. I roasted pheasants to perfection, and prepared memorable vegetarian dishes, almost converting some of our meat-eating friends, and reaped enthusiastic compliments and applause from my guests. However, the praises I received for that awful concoction surpassed everything I ever achieved with my culinary skills. That dish, by popular request, stayed on the menu until the house was completed.

"See Ma'am, you really know how to cook the way we like to eat..." Even Dr. Stangel could not top this praise. Apparently success is just as unpredictable as failure is. Or as the saying goes, necessity is the greatest inventor.

Another local dish I quickly learned was simple and always greeted with the sighs reserved for special works of art. Thinly sliced fresh cabbage was salted, then sautéed with a generous glob of lard until it had a nice rosy color. It was then mixed with *quadrattini* (fettuccini broken into smallish squares) cooked al dente and sprinkled with lots of freshly ground black pepper. Even I grew to like it; the taste reminded me vaguely of Chinese egg rolls.

When in Rome, eat as the Romans do, but when in Szabar, forget about the "pap", or the sophisticated sauces and the delicate herbs. Light and exquisite foods and the new cuisine are not known here, nor would they ever be accepted. The locals want the robust food, the kinds that would give indigestion to the rest of us. Bacon, meat, beans, sauerkraut, lots of bread, pasta with accompaniments (roasted potatoes and ground red pepper, or toasted breadcrumbs, or bacon and cottage cheese, perhaps roasted red bell peppers and garlic) are preferred. Everything is prepared with generous amounts of home-made lard; they render it themselves after they slaughter their pigs. Any self-respecting cardiologist would get clogged arteries just at the sight of it, but these people are healthy, strong and live a long and productive life. And of course, almost everything has to be spiced with hot peppers. One man told me, "Ma'am, if I don't sweat during eating, I consider the dish a failure." Sweating, of course, comes from the red hot peppers. We are not used to such robust fares and although I tasted the dishes I cooked, (and found them very tasty and satisfying), we preferred lighter meals. As a result, I very often I had to cook two meals: one for us and one for them. Theirs was the fare of hardworking people, for whom body fuel and strong muscles are a must. They eat in order to be able to do the extraordinarily hard work winter and summer. But the pharaoh's wife is happier with a salad and perhaps a piece of grilled chicken. (But the chicken better not be from Esther's barnyard.)

When I wasn't cooking, I was cleaning, washing, doing beer bottle patrols, or working in my garden that provided the produce for our meals. Now, that I was home and offered decent meals, the word was out that the food is good, and there is plenty of it. Suddenly it was quite possible to get workers to come and to stay on the job. In less than a week they lost their shyness and would inquire at breakfast what would be for dinner. Just like my children used to do.

Despite the considerable amount of work being done daily on our house, it did not seem that we were making noticeable progress. Laci, the carpenter, was still working on the windows and doors. Our house was totally open in every sense of the word. Most of our life happened outdoors or in the open spaces of the future living areas. There were no doors we could close at night.

When I was not worried about the completion date, or unexpected four legged, or flying night visitors, I could and did enjoy this unfinished, open part of the house. If God forbid, we would build again, I would add such a roofed, arched, heavy-walled and spacious space to the building. Granted, the rooms behind such a structure would be dark, but the experience of living in such a half-sheltered, half-open space was unforgettable. It was neither a porch, nor a patio, but it had its own sense of fine tranquility. The coolness and the playful interplay between sun and shadow and the feeling of being protected, yet in the open, reminded us of those charming Italian country estates. We discovered that large spaces lift the spirit and that there is an immense psychological value in non-utilitarian areas. The spirit is no longer confined and feels free to roam and to expand. Our "loggia" was the size of the entry, the living and dining rooms combined. It was magnificent. Years after the house was finished I still regretted having lost the space that carried the moods of romantic palazzos in Tuscany or the Veneto.

We selected sand colored, discreetly glazed octagonal ceramic tiles, imported of course from Italy, for the entrance and the dining room, and cream colored ones of similar shape for the kitchen and the back entrance. Both tiles were delicately smudged to give an antique, used look. The sand colored ones had the hint of coffee au lait, and the ones in the kitchen had the palest of orange. We picked the tiles out of a selection of hundreds and were jubilantly happy with them.

Not so Esther! She marched into our house with the self-assurance of an empress, inspected the tiles, then held her head in desperation and jeered at us.

"You should have taken me along when you looked for tiles. I would have caught this swindle. Can't you see? These are all seconds! You got the junk they couldn't otherwise sell. You don't pay attention and everybody cheats you. They can tell a kilometer away that you are foreigners and don't know beans about construction and stuff. How could you have been so careless, when you bought them? Look at the coloring; the tiles are all smudged. I hope you'll take them back instantly and demand your money back. They look dirty and used. Whenever you need to buy anything in the future, do take me along and I'll take care of your interests."

It was useless to explain to her that this was precisely what we wanted. She never heard a word of our argument. And we did not tell her that our "smudged" tiles cost almost twice as much as the "clean" ones.

She was our self-proclaimed guardian, not only because she was a few years older, but also because she was convinced that we are intellectually challenged. Unarguably she was a good person. She tolerated the chaos created around our house, and hers as well; put up with the noise and the dirt. The havoc created in her backyard cannot be described with polite words, and she could not let her chickens out of their hot and stuffy coops day after day, on account of the constant coming and going of the workers, who left the gate wide open. The hens retaliated by not laying any eggs while they were imprisoned. In the evenings, after everyone left and before the chickens decided that it was bedtime, she would let them free for a few hours, but then the stupid birds would fall or fly into the trenches that were dug out for various purposes. Since I would not touch them, it was up to the village children to retrieve them in exchange for quantities of chewing gum. Labor is cheap here.

Esther works much too hard. Life was not very kind to her, but her philosophy is to do the best at the moment, and cry later. Provided there is time left. She was a girl of adequate means, when she married a teacher, who later became the local school's principal. They built a nice house on the other half of our shared property, and she had an easy life staying home, raising her son and enjoying great respect in the community. Then one of those inexplicable things happened that was common during the horror years of Communism, and as a result her husband was taken away one night on some charge or another, was tried and sentenced to two years in prison. After this, things never got better, even after he was freed. The horror, the injustice, the senselessness of it all broke him, and within a few years after he was freed, he died of cancer. What little social benefits she received after his death were not nearly enough to live on, but too much to die on. Stubbornly she decided to do what everybody else was doing, and tried her hands at farming. She had a little vineyard in the hills and went ahead, all by herself, to work the grapes and to produce wine for a little extra income.

Viticulture is demanding and very hard, as she soon found out. The vine is an exacting mistress and wants full attention at all times. So Esther hoes and sprays, weeds and prunes, ties the vines to the support poles, and spreads manure. She scrubs the barrels (some big enough so she can climb into them) harvests, presses the grapes, watches the fermenting process, monitors the temperature of the cellar and adjusts it by either heating it with a wood burning stove, or cooling it by opening the doors. She watches the alcohol content and is attentive to the needs of the young wine. When it matures, she airs it by transferring it from one barrel to the other. Finally she sells it at forty cents per quart. She also raises chickens, ducks and geese for the eggs, the meat and the fat. In order to feed them, she grows corn. She dug up her large flower garden and planted vegetables to provide food for the entire year. Cabbages line the walkway to her house and snap beans and peas cover the garden fence where honeysuckle used to blossom.

When she feels ill from high blood pressure or physical exhaustion or ailments that she does not even know she has, she rests for a few hours after which she claims that she is well again. Before long, she is at it again, feeding the barnyard folk, carrying water to them, or lugging wood into her kitchen.

"This is the fate that was planned for me, and I have to make the best of it," she said. I looked at her hands that used to make delicate embroidery, but are so worn, cracked and swollen now that she could not sew on a button without considerable difficulty. The broken nails, the black criss-cross marks of innumerable injuries received while she repaired a fence, chopped wood, or did a great many other jobs not really intended for her sex, or her age, were the hands of a most miserable peasant woman. Her touch on my face felt like sandpaper.

Once I felt particularly sorry for her and exclaimed over her difficult life. She shrugged and her unbelievably blue eyes, the color of summer skies, danced with joy. "Well, it is true. I work hard. But then I think of all those city women, who have the same income as I have, but do not have a vineyard or a garden, and suddenly I feel lucky, rich and independent. Think of it, I was never cold or hungry, not even after I was left on my own. With the help of God, I can take care of myself."

I guess life goals, expectations and the quality of life are concepts as elusive and different as taste, culture and style. I could not help but wonder, how many widows of principals in the United States would consider themselves fortunate if at seventy-three years of age they would have to work from sun-up to sun-down the way she does. Would they consider it a rich reward if for all their efforts they could claim never being hungry or cold?

Even during the hottest days she is either in her garden, or at her cornfield, or up in the hill at the vineyard, until six in the evening. From the high elevation of my backyard I can see her in the evening as she moves down the dusty road toward the house, her hair tied back with a scarf, village fashion. She does not look any different from all the other exhausted, worn women dragging themselves wearily down the long road, too tired and exhausted to talk or to have emotions. I look at their bent backs and the sorrow I feel for their lot is deep, and black as the night. Something went wrong with the ancient curse. Women were supposed to bear their children in pain, and men were to earn the daily bread by the sweat of their brows. By some colossal cosmic mistake, these women had to do both.

By this time the table was set in the "loggia" for the evening meal and she came to join us gratefully and gladly. She was usually more dehydrated than hungry, and enjoyed the luxury of not having to do a thing, but sit and relax. At seventy-three a woman should have the right to a rocking chair and an easy day. Life is a bitch and then you die, was written on a coffee mug, I once saw somewhere.

These are her saintly sides, and seeing only these, I could love her like a sister. But then she wants to be an authority on everything, never mind if she does not know anything about it. This lady does not own a typewriter, does not drive a car, was married and had a child before she had electricity in the house, can't start a microwave for love or money, and gets frustrated by an electric mixer. Yet, she would look at me and tell me very earnestly what to do with my computer when it is suffering from its regular PMS.

Because she always ate everything I put on the table, I assumed she liked how I cooked. But after a while she had a standard comment about the food, including those dishes she never tasted before. "It isn't the way I make it...next time I'll show you how to do it right..." I then was subjected to her "expertise". The meat sauce for the spaghetti does not need any tomatoes. It is a grave mistake to put raisins AND red onions into the broccoli salad (never had broccoli before I introduced her to it). Fruit is unhealthy in the morning...olive oil ruins a salad...meat is never to be grilled...a steak must cook for at least two hours... I was also instructed that it is a mortal sin to deviate from the standard menu offered every Sunday, every wedding and every other state occasion. It starts with chicken soup (with homemade angel hair pasta) and ends with strudel and there is never any deviation. She was aghast when I had company and cooked a totally unorthodox menu. She was sure I'd end up in hell for defying tradition when I served chilled gazpacho.

During this summer I broke my old habit, and went to bed early each day. I was usually so tired that I was content just to stretch out on my back for a few minutes feeling how every inch of my body tingled in delight for being horizontal. A few minutes later I fell into deep sleep that lasted until Esther's rooster sounded the wake-up call, or the noise of the workers penetrated my dreams, whichever came first.

But I was happier than I have been during the last years. The house was shaping up and I loved it. And slowly I grew to like the village, its people, the view, our walks, my husband's exuberance, the rhythm to our life. Time was flying and although I did not want to talk about it, I had to face the truth: I did not want to leave, I did not want my former life any more. I tasted a sort of freedom and joy, and found it delightful. I was content and happy where I was.

The beautiful, smudged tiles were laid, the electrical wiring completed in the new wing, the sewage line and the water connected to the new kitchen, and the cabinets were in place. The refrigerator-freezer hummed reassuringly, the oven functioned, and I opened all the crates marked K for kitchen. All the dishes were in place, although I worried that without doors and windows somebody could slip in during the night and take it all, but my worries were superfluous. I also worried about a fully equipped kitchen that was wide open to the elements, and hoped that the extra wide overhang of the roof would prevent rain coming into the kitchen. But it was an unusually dry summer and the rain I feared never came. I promised Laci the sun, the moon and several galaxies, if only he would hurry with those windows and doors. He solemnly promised to deliver. But by then I was sophisticated enough not to believe a word of it.

In theory we had a dog to guard us, but Törpi as a protector and watchdog proved less reliable than Esther's cat, called Midnight, that shared the fate of Maria Leczinska, wife of Louis XV. She once complained *"Toujours coucher, toujours grosse, toujours accoucher"*, forever in bed, forever pregnant, forever in childbed. Midnight too was either in heat or pregnant. Still, in case of an intruder she would have fussed more than our excellent watchdog. Whenever Törpi was not sleeping, he followed my husband, staring up at him with those fabulous eyes, ate a gargantuan dinner and burped heartily as a closure. Then no matter what we did to him, how we closed the gates or tied him up, he always escaped and went after his nightly amusements. He returned in the morning, exhausted and very self-satisfied. My husband, the pearl of dog-trainers, never thought of punishing him, but merely asked with remarkable empathy, "Well, old boy, did you have a good time?" And I swear, Törpi told it all, and it was always good.

He was an exceedingly ugly animal, and although I was immediately designated to be his provider, he did not feel that he owed me any gratitude for the services, nor had he any love for me. I didn't complain, because the feeling was mutual. I tolerated him, but just barely. My husband tried his very best to make me see what a wonderful animal this beast was, but we just were not made for each other. Actually, Törpi was not made for anybody. He was an egocentric, sybaritic dog that refined hedonism far beyond the Greek concept. Like all creatures whose pleasure-seeking goals exclude everything else, he was totally worthless.

Our strained relation came to a satisfying end, at least as far as I was concerned. Esther wanted to visit her son, about seventy miles from us. My husband offered to take her to the railway station a few villages down the road. As I was busy and couldn't keep an eye on the dog, he went along for the ride. As soon as they arrived at the station, Törpi shot out of the car like a bat out of hell, took off between the tracks like a true tramp, and was never seen again. My husband called and called, but Törpi was otherwise occupied. The train came and went, but the dog did not return. His owner waited an hour, then went to a lumberyard to make some purchases, and went back to the station. Nothing. He then came home depressed and disconsolate. Despite an ugly sense of relief that we lost him for good, I felt so sorry for my husband that I wished the beast would return. My big boy lost his pet, and he was heart-broken. He perked up toward evening when he drove back to the station to pick up his sister, and hoped to find his dog sitting there patiently waiting for him. Fat chance. We never saw him again; however, there are a lot of dogs now in the neighborhood that look remarkably like him, fabulous eyes and all.

As the summer came to its close, I was more and more convinced that my sister-in-law would drive me mad. I kept reminding myself that the woman is goodness incarnated, and that she has not a single bad bone in her body. We messed up her life and her backyard. Her hens would be permanently neurotic on account of having been locked up for so long. She granted us bathroom privileges when ours was undergoing its several episodes of labor pains. Sundays she baked us vast quantities of strudel. Without her this entire building project would not have been possible. With her I had a good chance of ending up in a strait-jacket.

She told me what to eat, and how to fix it; what to wear and when to do things. Also how to do them. This would have been almost acceptable; after all, I was being introduced to a new world that was bewildering to me, but familiar to her. I needed some guidance. However, she also told me the obvious, such as to wash the tomatoes before I made a salad of them, to turn off the burner on the oven after I was done cooking, and not to wash the car when it is raining. She also monitored every one of my steps.

A typical encounter would be as follows: I am leaving the house in the morning with the shopping basket in my hand. She would pop out of her house, pretending that she was on her way somewhere.

"Are you going somewhere?" she asks. I nod silently, my lips pressed so tightly my jaw hurts, because if I would open my mouth an ugly sneer was bound to come out, such as, "Not really. I'm in the middle of taking a bath."

"Are you going to the store?" A second nod. What else is there to do in Szabar? Where would I go except to the store? With a shopping basket yet.

"Isn't your husband going with you?" Negative head-shake. I assumed that this too was obvious. And why would he accompany me to buy a loaf of bread and a bottle of milk, the only items I could buy in the local store?

"Well, all right. Don't walk on the road, you might get hit." Yes Ma'am. I drove all over the USA, Europe (at some places on the left side of the road), Venezuela, and parts of Africa. I traveled in cars, trains, planes, helicopters, boats, on donkeys, horses, camels, bikes, ski lifts. Also in taxis all over New York, Mexico, Italy, Greece, South America and the British Islands, (again, on the wrong side of the road.) I think I can manage to survive the few yards on foot to the store across our house in Szabar.

As her methods of driving me insane were crystallizing I could identify those that had the greatest effect on me. First, despite her youthfully shining eyes, ready laugh, and otherwise healthy attitude toward life, she also has a generous amount of negative streak in her. Every other one of her sentences starts with "jaj", which is an expletive of lament, or cry of pain. It is a red flag in speech; after the jaj one expects that calamity or disaster would be communicated.

Her second maddening trait is that she must always be in opposition. If I said "white", she would insist that it is black.

Third, she has to be informed about everything. The information has to be given in minute detail, and she wants to hear it several times in a row. After I told her something three times, she will act as if she never heard it, and make my husband tell it also. Three times.

And finally, she is convinced that she knows everything better than anybody, including those things she had not known a minute ago. It is her absolute conviction that the rest of the people were created totally brainless.

One day she brought over a pot of fish soup and asked me to freeze it. In the cooking pot. I explained to her why it would not work, but promised to find a proper container, and take care of it, as soon as the soup cooled. An hour later she returned to check out the soup situation, and caught me in the process of transferring it into the container. Instantly she was agitated.

"Now don't you break up the pieces of fish! Be careful! Jaj, watch the fish heads, so they remain intact. Jaj, you are making a mess, it will look like sop!" This was repeated about ten times, without variation. Now as far as I am concerned, the less is said about fish soup, the better. I was doing what was asked of me, and was happy enough to have found the container and was not overly concerned about the aesthetic appearance of carp heads. I was as careful as I could be under the circumstances, even though I would find it gross to have a head on my plate. It is bad enough to have to eat our fellow creatures, but I find it really disturbing when my supper is watching me.

"Jaj, you are making a total mess. I never even stir the soup, just shake the pot from side to side in order not to break up the fish," she continued her laments. To this I made the only appropriate gesture there is: I smiled and handed her the ladle. "You do it, Darling," then cleared the kitchen.

Another time she woke us at midnight. (Were you sleeping? Who, us? At midnight? Naw.) She announced that her son would arrive for a visit the following day (I never found out why she did not tell this earlier) and would I please take out her stuffed cabbage from the freezer, so she could feed him. I staggered into the kitchen and did as I was told. By next morning it thawed out. Visions of salmonella danced in my head, so I stuck the container into the refrigerator until the time she would come for it. The good woman was soon at our door claiming her food, and when she saw that I headed for the refrigerator she panicked, since she could never remember which side was the freezer and which the refrigerator.

"Jaj, you did forget to take out the cabbage, didn't you?" she whined.

"I haven't forgotten; it is in the fridge."

"Jaj, then it is not defrosted after all! Whatever will I give him now?" He is fifty and by the looks of him he wouldn't starve to death if he didn't receive food for three weeks. I kept my rebellious thoughts to myself and told her to take her cabbage. Actually, I wanted to pour it over her head.

"You should have taken it out when I told you. This is frozen solid."

Later in the afternoon I met her briefly.

"How was the cabbage?"

"Well, it was all right and not frozen. But it could have been at that. Who knows how cold your refrigerator is, besides, you did not tell me it was defrosting during the night. How was I to know that it was not frozen?"

I looked at her like a cobra does at her victim before she is ready to strike, then told her coldly, "Because I told you so. Damn!"

This unexpected expletive quieted her long enough so I could quickly put in a word edgewise.

"You know, Darling, I was married twice and I was spared both times from having a mother-in-law. Fate has a funny way of compensating though. In you I received four of them all at once."

She was terribly hurt at that, and after I have long forgotten my angry remark, she would ask me sadly over and over again, "Do you really see a mother-in-law in me?" And because I am basically an honest woman, I could not help but answer truthfully. "Not one, Darling. Four."

From here on she was much tamer, and our shaky relationship headed toward calmer waters. But it was a Pyrrhic victory and I felt bad for days.

"Why is it necessary to step all over people before they would leave you alone? Why was it necessary to show my claws before she was willing to go back to her corner?" I complained to my husband.

"You don't own that problem," he shrugged. "She was asking for it for a long time."

Once, when I was young (during Truman's administration) I attended a course designed to help young mothers raise their babies. The woman, who spoke to us first, had a delightfully dry humor. She reminded us that whenever we try to do a new thing, the first product of our effort is usually a failure and we throw it away. Out goes the first soufflé, followed by the first cake we baked. We throw out the first dress we attempt to sew, and even our first Christmas tree does not look right. The only thing we are obliged to keep is our first baby. It is against the law to throw it away, even if it is completely messed up. She was there to teach us how to do a better job with our soon-to-be-born-babies, because otherwise this child would haunt us for the rest of our lives. We have to do it right the first time around.

My sister-in-law was a first baby, and apparently her mother did not attend the same prenatal course I have. She is the living proof at age seventy-some that our instructor was right. And I can't even tell that excellent lady how right she was. Come to think of it, I too was a first baby.

CHAPTER FIVE

Somebody once said that it is possible to stop working on a house, but it is not possible to complete work in, on, or around it. Greater wisdom, as far as building houses, or doing household chores, was never spoken. While we rested during the night, the unattended jobs multiplied like mice, or like our workers around mealtime. Each morning I made a mental list of what to do on that day, but there was always an emergency that had to have priority over the planned tasks. By the first evening I was one job behind on my list, the second it was two, the third it was four, then eight and by the following day it multiplied to sixteen. The concept of geometric series stepped out of the textbooks, and stared in my face every morning. Soon the leftover jobs were more numerous than the ones I planned on any given day. The big finale of the Ice Capades came to haunt me. It is the figure when all the skaters form a long line holding hands, and skate around in a circle. They look like the turning blade of a windmill. The center figure is the axis and she is practically standing still, while the ones at the two ends can barely keep up with the turning line. I was that tail-end skater. There was so much to clean, haul, burn, paint, weed, cook, wash that I was barely able to keep up with the ever-increasing speed of this windmill gone crazy.

As if my jobs would not keep me occupied as it was, I fell in love with two handsome chairs we salvaged from the old house. Although the upholstery was hopeless, the frames were carved from good hardwood, and had a faintly oriental aura about them. Most good home magazine show at least four times a year how city dump rejects could be transformed into heirloom pieces. The magical promise was not lost on me. What Better Homes and Gardens can do, I can do too. Here was my chance to become creative, and I attacked the project with the reckless abandon of first love. A woman in the village reupholstered the cushions with upholstery material I found in one of my crates. The cloth looks like tapestry and is beautiful. She charged ten dollars for the job. Eat your heart out, Better Homes and Gardens, because I bet you could not come up with such a price.

The next step was to remove the glaring red paint from the woodwork, and replace it with a subtle stain to match the subdued colors of the tapestry. Somebody must have acquired gallons of red paint left over after spraying a fire engine, and in a sudden fit of artistic dementia, he covered the chairs, layer after layer with the powerful paint. I applied paint remover very generously, but the stuff would not budge. I repeated the application several times, and finally the paint seemed to soften. But if I did not scrape it fast enough, it would harden again and sit even tighter than before. I scraped with a spatula. I scraped with a wire brush. I prayed. Then I used foul language. Nothing happened. I was hot and dirty and horrible insects were feasting on my flesh in blissful security, knowing full well that I could not swat at them with my messy hands. But the paint remained. I believe I was in possession of the first and only paint that could withstand anything and would last forever. I had nasty burns all over my arms and legs from the splatters of the paint remover; my overalls and Reeboks were covered with globs of red paint.

After three days of fruitless laboring I managed to remove so much paint that the chairs actually looked smaller, but they were still quite red. Finally I took them to the cabinetmaker, which is what I should have done in the first place. He promised to sand it, probably the week after. In terms of Szabar this means that it might be ready for the graduation of my grandson. He is three years old.

Perhaps the project was futile from the start. Perhaps I should have searched for some black paint, left over from spraying a locomotive. Passed off as lacquer, it would have been appropriate for the oriental look of the chairs. If my heirs won't care for it, let them remove it, if they can.

I labored hard, because I wanted to be creative and wanted to make an heirloom piece, so that my descendants should remember me with tears in their eyes and deep appreciation in their hearts. "Look at this marvelous piece! I inherited it from my great-great-great-grandmother and she finished it herself, she was that talented."

But now that the chairs are finally finished and look quite handsome,

I am reconsidering this inheritance thing. I worked so hard on these chairs that I no longer want to part with them. I will have it written in my will: no coffin, please. Bury me, sitting up in one of them. Come to think of it, bury me with both. Let the heirs find their own heirloom pieces at the city dump, and let them refinish them by the sweat of their own brows.

The good news was that since I arrived in Hungary, the speed of construction was accelerating. The down side was the incredible schedule we had to follow. It seemed that everybody worked at two or three jobs to make ends meet, and we had to accept their complicated schedules. Some workers arrived at four in the morning, others at ten in the evening. The ones who arrived at dawn wanted breakfast at seven; the ones who started at seven wanted to eat at ten. Dinner was served in shifts, just like on a cruise. Foolishly I thought that I would never be able to look at food again.

I also learned a great many things about the social structure of the village that were never mentioned in my sociology classes. Some villages, especially in Europe, retain a rigid, medieval, closed-community thinking. Szabar is such a place. Here habits do not change, innovations are viewed with suspicion, and out of a long-standing habit they prefer their thinking to be done by somebody else: a political leader, the mayor, the clergy, the television, or the newspaper. Only seldom do they rise to an occasion and cause a change.

Their hospitality and kindness are legendary, visitors and tourists are absolutely enchanted by the reception, but at the same time they are politely and stubbornly kept at a distance. Since my husband's family lived here longer than anybody else in the village and he was actually born here, he was never considered a stranger. They like him, trust him, turn to him with every problem they have, so that there is a constant coming and going at our house. I even suggested that we post our office hours on the gate so that at least we could take our meals in peace. I, on the other hand, cause some confusion in their well-ordered world. I am definitely as foreign as they come. Everybody knows that I am different. I have a sauna and a waterbed. I eat strange foods. Strange, foreign people come to visit me. I keep odd hours, and I have a computer and a dishwasher. I have a pasta machine and my refrigerator makes ice cubes, and the garage door opens by magic when my car nears it. I am probably bad for the morality of the village. But since my husband is the favorite son, they have no choice but to accept his wife as well. I'm sure they make the sign of the cross behind my back. For Americans, who are on the move constantly and whose way of life includes the Welcome Wagon visits in the neighborhood, it is almost incomprehensible that a newcomer, although always treated with kindness and hospitality, would never truly become part of the community.

This xenophobia, by the way, is not just a local thing at Szabar; it is fairly typical of most small villages in Europe. Some of our friends own houses in Corsica, Madeira, Italy, Portugal, France, Spain or Greece, and they encountered the same polite resistance, which is usually so covered up that it took them years to realize its existence.

This attitude is well illustrated by one of our encounters with the village elders. They came angry and frustrated to see my husband about village politics in general, and the mayor in particular. They put up with him as long as they had to, but were worried that he would be reelected. Since the mayor and his wife are related to more than half the village, their kin would surely vote for him in the new election. Our visitors wanted to have a strong candidate to run against him, but could not agree on a choice. Finally my husband suggested a person for the position, who was moderate, fair and honorable. No Einstein in disguise, but he was still smarter than the incumbent, or any of the candidates suggested by the village gentlemen.

"Wouldn't do," one visitor grumbled. "Nobody would vote for him."

"Why is that? He is the best choice of the lot," my husband argued with genuine surprise. "What's wrong with him?"

"Nothing. He is a good man. But he is not local. Sort of Johnny-come-lately'. People would never trust him."

"Where did he come from?"

"Can't rightly remember. Was a long time ago when he came here. Maybe thirty years. Maybe more."

"He lived here for thirty years, married a local woman, raised four children to adulthood here, and he is still not considered a local?" My husband was incredulous. "Hell, how long does one have to live here to be considered a local?

"That I don't know. But more than thirty years."

As I said, changes come slowly to this village.

During that summer an elderly woman died in the capital, but was to be buried in her home village, Szabar. We did not know her, but her daughter lived in Germany, and we were close enough to her to attend the funeral of her mother. For some reason Esther's news network did not work properly on that day, and I found out about the funeral and the arrival of our friend from Germany only, when the church bells were already ringing for the requiem.

I jumped into the shower and slipped into the only dress I could find, a plain, medium-blue, sleeveless linen shift. I am usually very self-conscious when I have to wear a hat, but it was 99 degrees in the shade, and the thinning ozone worries me, so I added a very large, black straw hat to my outfit. I felt eminently silly in it, and hoped the mourning congregation would be so deep in their grief that they would not notice my silly hat. I was not trying to put on airs, but I do have a fair skin, and had no desire to be nuked in the midday sun.

We arrived at the cemetery just when the coffin was placed on a stretcher with rubber wheels, like the gurneys that they use in field hospitals. We followed it to the grave, which was already dug. There were many prayers and songs and several people delivered lengthy eulogies. Everybody was dressed in long-sleeved, heavy black things that looked like wool, and I was getting worried. The ceremony was much too long, and I feared some of the older people standing in the relentless sun, would be next in the grave, because an epidemic of heat strokes seemed inevitable.

The prayers droned on, and the heat was so intense that the surrounding tombstones felt hot to the touch. I was the only one who was dressed sensibly, and also the only one who stood in relative shade under my ridiculous hat. I was marginally aware of being scrutinized, but I figured some people have not yet seen me, and their curiosity was stronger than their bereavement. After all, we were celebrity: who else destroyed a bed in Szabar, and who else wore a hat the size of which would only be appropriate for a movie star in the top payroll category?

Finally they lowered the coffin into the grave, and I thought this concluded the ceremony. But not so. The priest turned his gaze toward heaven and started to pray again, then threw a shovel of earth on the coffin. Still praying, he handed the tool to the daughter of the deceased, who did the same. The shovel went from hand to hand, and everybody participated in the task of burying the dear departed. I don't think I can ever forget that hollow thud, or the slight echo as the soil hit the coffin.

Death, as a philosophy, or even as one of the unavoidable facts of life is one thing; but to witness how somebody is irrevocably buried into the grave, shovel by shovel, is something else. I pulled toward the safety of a large tombstone, because I simply was not about to throw a shovel of earth on that coffin, which was slowly disappearing under the mound of dirt. I didn't even know her, but the experience was shocking. I could not imagine the agony if someone I loved would be inside that coffin. With this ritual, which seemed macabre as far as I was concerned, the finality was effectively spelled out.

After all the funeral guests had a turn with the shovel, four young men finished the job, while the congregation murmured "Hail Mary" and "Our Father" until the last shovel of soil was in place. They stuck a wooden cross into the finished mound, piled the mostly plastic flowers on the grave and we were finally free to leave.

"You OK?" whispered my husband as he joined me behind the tombstone.

"Not quite. Promise me anything but give your assurance that I would be cremated and not buried," I whispered back. "This was a claustrophobic horror. Lock the box, lower it six feet, then pile a ton of dirt over it..." I shuddered. "I don't want to be put down there, and I won't let anybody do that to you either." He gave me a look that assured me he fully understood what I meant.

During our walk home, I chided Esther for telling everybody the story of our collapsed bed, so that even during this solemn occasion I had to endure being stared at.

"Oh, Dear, it wasn't the bed at all. You got stared at, because you were so inappropriately dressed."

"My hat! I knew it," I cried.

"There is nothing wrong with your hat. It is black. But haven't you noticed that everyone, except you, was in deep black as a sign of respect to the deceased and her family? Yours was blue. And sleeveless on top of it."

I told her that I don't own a black summer dress.

"Everybody needs mourning dresses for all seasons," she replied. "You better see to it that you have some handy."

I pointed out that it appeared to me pretty stupid to risk a stroke, and besides, I did not even know the deceased; I merely attended because of my friend. Empathy and respect are one thing; frying in a long-sleeved black wool on the hottest day of the year is quite another.

"It is not a question of heat or knowing the one who died. To wear black at a funeral is our custom, and if you want to live here, you must accept it instead of trying to change it."

She was right, of course, and I felt like a four-year old being chastised. Physicians consider the skin to be the outside boundary of the body and self, I reflected in humility. They know that the skin by its color, texture and temperature, or by the appearance of allergies and rashes of all sorts, are often manifestations of inner stresses, unresolved conflicts and frustrations. The skin shows not just the state of health, but often the state of mind of the patient. As civilization added clothing as an extra layer to the body, the boundary was extended. We often express our emotional whereabouts through the dress we wear, be it at a wedding, funeral, church service, the opera and the theater, or any other special occasion. At the University of Dayton, where I earned my second master's degree, the students used to dress formally for the final examinations. I suppose it was a way of paying respect to education. I should have known that a blue shift does not properly show bereavement. And if I felt none, I had no business attending the funeral.

We walked silently the rest of the way as it dawned on me that indeed, I would have to learn to adjust. When I agreed to move to Szabar, I stepped out of the twentieth century and left my world behind. I did it out of my free will; nobody forced me. I should be thankful for having been given a home, love and security. I had no right to be critical of their ways. I had the responsibility to conform to their customs and expectations, at least as long as I was on public view. It was as simple as that. I should have been more careful, and should have paid more attention to my new environment.

I was on my way to learn a great deal, not just about the village, but about myself too. Not all of it was pleasant discovery. First of all, I was a fool, of course. Prior to our arrival I almost succeeded in convincing myself about how I yearned for the simple life. I had idealistic visions of Earth Day, and the resurrection of Mother Earth. I reread Walden again. But in truth, on my second reading I noticed the obvious, which seemed to be insignificant the first time around, namely that Thoreau did not make a life program out of staying at Walden Pond. He returned to civilization within two years. Not that it detracted any from the most important thing he had to say, namely that it is possible to have deep joy, and not just mere contentment in life. But the fact remains, that his was just a temporary experiment. On the other hand, I was in it for good.

Still, I felt pretty pure and noble when I planned our future life minus the sins of a wasteful and throwaway society. Going back to basics and the simple life was the thing to do. But as we were working on the house, it became apparent that I was fooling myself in a big way.

First, I was not really willing to go without the things that make life beautiful or comfortable. This was clear enough on that first, memorable day at Szabar when I attempted to do the laundry the way the natives do it. It was also soon obvious that the simple country-life, which we were about to embrace, was far more luxurious than what even the wealthiest of our Hungarian friends enjoyed at the time. It was they who were living the simple life; we were not.

"Man, you don't need an updated fuse box here," the electrician grumbled to my husband after he surveyed our vast collection of power-driven machinery. "You need a damned power plant, that is what you need with all this crap."

How could I dare pretend simplicity, while I insisted on a second bathroom, a string of extra rooms, including two guest apartments with their own kitchenettes and bathrooms? Didn't I bring a sauna cabin? Didn't I insist on an automatic garage door? Wasn't there a washer and drier on the van? Didn't I own all the convenient electrical appliances ever manufactured? Didn't we plan for a full-time housekeeper? Whom was I trying to kid? I had lofty dreams of Walden Pond, but settled for Dallas or Hollywood.

There was a market in the town of Keszthely with produce most people would not consider buying: wilted, half-rotten things having long lost color, vitality and vitamins. Worms were having obscene orgies on slimy mushrooms. Women, carrying their ubiquitous wicker baskets were rummaging among this garbage to find something that could be resuscitated to make it into an edible meal. And nobody screamed about the quality, or the lack of it.

I recalled the market in suburban Atlanta, where my daughter Christina took me shopping. It takes real doing before a food market impresses me, but that one did it to me. I grew unused from seeing such plenty. There were at least eight different types of fresh green beans, at least eighteen sorts of salad greens, mounds of crisp, fresh vegetables and fruits artistically displayed and in order to keep them fresh, they were periodically sprinkled through a network of tiny overhead pipes. There must have been ten dozen different types of breads and rolls, hundreds of convenience foods. A shelf, as long as one of the walls, was packed with freshly prepared take-home foods, pasta in every imaginable sauce, miles of salads and roasted meat to satisfy every preference and diet. There were endless varieties of coffee, tea, spices, and condiments. Fish, lobster, oysters, mussels were offered live, or bedded in crushed ice among wedges of lemons; a wonderful still life, created by artists, for the shopping pleasure of the housewife. Caviar of every price category was displayed next to smoked eel, trout and salmon along with everything else only a gourmet could imagine. It was mind-boggling, almost obscene in its shameless opulence in the middle of a world that is not able to solve the problem of hunger. I was totally awed and very uncomfortable.

But at Keszthely, as I considered a cucumber that was so life-worn and limp that by a slight movement of my wrist I could bend its one end to the other, I quickly forgot the discomfort I felt in that Atlanta food emporium, spread out over several acres. I wished there could be some middle road between starvation and unimaginable opulence.

What I saw here at Szabar was not the noble Walden. I did not really see the romance of a wonderful life the way God created it; I saw plain and painful poverty in the form of little old women, broken and gnarled, offering three heads of garlic or a bunch of lavender they grew in their small gardens. I saw women, well over seventy working from sun-up to sundown in their gardens and vineyards, so they could supplement the miserable social security checks that could not possibly keep them alive. There was simplicity and frugality in the way Esther washed and line-dried every plastic bag or strip of silver foil, so she could reuse them, or when she calculated in February how many eggs to put under the hens to keep her in eggs and some meat for the coming season. What I saw around me was not idyllic; it was harsh.

After dissecting my weaknesses in this way, I took the glasses out to the "loggia", where my husband was waiting for me and for the drinks. So where was the simplicity? Did Thoreau celebrate his sunsets with cocktails, tinkling with freshly made ice cubes? Our life in Szabar already was much slower and calmer than it was before, and I loved that. But it was not simplistic, not even in that half-finished house. And I was eagerly looking to the future and did not wish to give up any of the luxuries we had. If this was contradiction, so be it.

We clinked our glasses in quiet contentment, and in my new, take-it-easy attitude I shrugged off the uncomfortable thoughts. During the great transitions in my life, I accumulated some complexities and unresolved conflicts. I was poised between the desire for an uncomplicated life and the need for comfort and ease. Assuredly, this is a most difficult contradiction. But the evening was velvety, the sky immense, and we were absolutely happy. Heaven has touched us, and it was not the time to think heavy thoughts.

Of course, some of these comforts that made me uneasy at the moment, were still way off, somewhere in the misty future. The house was actually not fit to live in, and people never stopped marveling how we could stand our life in what looked like a battle zone. We still had no windows or doors, so that cats, dogs, ermine, martens, mice, mink and people could freely come and go, and they did. Swallows built their nests in the living room, and taught their young to fly over our heads. We lived with our garden furniture, which (dare I say?) was mostly made of plastic. In a less happy mood I worried about the snail's progress our house was making toward completion. Suddenly it appeared that Christmas was just around the corner.

The heat was almost unbearable that summer. The temperature hovered in the upper nineties and not a drop of rain fell. The gardens suffered and the crops in the fields turned brown and then they dried completely. Only the cool breezes in our huge "loggia" made life not only tolerable, but very pleasant.

We were told not to use city water for sprinkling. Fortunately, this was the time my husband discovered that we had an abandoned well on the property. Without wasting any time, he called a technician to check it out. The upper part of the well was almost clogged up with dirt. The thick mat of refuse was made up of leaves and other material and was supported by some planks, which somebody once pitched into the well, and now were wedged crosswise in the shaft, about seven feet down. But underneath the mess, at a depth of seventy feet, the well had a marvelously rich supply of clean, fresh water. It took two days to clean it out, and to build a secure housing over it, but by the third evening a pump was lowered. As we sat in the darkening loggia with our glasses of wine and a few candles giving flickering, subdued light, we listened to the cooling sound of water sprinkling over the thirsty soil. Nothing could have sounded lovelier.

In spite of the disorder and the many inconveniences, we had a fore-taste of heaven. If only we could hold our own until the happy day when the last craftsman would clear out of the house! We hoped that this would be before we turned one hundred years old. We were dream-ing of the times when the turmoil and the hammers of workers would no longer beat the rhythm to our lives, when the counterpoint would not be the whine of the saws, and the refrain would not be sung by the groans of the medieval cement mixer. I was yearning for the day when I no longer would have to cook for half the village.

The stress that was our fate during the last years was dramatic. In a relatively short period of time we had to face retirement, losing a pro-fession I loved, a total restructuring of our life, separation from family and friends, building a house, adapting to a new culture. All these are considered major stress factors. Yet we resisted the temptation to cave in and were doing well. Stubbornly we refused to be eroded. Attrition was not an option.

My older daughter, Christina, a veteran of stress, admonished. "Watch for the first bad signs, Mom. You know you reached the end of the rope, when you start snarling at each other." We haven't done that. We yelled at the workers, the drought, the rain, the mud, the deliverymen, the mosquitoes, even at Esther, but not at each other.

But secretly we started to wonder, how long would the healing smile last and when would the time come when "enough" turns into "too much". How many times can we run into a brick wall at our age, and not be-come casualties? We worried about each other with a new, groping, searching concern. This was a new modulation in the old love song. We tried not to intrude, but the watchful worry was everywhere. How do you feel? Did you have a good night? Don't you need a short rest? What would you eat? We were suddenly beset with all the unspoken worries. He looks a little pinched today…She is so pale…Were his pants always so loose?…This road is almost level, why is she panting?… And then at night, when the other is sleeping so terribly noiselessly, there is this tentative, embarrassed, careful reaching across the double bed. Softly the hand hovers, as if the intent is just to caress, just to touch flesh, like in the old days. Then the hand moves gently and comes to rest on the face of the other. There is a small stir and a quiet, happy moan of acknowledgment. Then we smile sheepishly in the dark and go back to sleep with immense relief. How silly it was to think that there was no breathing! And so the cycle closes. We used to get up countless times during the night in the past to listen to the breathing of our babies. The babies are now grown, and even their babies are grown, but the ancient and urgent fear about each other's breathing is left. Please, do keep on breathing, and let's stop counting the days, as time flies by. One day we are giants and nothing can stop us from conquering the world; then overnight we become so fragile and weak that we find it hard to unscrew a baby-proof bottle of cleaning fluid. We attempt to protect and to shield each other from the inevitable, which comes so soon, so very soon. And we are not ready for it yet.

In spite of my culinary efforts, the construction seemed to slow down toward the end of the summer. We had problems with every phase of the building. Our workers, never having seen the Leaning Tower of Pisa, did not share our distrust regarding slanting walls. With a religious conviction of the kind the Crusaders displayed, they refused to use levels or plumb lines. Real men are no different in Hungary than in the rest of the world, but in addition of not asking directions, they also refuse to look at blue prints, created by highly paid architects. Sometimes, halfway through a job, they would come up with unexpected, divine inspirations, and with bewildering speed they would do things differently and incorrectly, without consulting first with the architects, or us.

None gave us more grief than the plumber, or I should say plumbers, since by the end of the summer we hired four and fired three. Just like the great love, or the fish that got away, in retrospect the plumber that we had before the present one, always looked better. I was very near the verge of losing my mind with all the mistakes they created in our waterworks, but finally, just before I was ready to return to Germany, the Last of the Plumbers completed the major work. The pipes for the master bath were laid. Of course, it goes without saying that in doing this, he destroyed every wall in the vicinity of the new kitchen, both baths and the utility room. At this time it seemed that our entire life consisted of tolerating the destruction of what has been built before. He asked for a king's ransom for the job and I balked. However, my husband was of the opinion that we should give him all our money, and everything else he asks for, just so that he is out of our house once and for all.

Understanding perfectly well how we felt about him, the plumber, clutching his bundle of money gleefully, was gone before I could wish him leaking pipes for the rest of his life. No doubt he laughed himself sick for getting paid for a job that should have been condemned.

The smell of the exhaust fumes from his Trabant was still in the air, when every one of his newly installed pipes started to leak. I kept mopping the kitchen and the bath, but after lugging the sixth bucket of water into the yard, I admitted defeat. There was nothing else to do, but to shut off the water main. I would have loved to stuff his scrawny body into the pipes to stop the leakage, but this was no time for revenge. We had to swallow our pride and beg him for a return performance.

The Knight of the Holy Drain had to be asked ten times before he would consider lowering himself to visit our humble abode. In general his attitude was, "Give the pipes two aspirins, and call me in the morning." Of course, he did not have a phone, so we kept sending him telegrams, and pasted notes on his front door. May he and his kind be condemned to a dripping boiler room for the rest of eternity. Finally he did come and stopped the leakage, temporarily, as we were soon to find out.

But not all things were devastating. One day we were picking sour cherries in Esther's vineyard, up in the hills. In the quiet, sun-soaked afternoon I had a vision of the Golden Years to come. Way below on the road toy cars were moving, but their noise did not reach us. The silence was deep and absolute and the sounds of Nature made it even more so. Crickets played their tireless music, birds called, insects hummed. We were dropping ruby-red berries into our wicker baskets and felt deep contentment in doing this totally mindless work. The village was far below us and behind its red roofs the Lesser Lake Balaton shimmered in blue haze. We did not talk, but knew without words that if this is how the end of our life would be, it was certainly worth coming this far. The affairs of the world dropped away. Miraculously the economy, international affairs, political concerns, the military draw-down, the promises of DoDDS, and the major trade agreements rolled on as always, without our having to worry about them. We have not read a newspaper in weeks, and did not know where our radio was packed away. We remembered the Fourth of July a full week after it was gone. As far as that goes, we might have been living on another planet, and it was good. Ages ago, when we were rushing ahead in the passing lane, we missed what was important. Now the safety belt was unbuckled, the demon car parked, and suddenly we were able to experience the world with all of our senses. It was a full life, and it promised absolute peace.

Toward the end of the summer, we bought a dog, a kuvasz, and named her Borka. She is snow white, a Hungarian breed of great antiquity and elegance, used for centuries as a guard dog. She was a fluffy butterball when we bought her, but in less than two days she developed into a white monster of fearsome reputation. Her growl and size inspires instant respect, and nobody enters our house without her approval. She seldom approves. Nobody, including our cleaning lady, can touch anything that belongs to us. This caused quite a problem when she tried to remove the vacuum cleaner from the closet, or wanted to take out the garbage. Borka also disapproves with an angry growl when a lady visitor wishes to leave with her purse and coat. Borka, somewhat more fierce than intelligent, is never absolutely sure whether the purse belongs to the visitor or to me.

From the beginning, she preferred to sleep all day and have company all night. Of course, staying awake at night was in keeping with the character of a conscientious guard dog, even if she was only at the stage when she was still mortally afraid of Midnight, the cat, which by now was totally worn out by her maternal cares. However our life style was such that we actually preferred to sleep at night. She could never quite get over this oddity of our character.

Borka was born with outstanding psychological gifts. She could sniff out at once who the sucker was (both of us) and how to get what she wanted. Despite her fearsome size, she was (and is) a very light and picky eater. I read how much a dog her size ought to eat, and was constantly worried that she would starve to death, because she ate so little.

One day I made an omelet for her breakfast, and my husband announced in his Very Supreme Court Voice the verdict. "Now that's the limit. Spoiling must stop here. How can a grown woman forget the difference between man and beast?"

On the other hand, Borka wanted to take a stroll at three AM, and this man of very strict principles actually took her out. It was my turn to mandate what the absolute limit of spoiling would be. How can a grown man be manipulated to such a degree? By a bitch, no less.

It was almost time to fly back to Germany, and we decided to give ourselves a few days of rest. We got into the car, taking Borka with us, who just loved to travel, and we drove randomly around Lake Balaton.

"It looks as if the Creator was dissatisfied with His designs, and kept throwing away all the models," I rhapsodized. "Each of these mountains has such an odd, individual shape, but they are totally incongruous. They have nothing to do with each other."

"I think that aesthetically they look all right," my husband decided, "But I agree that the Creator might have changed His mind during the process of creation. They were originally volcanic mountains, and maybe He realized, just in the nick of time, that mankind couldn't be trusted with fire. He then destroyed them, or blew them up, or just threw them away."

"I'm glad he discarded His models right around here. They are beautiful, don't you agree? Their youthful fires cooled, their rough edges eroded, their slopes mellowed into vineyards, they now slumber peacefully in the late summer sunlight and dream about their turbulent youths."

"Just like you and I." Was there a wistful tone in his voice?

Below the hills the great lake spread, changing its color by the hour. Sailboats were gliding on its surface in the lazy, golden afternoon, and small villages huddled at its shores, where the last tourists were still shopping for souvenirs. We parked the car and walked around the ancient settlement of Szigliget. For a while we considered the steep walk up to the ruins of the fort, from where the view must be spectacular.

"You were the one, who talked about youthful fires cooling," he panted after a short while. "Mine is about to go out completely, so let's not insult our cardiovascular system. Wouldn't you agree that the view from here is just as great?"

I agreed. We found a lovely inn on the hillside and sipped our wine in full view of the lake and the ruins. Borka dozed at our feet. Our meal of tender, grilled lamb chops was superb and we chose a wonderfully aromatic, garlicky cucumber salad in a light cream dressing, flavored with fresh dill to go with it. Later we spent time in an antique shop about which my husband was not especially thrilled. He, of the practical mind, is convinced that half of our household stuff ought to be discarded in the first place. He thinks it irrational to buy things of no practical use, when even the practical things are only occasionally used. I, on the other hand, am ecstatic, when I can touch old scales, lamps, copper dishes, bottles and jugs. I used to lug home old dishes from Sicily, Belgium, Portugal and a dozen other places. We did not leave empty-handed from Szigliget either.

"I'm not complaining," he said complaining, "but I wonder what takes more energy: to climb up to the fort, or to lug all this stuff to the car?"

We spent a day at Zalakaros at the thermal pools, because I was intrigued about the underwater massages, whirlpools, and the swift current that whips the swimmers around the pool at a speed way beyond what an Olympic gold medal winner could produce. A century ago Zalakaros was about as insignificant as Szabar is. Then an American concern started a search for oil in the neighborhood, but instead of the liquid gold, they hit on hot water at many places, where they drilled, including in Zalaszabar. Disappointed, the geologists turned their attentions elsewhere, and the settlement would have sunk back into oblivion if it were not for the far reaching vision of a few. The unexpected natural resource furnished a tremendous supply of hot water with the same healing elements that the thermal lake Héviz has, a few miles east of it. In a relatively short time the first set of pools were built at Zalakaros, and hotels sprang up like mushrooms around it. The vision of a few turned into a flourishing year-round resort. Americans are usually surprised to find that London is located about on the same latitude as Newfoundland, and that Venice is located farther to the north than Cleveland is. And although latitude is not the only factor that influences climate, still Europe offers relatively few winter vacation spots for the non-skier and so these thermal baths in our neighborhood quickly acquired an excellent continental reputation. Héviz and Zalakaros soon turned into favorite vacation destinations for Austrian and German guests.

To compare notes, we also went for a soak to the hot water lake at

Héviz, a town tucked away in the valley, just a few miles from us. The lake, the largest thermal lake in Europe, is more than warm water; it is an experience. Two carved griffins guard the entrance, and a long, glass-covered boardwalk over the water leads right into the middle of the lake into a structure built on stilt. It houses the dressing rooms , showers and rest areas. Here a fair-sized area of the lake is enclosed , so that even in the harshest winter it is possible to step into the lake without getting chilled. The enclosed area has gates, so the bather can swim through them to the outside to enjoy the rare pleasure of a good swim in warm water while the snow is falling.

The lake at its deepest point has a twisted cave, the shape of a cornucopia. Here the waters of several cold and hot springs mingle to the perfect temperature of 33° Celsius before coming up to the surface, where it cools just a few degrees to a pleasant and constant temperature. The amount of water bubbling up is so profuse that the lake exchanges its entire content every thirty-six hours. The bottom of the lake is covered with a thick carpet of peat, rich in sulfur and radium, and is said to have outstanding medicinal properties. People afflicted with various diseases of the joints, muscles and bones are enthusiastic, and tell stories about its benefits, which almost verge on the unbelievable. This is probably why Buzád and his men frequented it a thousand years ago. Both horses and men must have suffered from the long rides, especially during the winter. Man and beast alike must have found wonderful relief in the warm, healing waters.

The weather was perfect on that late summer day, and we left the shelter of the bathhouse and swam out into the open lake. The water was the color of emerald, but then it changed to the deepest blue, as if a magician was busy entertaining the bathers from some hidden workshop. Thousands of purple lotus blossoms made a spectacular carpet near the shores. The Japanese stood around in crowds with their expensive cameras to get a picture of these wildly contrasting colors.

After our swim we indulged in a complete body massage, a luxury I always associated with top-earning movie stars. It was so relaxing that I promptly fell asleep and only woke with a start, when I heard myself snore.

"Having a little snooze?" the masseur wanted to know. "That's the way to do it. The more relaxed you are, the better it is for you." I was on my way to embrace the hedonistic way of life.

Refreshed and pampered, we walked around the lake in the lavish flower garden, straight out of the Arabian Nights. People, just as relaxed as we were, strolled around. They talked and chatted in the manner of people having a lot of time, and no worries. It seemed, that time stopped and wonderful eternity had begun. The shadows grew long, and soon exciting food fragrances mingled with that of the flowers. Slowly the lights in the park were lit, and we chose a restaurant with the most potential. Our dinner was by candlelight, and accented with soft gypsy music.

"I don't ever want to leave," I whispered. "This is better than I ever thought possible."

I was unfair to him. He could not alter the situation, and here I was burdening him with my unwillingness to leave.

Life was becoming complete, exactly as I always wished it would be. The sharp edges were disappearing, and every day resembled more the dream we were trying to achieve. Zalaszabar was no longer just an inexpensive place to while away the remaining few years of our life; it was turning into the very place we always wanted to have: peaceful, tranquil, comfortable, but within reach of all the good things and the cultural gifts we both craved.

I often thought about the advertisement I saw a few years ago in a glossy magazine. I forgot what it was promoting, but I remember the magnificent palace shown, with every comfort imaginable. In front of it stood an attractive couple, the swimming pool and tennis court just visible to the side. The caption asked in effect, "if this is where they live, where on earth would they go for a vacation?" I no longer remember the answer the ad gave, but I know our answer would be: thanks, but we'll stay right here. We lost the desire to go anywhere. The wonderful places on this planet no longer call us. Well, maybe with the exception of Cleveland, Atlanta, Charlotte, and Ramstein-Miesenbach.

We celebrated the last day of my vacation up in the hills with friends. We have a piece of land there that my husband bought for me during the first week we ever stayed in Hungary. At that time we took a long walk in the hills, and arrived at this spot that must have fallen down by accident from heaven. It was on the highest point of the hill and offered a breath-taking view of the lake. It is a fairly large tract of land, but of no practical use, since it is on a steep hillside with numerous ravines on it. Only the very top area at the roadside is more or less flat. It has some stately walnut and chestnut trees on it, and a number of delicate almond trees, but otherwise it is a luxuriously useless piece of beauty.

"If this place were mine, I would never leave," I sighed, and meant it. Before the end of the week, my husband bought it. This only shows how careful one must be when making promises or wishes. Since that day, we did a few things to it, but were always careful not to destroy its original, natural beauty. We added a few evergreens, a living fence, a covered arbor to shield us from the sun while eating, a barbecue pit, and a deck on stilts so that we should have a comfortable place to watch sunsets and the gathering dusk. All of this blended well with what has been there before, and soon the grapevines going wild almost hid the man-made structures.

The day was perfect, the breeze constant and Borka ran around like the dizzy puppy she was, and in the process picked up every burr there was, until her snowy fur was speckled, and she looked like a first cousin to a Dalmatian.

While I sat the table on the deck, Zoltán prepared his famous *cevapcici*, little savory sausages, which he encountered during a vacation in one of the Balkan countries. These are made from triple ground meat, flavored with garlic, thyme, black pepper and surprisingly a dash of baking soda. Since this was to be the day dedicated to the garlic god, my husband marinated slices of turkey breast in milk that had a generous amount of that powerfully fragrant ingredient, and some salt. Géza, the one blessed with the talent of making perfect fires, was busy at the barbecue pit. Erika offered her special salad of corn, pineapples and other unlikely ingredients, while I lifted from the cooler my own specialty, a pasta salad in light creamy sauce, flavored (with what else?) garlic and quantities of roasted red bell peppers, sprinkled with Parmesan. Clara fixed the cocktails, which she flavored with a dash of woodruff to make it memorable.

I have not encountered woodruff until I came to Europe, where it is an absolute must, especially during May, when everybody, especially in Germany, ritualistically drinks May wine (Maibowle). This drink, concocted of white and red wine, a dash of orange liqueur, fresh strawberries and champagne, cannot be served without a sprig of the herb, which gives it that particular aroma. The herb's Latin name is *Asperula odorata*, but the Germans call it *Waldmeister*. During May huge bunches of woodruff are sold at every vegetable stand. To tell the truth, the weed looks limp and useless. When I first saw it, I was disappointed; its fame was better than the real thing. It had no fragrance and it looked dead. However, once it is dried, it becomes a thing of wonder. Its fragrance is like freshly mown meadows; it carries the hint of sunshine, morning dew, exciting herbs, and wild flowers. Although I never saw it before, still the fragrance appeared familiar, reassuring. Some tobacco factories even use it to give an extra fragrance to some of their products. A sprinkling of it into the glass is enough to be transported into ancient gardens that probably do not even exist, and recall dreams that only gods have. Since woodruff can only be bought during a short week each year, Clara solved the problem neatly. She bought enough of the herb to fill a big jar with a tight lid, then poured vodka over it. After a while she strained it and had enough woodruff -flavored vodka for the entire year. A few drops of it go a long way and she can create the mood that belongs to May in a snowstorm in February.

The men brought the freshly grilled food to the deck and somewhere below, in one of the trees, a pheasant called, probably complaining that he was not invited. We were well fed and mellow; conversation slipped into comfortable channels. Surprisingly, we talked a great deal about food.

"I read somewhere," Zoltán said, "that the French are the absolute gourmets, which is evident from the fact that they talk about food before they eat, during the meal and also afterwards. I think we have reached that level of sophistication." No argument was offered on that point. Much later we decided to take a walk in the hills. Borka understood this immediately, and even before we were ready, she was panting with anticipation.

But we progressed very slowly. First we had to pass Pista bácsi's wine cellar on our way, and he spotted us immediately. Naturally, we had to stop and taste his wine and wish him well. "The moral code of our ancestors prescribed, that all friends and strangers passing by, must be offered a cup of friendship," he explained, as he poured the second cup. Less then fifty yards later we were halted by Gergely bácsi. He saw us when we entered the other cellar, so he was all prepared, and the wine was already on the little table. It was an excellent wine, and foolishly we accepted a second glass. By the time we reached Imre bácsi's old, vaulted cellar, we felt no pain.

"We either have to make our walks at midnight, when all the good people are fast asleep already," giggled Clara, "Or accept cirrhosis of the liver as an alternative."

"That is a long way off yet," hiccuped Zoltán. "Our immediate problem is how to reach the village without making absolute fools of ourselves…"

"It is so good that you moved here," confessed Erika in alcohol induced emotionalism. "You two are much older than the rest of us, and it is so good to see that you are happy, and have so much fun. I used to be afraid of old age, and all that it brings, but not any more. When I think of the two of you, I always think of good times coming and it is so reassuring…"

"I beg your pardon, Ma'm," argued my husband trying to look stone sober, which he certainly was not, "but who the hell is old here?"

Back home I found a letter from my younger daughter. As soon as my guests left I took it to the loggia and knew I was in for a really good time. I love her letters.

"…Lexie (her youngest daughter) has a new best friend. They are exactly alike. Her name is Justine and her mom and I cannot believe how alike they are. Together they are hell on wheels. We have to limit their togetherness for fear they would start a political uprising. Or build a rocket to Mars. Or figure out a way to get arrested….Nikkie (her eleven-year old) is at camp this week. She cried when we left her, but swore that she wanted to stay. Sick puppy. I wouldn't have stayed in that moldy cabin for anything. Bathrooms up the hill and over the woods in the next county. No way. But to each his own. Anyway, I love summers. There were times this winter when I really didn't believe it would ever get warm, but it did and it is great. I am one of those mothers who adores having her kids at home, because I like children so much more than babies. Babies don't have humor, joy, or opinions. They don't want to wear rhinestones with corduroys, or dark blue nail polish. Babies just sit there, and either cry or go goo-goo-gaa-gaa, or fill their diapers. I always cry when the girls have to go back to school. They are so much fun, but they are growing so quickly. I know the time is coming very soon when they would rather be with their friends than with me or Mike, and we both dread that time. So we are trying to do as much with them as possible now, while they both still think that we are cool. We are having outings planned most days and this is so much better than having babies. I feel sorry for parents with shitty kids, 'cos mine are so great..."

Considering all the good things that mankind could be given, I am convinced that the joy of seeing one's children happy and settled must be the best gift. Only this can give the peace of mind to aging parents, so they can turn to their own life and fill the remaining years with content. Freed from the worry about the children, and being secure in the thought that they found the goals in their lives and are happy, makes it possible to soar into the possibilities that are open to the seekers even at our age.

CHAPTER SIX

On my arrival in Germany, I found my uncluttered attic apartment in comparison to what I left behind, almost healing. It was shabby beyond words, but organized, and I could find my things. And I did not have to cook gargantuan meals; if I wanted tea and toast for supper, nobody objected. Surprisingly though, even after all the work I did during the summer, I felt very strong and confident. I knew that I would cope with whatever the year brought. I would teach, if that is what they want me to do, and it won't be so bad. The man at the Regional Office was probably right when he said that teaching is less stressful than administration is. After all, you were only expected to do a job for which you were trained (even if this training happened, like in my case, sometimes around the Middle Ages), and the responsibilities and unexpected situations were far fewer, the solutions easier. I would not have to work eleven-hour days any more. My husband would soon join me, and we would live like a normal, aging couple. During the winter months we would be preparing and waiting for the summers, when we could escape to the Paradise we were creating for ourselves. The months between vacations would fly by, and in a few years we would retire for sure. A piece of cake, as my students used to say.

As always, Christine arranged the first working day for the returning teachers with the flamboyant style that was her very own. "No CEO of a major concern would consider calling her executives for an all important organizational meeting in the cafeteria of the plant," she announced haughtily. "And none of those guys has a staff with as many degrees and college credits as I have," she added proudly. "Would I give less to my staff than what Detroit offers to its?" Since the humble school budget did not allow for grandiose plans, she shrugged in the manner of a Spanish Grande, and paid for it out of her own pocket. So it happened that while hundreds of thousands of faculty members in schools all across the nation met in cafeterias and smelly gyms for the conferences and orientation before school opened, Christine's staff got into cars and drove up into the hills to a medieval castle. No organizational bigwig would outdo her. As far as she was concerned, her teachers deserved as much as auto-makers, or chain-store managers. She rented the entire castle, lately turned into a restaurant. The Hall of Knights was converted into a conference room and it looked only slightly incongruous when it was set up with computers, overhead projectors and flow charts.

Before the real work began, she first hosted the breakfast for well over a hundred guests, primarily for returning staff members. But she also invited the base commander and his wife, other leading military persons, the new superintendent and his wife, the officers of the PTA, and the representatives of the Teachers' Union.

The breakfast room was an addition to the old structure, very light and airy. It seemed to be floating above the vineyards where the leaves were turning golden at this time of the year. The window seats were upholstered in bright chintz, there were masses of flowers and fruits everywhere, and the braided rugs softened the harshness of brick, stone and ancient weapons displayed on the walls.

The food was served buffet style, and even as teachers were lining up with their trays, they were already arraying themselves into intimate little groups as they discussed their vacations stateside, or at some fabulously exotic place. The new superintendent, the other dignitaries and Joyce (who despite the prediction still had her job) were already seated at the large table reserved for them. Christine, the perfect hostess, was moving about, greeting her guests and spreading good cheer. Briefly I glanced at the "executive table", and remembered that in previous years that is where I too used to sit. I stopped for a moment, tray in hand, to observe my emotions. Does it hurt to be denoted and be closed out from a circle to which I used to belong? I was honest to myself and admitted that it did. For a moment I was keenly aware of the injustice, but this passed quickly, and I asked the next question. Would this destroy me? I almost laughed out. Of course, it wouldn't. It hurt my pride tremendously, but did not touch my inner self. The thing that hurt me more than my pride was that I was out of my element. I knew every person in the room, except the new-comers, but they were not really friends. Christine discouraged Joyce and me to be too close to those, whom we had to supervise. She thought that even if we could be unbiased in our judgment, it would cause other teachers, with whom we did not associate closely, to be suspicious of those who would be considered our friends. During the years we mostly associated with other administrators, but I no longer belonged to them. At the same time, teachers did not know where my loyalty was, and felt uncomfortable with me. I was in limbo between two worlds. The groups of teachers closed, and I was not invited to sit with anyone.

When I was six and my sister barely three, we moved to a new town after our parents divorced. My sister was too little to care, but my mother and I were devastated and lonely. After a while, with the resilience of children, I decided to reorganize my life. Children heal faster than adults; or perhaps it is less traumatic to lose a father than it is to part with a husband and lover. Our new home was located at a beautiful public park that had, among other things, a well-equipped playground.

A few weeks after our arrival I marched out with my nanny to this new territory. She sat aside from the other nannies, because she was German, and could not communicate with them. In a way she was as much of an outcast as I was. But I gathered all of the bravado (which of course, I did not really have) and approached the group of children who were busily playing in the huge sandbox. I stood and watched them for a space of time. This initial silence is considered polite and quite appropriate for the sand-box society, but eventually I took a deep breath, stepped closer and introduced myself.

They looked up morosely for a second, without saying a word, then turned back to their castles in the sand. I was caught off guard. They did not follow the rules, one of which was that if I tell them my name, they have to tell me theirs. Up to now this was the modus operandi, but here it did not seem to work. I am not one to give up a plan lightly, so I approached it from an other angle.

"Your castle is very nice. May I play with you?" Again they looked up with cold stares, their faces closed. Recalling those hard, indifferent gazes well over half a century later, I still can't remember animosity or hate. None of that. I could have defended myself against that, but what I saw was far worse. They were dispassionate. They spurned me on account of being a zero, a nobody, an excess. Their unsmiling faces, the uncompromising rejection in their eyes were unambiguous. I committed a horrible faux pas by intruding to a place, where I was not wanted. This shamed and frightened me.

"No, you can't play. We don't want you. Go away." The fragile little girl with the blond braids spoke for them all.

At that time I was still hurting from a far bigger rejection, and I was terribly vulnerable. I was in no condition to laugh it off, or to defend myself with the repartee any six-year old worth her keep would have given under similar circumstances: "Go away yourself. I didn't want to play with you in the first place, and your castle is ugly. So there." I could not say it.

Instead, I just stood there in my humiliation, because this new experience of a categorical exclusion took my breath away. Yet I was brave enough, or proud enough, to stand there for a little while yet. Not wanting to play with me was one thing, but chasing me away from a public place that was next to MY home (I already had some proprietary pride) was quite something else and unacceptable. I would leave, when I felt like it, not when they ordered me. Eventually I turned, and went back to my nanny. We left the battlefield defeated, but heads held high.

That first social failure, coming so quickly after our father's rejection, scarred me for life. Standing there with the tray in my hand I was once again a six-year old, and immensely hurt, because nobody wanted to eat with me. Luckily I found an empty table by the window. A moment later a lovely woman dropped her purse on the seat next to me.

"Mind if I join? My name is Debra, and I am a reject from another school. I don't know a soul here." Soon we were deep in conversation and I totally forgot my rejection and the initial bad feelings of the morning. She was great company, bubbling with excitement, and full of fun and ideas. It was a few weeks later when I found out that she was the new superintendent's wife.

After the big breakfast I was not at all hungry at midday, and instead of lunch I took a walk. Few things can soothe me more than a clear, golden autumn day. And I was in need of some soothing. In the area where we lived in Germany, fall comes a little earlier than it does in Ohio. By the calendar it was late August, but the air was already fresh with just a hint of the cold that was lurking around the corner, although the sun had plenty of heat yet to make the day warm and pleasant. At first glance the leaves of the trees still appeared green, but they were of a less vivid hue; the edges and the tips were curling in dry brittleness, showing in yellow and bronze where the damage was done. The leaves of the vines already turned into gold that contrasted in artistic abandon with the intense blue of the sky of that deeply burning color that only the genius of Marc Chagall could duplicate in his stained glass windows in the church of St. Stephan, in Mainz.

The road from the castle led directly past the vineyards, where the grapes hung heavy and ripe, then narrowed into a path, which disappeared among the trees in the forest. As is customary in Germany, benches were placed at points, where the view was the best, and I sat down on one of these. Elderly couples were walking past me, talking, laughing, and being happy. Many had their dogs with them.

For the first time in my life, I felt true envy. I too wanted to be free on such a wonderful autumn day, and I too wanted to walk in the woods with my husband and Borka. There was something complete and wonderful in the carefree chatter, and easy laughter of these elderly people as they enjoyed the lovely day . The passages, dominated by work and worries, were behind them, and they possessed the gift that helped them extract the best of every day. I could just see them at home, right after the breakfast dishes were put away. *Frau* Müller would say to her husband, "Heinz, today the weather is truly beautiful, let's take Fido for a long walk. Let's invite our neighbors to come along, then have coffee and *Kuchen* later at the castle…" I sat there alone, yearning for this simple joy, which suddenly seemed very far away. I thought the sunshine was dimming a bit.

Life fell into a pattern of sorts. I found teaching terribly hard, since I have not done it for so long, and forgot the routines. I had to work out each lesson first, invent some creative exercises, construct teaching aids, think up motivational gimmicks, make fair and good tests. When I was a teacher, I gradually built up a large collection of these, and all I had to do was remove them from the file when the time came around for it. Now I had nothing. I worked long, long hours into the night to create the things to make a lesson clearer, to explain fractions, sentence structure or the location of the planets. Pauline, one of the most talented of the teachers on the staff, was the only one who thoroughly understood my difficulties. She was the only one who rushed to my aid and shared her supply of teaching aids. Without her I probably would have sunk during that year. I was always under stress, and mortally afraid that I would forget something, like counting how many children wanted to have lunch, or wanted to buy milk that day, or some other thing, which an experienced teacher routinely does without even having to think about it . I also suspected, that as ex-supervisor, I was probably watched very closely by my fellow teachers, who would have been very happy to catch me in some error.

Andrea's letters kept me afloat.

"…Dearest, I'm so glad August is gone. Braces, Bifocals, Biopsy and Bad Gum Surgery. I had the gum surgery and the biopsy done the same week. On Friday Mike remarked that I needed a haircut. I promptly burst into tears and told him that I didn't want to be cut any more, anywhere that week. He didn't get it. You are right, Mom. Men do think differently. I adore my husband, but he is useless in a crisis. He kept patting my arm and kept saying idiotic shit, like 'try not to think about it.' How inane…Otherwise life is great. When are you coming? I could dysfunction, you could whine about your sister-in-law or your job, and we could both guzzle port wine…We could also scandalize all my friends, who think it is abnormal to love your mother so much…"

But things turned out so very differently from what we planned and what we wanted. In November I became ill. Although the house was still in no condition to be abandoned, my husband cancelled all crafts-men, locked up and flew to Germany to be with me. By Christmas I was released from the hospital, but it was obvious that my attic apartment was not the place to recuperate. We moved into our tiny, but lovely apartment at his daughter's house, where I was spoiled, and somewhat insulated from all worries. As far as I was concerned, I felt fine, although still a little fragile, and could not imagine that I would ever be able to carry the workload I used to have. By March my doctors shook their heads in that strange worried way doctors have, and in May, consider-ing my condition, my age, and the situation in which I would be strug-gling, decided that I should quit, permanently. So, after all, I too be-came part of the statistics, a faceless figure, who eventually eroded, ex-actly as it was predicted. I applied for medical retirement, and although the considerable financial loss I would have to accept in the bargain hurt badly, we both realized that this was not just a necessary, but prob-ably the only step to take. The medical retirement was granted, and I swear that the sound of heavy stones rolling off my heart could be heard for miles. Even more than my doctors, I was fully aware that my working years were up, and I was in no condition to continue what I have done before.

"You see, I told you that you'd leave," his daughter said. But it was not that imminent yet. I stayed in our little apartment at her house for a few more months, while my husband flew to Hungary to complete the house and to find a full-time housekeeper. I was able to join him in November, a full year after I was taken ill.

CHAPTER SEVEN

Christmas came, the first one in our new home in Hungary. I had very ambivalent feelings about it. My family was thousands of miles away, and the phone, promised a year ago, was still just a fantasy. We wouldn't be able to call anyone.

During the year of my illness very little happened to our house. Although we now had doors and windows and the kitchen was completed, very little else was done to it. The old section of the house had electric heat, but the new addition, which was to be heated by oil and later by gas, was freezing cold with that bone-chilling dampness that new houses with very thick walls have. The big furnace was already in place, and the radiators were on the walls, but some mysterious parts of it were spread out in hopeless heaps on the unfinished cement floor in the living room, along with an assortment of other building material. We were still living in the middle of a construction site and my doctors would have had a fit if they could see it. It totally lacked the spirit needed for a proper holiday.

Stubbornly, I wanted the first Christmas to be exactly like it used to be, with holly and ivy, boughs of evergreens, a grand Christmas tree as tall as the ceiling would permit, good cheer, happy people, a blazing fire, lots of snow and superb food. That was the dream. Reality was not quite like it. I was close to tears every time I heard the tearjerker on my tape, "I'll be home for Christmas…" The imminent depression that was about to overtake me, promised to be catastrophic in scope. Our home was not festive; it was not even a home. It was a warehouse, or Baghdad after the Storm, or a building site after a hurricane hit it.

"I'm not going under," I promised myself fighting tears as I supervised Agnes, our new and wonderful housekeeper, as she and two young gypsies put up thousands of tiny white Christmas lights on the bushes and trees around the house. At least the outside should look, as it ought to.

I switched on the lights and the magic was instant. In the dark of the night the ugliness disappeared and the garden turned into a blinking Christmas fantasy, worthy of Walt Disney. Szabar, like most Hungarian villages, is almost totally dark after the sun sets. Only a few streetlights bear witness to the fact that people actually live here. Windows are shuttered, and the frugal people would never consider leaving an outside light burning. The villagers have never seen anything like our lights. They made pilgrimages to our house, and invited friends from distant places to see the wonder.

"America came to us," they commented, because sometimes they saw wonders such as this on television.

"Is this the house of Father Winter?" a little girl wanted to know. She was raised in Communism, where Santa Claus was a *persona non grata*. But because children would not conform to the new ideological norms, Big Brother had to compromise and had to allow Father Winter to take the place of the saintly gentleman.

"Is it Christmas yet?" a little guy bundled up in a purple snowsuit wanted to know.

I always went way out for displaying Christmas lights, but never before did I get so much satisfaction or joy out of it as in Szabar. Without realizing it, I gave a marvelous gift to our village. (Years later lights began to appear here and there, until almost every house now has some sort of a decoration for the holidays, but at that time this was a miraculous novelty.)

On the day before Christmas, heavy clouds were banking on the northwest horizon, a sure sign for some big weather. As far as weather and a white Christmas were concerned, things looked promising. I could already sniff snow in the air, and was thrilled. What could be more wonderful and romantic than be snowbound with the man one loves? Who cares about a half-finished house when the wonderful white stuff falls gently from the sky? The snow would also cover the hopeless and depressing mess around the house. Maybe I could even forget about the things that were missing during this Christmas, such as a civilized home, and the merry crowd we always had during the holidays. In other words, no family, no decent house, no warmth. I even had to give up the dream of a blazing fire, since the fireplace was still in its planning stage. My only guest would be Esther. But I forged ahead anyhow.

With the help of Agnes, I concentrated on the dining room, the only truly livable place in the house, the only room that had everything, including floors, and was not scattered with crates and furniture waiting for the completion of the house. We decorated the tree, all in pink, silver, and lace. It turned out to be truly beautiful. Freshly starched linen covered the table, set with Wedgwood china, Waterford crystal, and Norwegian pewter. The centerpiece, created by Agnes, a trained florist, was an art work of pink carnations, candles, and silver spruce complementing the color scheme of the tree. We tied silver ribbons on the stems of the champagne glasses.

It was picture perfect and very artistic, except for the arctic temperature, which despite the discreetly placed heaters, never climbed above the fifties. Oh, my kingdom for a working furnace! Because of the glacial temperatures, I decided not to dress for the Christmas Eve dinner. Actually I put on every piece of clothing I could find. Christmas Eve, back home, was a formal occasion, the best day of the year. It was family tradition to wear evening dress for the meal, which was the overture for the long celebration to follow. But Agnes and I looked like a pair getting ready for an ascent of Mt. Everest. I wore a heavy sweatshirt over thermal underwear, heavy pants, topped with my husband's oversized sweater. Woolen stockings and lined boots completed my haute couture. This was not the proper attire for an elegant evening, and I did not fit among the crystals, candles, and flowers. But at least I was not shivering, and still had the use of all my fingers and toes.

"You going somewhere?" The man of the house had the nerve to ask as he surveyed my attire.

I prepared a traditional Hungarian Christmas Eve dinner that starts with a creamy wine soup, then mushroom-filled pancakes and a salad for the first course. For the main course I prepared the irresistible carp dish, the food for Christmas Eve. On a bed of thinly sliced potatoes, layered with thin slices of onions, green peppers and tomatoes reposes the carp. This is baked in the oven with copious applications of a mixture of fried and crushed bacon, sour cream and red pepper.

Carp in Hungary is a different experience from carp in Ohio. Here they live in clean, fresh water with only a limited food supply, and they must share their living space with fish that have no compunctions about gobbling up their fellows. Hence, the carp is forever on the run and it is a sporty, solid-bodied fish without the easy fat, soft flesh and muddy taste of his relative, which lives an easy life at unmentionable places, mostly where the Cuyahoga river meets Lake Erie. The bigger specimens reach a venerable size, and their flesh is as dark and firm as that of beef, the taste is delicate and flavorful. The fragrance emanating from the oven was tantalizing. My husband worried that I worked too hard.

"Don't knock yourself out," he warned. "Counting Agnes and Esther, there will only be the four of us."

But I wanted to do it right, although even I could see that it would take extraordinary magic to change our house into something wonderful. The dining room with its festive air seemed to emphasize the bleakness of the rest of the house. Even with the lights dimmed, I could still see over the fine china, across the entry, the large mounds of clay, tiles, sand, boxes with wiring, and all sorts of things that really do not belong in a cozy living room. But I was not about to ruin our first Christmas with whining and tears, so I bustled about in my best Pollyanna manner, oozing good cheer to the point where I started to loath myself for all the insincerity.

In the midst of all this I answered the doorbell and faced a ball of mistletoes, huge like a third of my dining room table. Behind this incredible bough I saw Joska, our favorite gypsy, our all-around man.

"You said you'd like some mistletoe for the holidays. Well, this thing kept begging to be cut, so here it is, and a merry Christmas." He was delighted with his gift; I was somewhat shocked by the size. We could barely drag it through the front door. He must have been risking life and limb to get it for me. When my husband saw the tip I gave Joska, it was he who was then horrified.

"Just wait! When the rest of his tribe hears how much you gave, in an hour we'll have to deal with an entire forest! They'll be running us down with mistletoe."

The next person who rang our doorbell was the one and only florist in the village; she handed me a box of long-stemmed red roses that just arrived from Budapest. It was my husband's Christmas gift and I was almost speechless with delight.

"Don't just stand there waiting to be named Miss America," he teased. "Roses self-destruct within minutes, so give them to Agnes. She can lengthen their lives by about three minutes if she puts them in water right away."

The third time the doorbell rang, we had a surprise so great that had Santa Claus himself been standing there, we could not have been more shocked. Bundled up and with a toolbox in his hand, there stood our furnace man. He promised time and again to come and connect whatever had to be connected between the furnace and the radiators, but like all other promises in this land of hopes, this too remained a promise only.

By this time I was almost resigned to be constantly cold. I read somewhere that low temperatures lengthen life, and that cold excites the creative and intellectual powers, so I accepted the prospect of having a long, creative life, always just a few degrees this side from being frozen, while having deeply intellectual thoughts. I was just making progress in brainwashing myself that cold is beautiful, when the furnace man decided that he could not face the feast of love, while picturing us frozen in each other's arms. He drove eighty miles on Christmas Eve to make sure that we would have heat during the holidays. This nation is full of contradictions and surprises.

He took up his position in front of the furnace and while he did his thing with the stubborn cables that refused to behave according to the owner's manual, my husband hovered about him with the excitement of a new father, whose wife is about to give birth. Practically wringing his hands he asked every minute, "Is it OK? Will she make it?"

Agnes and I tried to make use of the unexpected bounty of the mistletoe in our so-called living room by covering with it some of the unspeakable mounds of building material, which were stored there for the fireplace to be built some day. I only interrupted my work with the wires and pliers to run into the kitchen to pamper the carp in the oven. The wind had stopped, the temperature dropped and the low clouds promising Christmas cheer burst forth, but not with snow.

I stepped out into the portico to tie some mistletoe and red bows to the outside lamps, and all but fell on my face. A killer ice-rain was falling. The walkway from the garden gate, the road, the trees, the roofs glistened with an inch of treacherous ice. The electrical wires, coated thickly with ice, hung ominously, ready to snap any moment. There wasn't a person or a car out in the ice-rain that crackled and rustled as it hit the already solid ice on the road and the roofs.

I went back into the glittering dining room and put another place setting on the table. With Agnes we figured out an acceptable sleeping arrangement for the furnace man; not an easy job in our disaster area. Christmas or no Christmas, I was not about to let him drive eighty miles in that mess.

In another hour the furnace was finally coming to life and for the first time blessed warmth flooded the house. Esther conquered the few yards between her house and ours by tying old rags to her boots, and used a broom for a walking stick in order not to slip and fall.

As we sat down to eat I gave thanks, because unlike the furnace man's family, mine at least knew where I was, and I knew where they were, even if I could not call them.

At the end of the meal, my husband poured the champagne.

"Here is to Christmas, to joy and happiness. And to every member of our family, with whom we now connect, if only in spirit." I was close to tears as I thought of my loved ones, and imagined how they gather around their trees and think of us, and feel the same longing pain. Holidays can be terribly trying. I once worked in the emergency room of St. Luke's hospital in Cleveland, and it used to amaze me that the worst and busiest day of the entire year was not New Year's Eve, as one would expect, but Christmas Eve. I could see why.

"Don't get emotional," my husband warned me. "I know exactly what you are thinking about. But your children are still hours away from gathering around their trees. Because of the time zones it isn't even noon there. They are at this moment losing their minds, rushing about with last minute things to do and wishing that the day would end quickly. Happy Christmas to us." Once again he got me out of my private black hole, and just in time too.

We also toasted our furnace man, and told him how sorry we were that he could not be home with his family on Christmas Eve.

"No big deal," he answered. "Our children are still very little, and don't know the difference. The wife and I don't make much out of the twenty-fourth. For that matter, even the twenty-fifth is only marginally interesting to us. The Communists trained us not to celebrate Christmas, and we have not yet developed this new habit."

"Nevertheless, we are deeply grateful for the heat," I told him. "It is the best gift we could have received. There comes an age, when one can go without food perhaps, but not without warmth."

"It was my own decision to come and I am glad I did. This evening was awfully nice. Sort of crazy, yes, but unforgettable. I never participated in such a celebration, but now I wish it could be part of our life too. I guess man must have some holidays in order to be able to tolerate the rest of the days." He drank some of his champagne, then placed the fluted glass next to his dessert plate with great care. "It is awesome that this half-finished, cold house did not break you. Others would have fled, maybe to a hotel. Or given up completely, and just nixed out the holiday. But not you. The side of the house that is heaped up with shit did not keep you from having candles, flowers, crystal and a fine meal in the other half. In the middle of this mess, you created peace and beauty. This takes some doing. You made a point, and I only wish that when I'm your age I'd be as strong as you are. I'm not so sure that I am that stable even now."

Despite my initial fears and dismal premonitions about the holiday I too felt peaceful and content. We each gave the other something that we could cherish and created a bond that we all valued.

We still had no draperies and through the large, arched windows, we could see the hundreds of tiny white Christmas lights shining like little gems on the silvery, ice-covered branches outside. The pink and silver candles burned peacefully on our table, and the house was filled with the rich aroma of freshly perked coffee. One of the red roses dropped a petal, and somehow even that was beautiful and poetic.

CHAPTER EIGHT

I was not feeling well just after the holiday and when our doctor came to see me, he looked around in speechless amazement.

"I hope you realize that this environment is not particularly conducive to getting well soon," he declared. "Why don't you move to one of your children while the house is completed? Or take a long vacation somewhere." Yeah, sure. For the next decade, or so.

I always loved the suggestions of doctors, because they were almost poetic in their silliness. "Take it easy," "stay in bed for a few days," (with three small children in the house), "go on a vacation," "lose some weight", and "fly to the USA for a few months." Translated: you are clearly in a mess, and it is all your fault. Do something reasonable to get out of it, which is why I'm giving helpful suggestions. If you won't follow them, you can't be helped. In that case, quit bothering me.

In a way doctors and plumbers have a lot in common, whether they realize it or not. A good example was the newest disaster in my kitchen. The pipes connecting to the washer, the dishwasher, the sink and the main pipe were dripping once again. I had no choice but to drive to the next town and call the despised plumber. I hated to do it, but necessity can be a tyrant, and it can force a woman to do undignified things, no matter how she hates to do them. I tried to use the proper shade of tone between polite humility (in order not to offend him) and assertiveness (in order to get him to come and see my ailing pipes).

"My pipes drip. I can't empty the pails under them fast enough," I explained the symptoms.

"Pipes drip. That's what they do. No big deal. Call me when worse happens."

It did. When health and pipes go very bad, they seldom get better without professional intervention. A few days later I entered the kitchen and found it two inches under water. My beautiful Italian tiles were submerged in water. It was as frightening as the first autumn flood on St. Mark's Square in Venice, and my kitchen had a sick resemblance to the hotel lobby of Europa-Britannia. That too was covered ankle deep with the once blue waters of the Adriatic.

During the time we waited for the plumber's appearance, we had to keep the water-main shut off. It was most inconvenient, to say the least, especially when I had to wash the dishes, or do the laundry. Maybe come spring, I could do all of this in the yard, or perhaps carry the stuff to be washed in the Zala River, two miles down the road. That, at least, would be romantic and picturesque. I could pose for tourists. What a scoop it would be for them! Local color: "Woman at the River". But in the middle of winter it was neither romantic, nor practical; also, there were no tourists during that season.

By now I felt totally intimidated by the plumber, but since he still didn't show, I sent him a telegram with the international message of S.O.S, although I really wanted to change that last letter. It would have amused me to get even with him in this manner. I recalled the anger of a woman at St. Luke's Hospital one night. She brought her husband to the emergency room, where I was employed as a receptionist. I was a layperson, but even I could see that he was suffering from a heart attack. I put him immediately into a treatment room, put in a triple page on the intercom, and only after I saw doctors and nurses flying down the hall, did I go back to the reception desk to fill out the admission form. I scribbled down the symptoms I observed, just as I was trained to do. To save time I abbreviated "Shortness of Breath" into its initials, whereupon the wife, who closely watched my writing, almost bashed my head in retaliation for the supposed insult. Wanting to change my message of S.O.S. to S.O.B. to the plumber only proves that this construction ordeal was reducing me into an immature child, ready to fight with childish weapons.

Venetians can't do much about their periodic flooding, but I believed that water coming through a main pipe ought to be easier to fix than water coming in with high tides. A week later he came, but showed very little compassion. My troubles were not his concern. He took out his stethoscope, listened here and there, his face turned grave and noncommittal.

"You should have called earlier," said the Voice of Doom, ignoring the fact that I was pleading with him every day of the week. "The leak metastasized all over the lower pipes. Now it needs serious intervention."

I was willing to sign on the dotted line to relieve him of all responsibilities should the operation fail, but then he announced that surgery would be impossible until we found the proper pipes and fittings. He made it clear that he would have nothing to do with finding the needed parts. That was our problem. He'll do the operation, but we had to secure the organs, the sutures and probably the surgical instruments as well.

"How am I to find these things off-season? You have the connections, you know where these things could be bought…"

"I haven't the time for details. And I can't do a thing without pipes." His voice had a dead finality to it, and I knew I lost the argument.

During the summer lots of Germans and Austrians are building vacation homes in this vicinity. The greater demand provides greater supplies. But try to get a pipe off-season!

"I'd trade my mother-in-law for a good water pump," our neighbor swore. "I can't say I'd miss her, but sure as hell I can't exist without a pump." I was willing to trade Esther for some pipes.

I have no relatives who are plumbers, but my father was a physician. Sometimes I worry how he is explaining his profession to his Maker. I am sure he too must have uttered plumber-style statements to worried family members, such as "Continue administering the medication, and if the need arises, call me in the morning." Then in the morning: "You should have called me sooner." It is indeed strange that no matter what goes wrong with health or pipes, the responsibility is always lobbed back right into our courts.

After decades of experience, I finally know my way around doctors and plumbers, but the builder of fireplaces was a new specimen that I have not met before. If at all possible, I would like to avoid the experience for the rest of my life.

January brought snow, cold weather and new hopes for the fireplace to be built. I was eager and highly expectant, which had nothing to do with wanting a cozy fire. The furnace was working superbly, and shivering in the unheated house was history. But by now the novelty of having piles of building material in my living room has worn off. The building of the fireplace was imminent (so we were told during the entire year) and we had to keep the material for it indoors to keep it all from freezing, or from getting them wet. Borka liked the mess well enough, and periodically buried her chew toys into one of the piles, but the rest of us just about had enough of it. We still had to walk sideways in the rest of the house because of the piled up furniture and boxes. I was also very uneasy about the rolled up oriental rugs among the damp piles of sand and was sure that sooner or later one of the paintings, propped against the stored furniture, would fall and be damaged. And last but not least I worried about the endurance level of Agnes. Her apartment was still nothing more but the walls and a roof, so she was housed temporarily in the future butler's pantry off the kitchen. I couldn't visualize life without her, but in all honesty I would not have blamed her if she left us, without notice. There are few people, who would have tolerated that situation for any length of time, be it for love or money. Agnes was that person.

We were so close to completion, and have lived so long in chaos that our patience was wearing thin by now. During the summer, when the weather permitted us to live outside, the situation bothered us less. But when the weather turned mean, being cooped up in a wild construction area was quite another story. Béla the mason, Laci the carpenter, Feri the painter, and Miska, who was to put down the wooden floors, were all brimming with sympathy, but they could not do a thing until the fireplace was built. But that was another hurdle we had clear first.

The saga of our fireplace started as soon as we made the plans for the house. I probably have a touch of pyromania, because I am endlessly fascinated with the blaze. When I watch a movie and there is a fireplace going in the background, I completely lose track of the action and stare only at the fire. We had a fireplace in Ohio, but none in Germany, and I missed it keenly. I had to have one in this dream house of ours.

We soon found the man, highly recommended, who seemed a true professional in the land of fireplaces. But soon it was obvious that we did not speak the same language. I had visions of a great, open fire pit and he was talking of a tile stove.

Tile stoves are uniquely European, and singularly attractive, some even spectacular in their own way. But that was not what I wanted. A tile stove is an intricate, rather large structure, made of special, heat storing bricks that are carefully built to form mazes on the inside, through which the smoke and the heat go up and down and around, before exiting through the chimney. In this process the interior mazes are heated. In turn the stored heat is radiated into the room evenly and pleasantly, up to twelve or more hours, depending on the size of the stove, long after the fire has gone out completely. The outside of the stove is shaped into intricate architectural structures, then covered with glazed tiles. It is a rare delight to lean against the warm tiles on a cold day. The drawback is that because of the mazes and the erratic way of the smoke, the small door of the fire pit must be closed at all times if one does not wish to die of smoke inhalation. The heat, generated by just a few logs inside the stove, is great, but the fire is not visible, or just barely.

My pyromaniac heart was set on an open fireplace, big enough for a blazing Yule log. Moving flames have an endless fascination for me; I love the deep silence of a winter evening, punctuated by the sound of crackling wood. It is deeply satisfying to walk into a room, where the living, yellow and red flames reflect on polished furniture, mirrors and china. I would love to have a fireplace in every room, including the kitchen, and the bathroom. On the other hand, there is a limit how long I can admire a shapely pile of tiles, no matter how artistic.

Our fireplace builder could only think in terms of tiles and units of heat calories. For him the fire itself was only interesting from the point of view of how to solve the problem of vents and flues through which the smoke and heat would travel. For him the fire was the means; for me it was the end. Indeed, we had very divergent visions.

Finally we decided that it was better to have a good tile stove than a bad fireplace, but insisted on a compromise. He had to incorporate into his design a large, fireproof glass door, through which the fire could be seen. Before he could voice the usual objection that there is no such thing, we assured him that we would furnish the fireproof glass from Germany.

"No problem then," he agreed upon hearing that the glass question was solved. This seemed to be his greatest concern.

The walls of our house were not up yet, when we visited the designer, and delivered the precious glass so that his specialist could fit it into the frame. We also wanted to select the cover tiles. He personally escorted us into the workshop, where mountains of tiles were produced for just this purpose.

I hated them all. Having seen some spectacular, truly artistic examples of faience in old homes and castles, I found the selection in the factory boring, the colors unacceptable and totally out of sync with the color scheme of our furniture, drapes, rugs and my wardrobe. At this point even a Franklin stove started to look good. Not only was I denied the fireplace of my dreams; I was not even getting a glazed tile stove of which I could be justly proud. The focal point of our living room would be an ugly, unimaginative mountain of tiles the color of chicken poop.

We were just about to leave in disgust, when I saw in a corner a small pile of partially broken pieces of rare beauty. It was exactly what I had in mind. There were about a dozen pieces among the debris on the floor, and unlike the rest of the plain tiles in the shop, each of these had three-dimensional figures of knights, kings and sailors, each different and wonderfully imaginative, yet very simple. I was fascinated and could not decide if they were classical, modern, or primitive in style. The figures on the graphite colored pieces might have been warriors in ancient legends, the crew from the ship of Odysseus, could have been copied from tombs of extinct civilizations, or could have hailed form the Ludwig collection of modern art. At any rate they were the products of a rare artist's unusual imagination, executed in exquisite taste and proportion. They were perfect, and despite their attention-commanding beauty they were subtle with the discreet sheen of pewter on the dark blue-gray glaze.

"*Eureka!* I found it," I almost screamed. "Our search ends here. This is what I want; nothing else would do."

"We don't make them any more," came the laconic answer. "They were designed by an artist, but people did not take to them. They thought that it was too extreme and too expensive. That particular glaze is a tricky one to fire anyhow, and the artist handed us a staggering bill. We stopped producing them after we lost a great deal of money on the venture."

I was being stubborn, and the builder was astute enough to perceive that he arrived at the proverbial brick wall. Leaving us in the drafty production area, he left on a discovery tour, and came back with the news that indeed he found the clay forms for about half of the designs. They would custom make them for us, if we insisted (at a special price of course), but since that particular graphite color needs a higher than usual temperature in the huge kiln for the final firing, we would have to wait until enough orders came in for that color.

"Don't get your hopes high," he warned. "Not many people want this gloomy graphite tone in their homes. The wait might be long. Even a year, or longer."

I wanted the tiles so much that I was willing to wait. Also, in my heart of hearts I did not believe that it would take that long. Six months later, glaring at the mess in the living room, I realized that the man was not exaggerating, and I started to wonder if the tiles were really worth all the waiting. Then miraculously the day after that memorable Christmas, a telegram came. The tiles were ready to be picked up. Immediately of course, since they did not want them around during their January inventory. The telegram also said that the three men, who would build our stove, would appear at our house on the first Monday in January. We were hysterical with joy. Our happiness lasted twenty-four hours.

My husband, who by now was careful about every promise, drove the following day the fifty-five miles to confirm the content of the telegram. But there was no mistake; the promise was carved in stone. He made a careful list of all the things we would need by Monday. In a week we would have a blazing fire and we could devote our energies to selecting floor coverings. He was already at the door, when as a gesture of politeness and good will, he offered to take back to our house the glass door for the stove in order to save the workmen the trouble of lugging it.

"Oh, well, the door" the designer sighed, and looked tragic. "There is a little problem with it." I knew it, my husband thought, they broke it.

"The door you want is very large, and the heat behind it will be very intense," the man explained.

"Therefore...?"

"Therefore, we must count with a considerable expansion of the frame that holds the glass. The glass might drop out of the frame."

"So?"

"So you need a cast iron frame."

"Fine. I figured that much. Do it."

"Can't. The company that makes the doors for our stoves has molds only for the small doors. Nothing as unusual as yours."

Making the mold for a large door, like ours, provided they would be even willing to do it, would take a long time. Maybe a year, he explained.

"So why didn't you tell us this while we were waiting for the damned tiles? The door could have been ordered at the same time the tiles were." My husband is a saint, but he too has a tolerance level.

"As you know, the problem did not come up before this," the man explained patiently. "At any rate, it is not possible to start building the stove until you have the door."

"Then your telegram made no sense, because it is out of the question to start building in the foreseeable future."

"That is correct."

"This is extremely ridiculous, don't you agree? Somebody ought to be able to make us a cast iron door frame," my husband yelled. He was almost, but not yet completely, out of control. "Man acquired the skill to work iron right after the Bronze Age. That's about a thousand years ago, man!"

The designer shrugged again with a noticeable lack of interest. He had no idea where the door could be ordered, but for an extra charge he would be willing to redesign the stove with the smaller door. I knew that this was exactly what he wanted to do all along.

I was furious and considered murder, but my husband was already working on Plan B. And indeed, after two days of searching and networking, he found a foundry two hundred kilometers away. Three phone calls and a personal visit later, they promised to do the job in a week.

The frame was ready not in one week, but two; yet we were happy. Esther's grandson, who lives in that town, was due for a visit here, and he offered to deliver the frame to us. A day before he was to arrive, a telegram came from him.

"Did not pick of frame. Stop. Strange angles, a geometric puzzle. Stop. Come see it."

What strange angles? It was a simple rectangular shape, what could go wrong with it? This was Friday and the office of the foundry was closed through Monday. My husband drove there on Tuesday and found that the frame indeed was very strange.

"Can you explain?" he asked in disbelief.

"Of course. While tempering the iron, a five inch chunk broke off at a corner," the foreman explained. "To make it look balanced, we filed off five inches from the opposite corner."

"And through this brilliant maneuver you made the frame totally use-less," my husband fumed.

The man, who did the job, was indignant. "There is nothing wrong with it. It looks perfectly alike on both sides and this unexpected design makes it prettier. I can't imagine that the quality of your life would diminish by the fact that the corners are filed off."

As far as I was concerned, at that point I would have engaged in an activity that is punishable with at least life imprisonment. And yes, the quality of life would not just be diminished, but totally wiped out, as smoke billowed out at the two filed-off corners of the door. One of the peculiarities of the tile stove is that the minute the door is opened, smoke which is snaking in a confused manner inside the mazes, finds immediately the path of least resistance, and without wasting time, streams back into the room. The openings at the two sides of the door would make it possible to smoke the Easter ham in the living room. Every child knows that. I do admire my husband's self-control. He negotiated the issue without bloodshed, so that as we turned the calendar to February we finally had our frame with the glass in it. On the second Saturday of the second month, our three stove-building men were ringing the doorbell, as promised. Who said that things couldn't be done? All it takes is time, patience and money.

They were a nice trio, who apparently liked each other and enjoyed working together. They also ate and drank a great deal more than one would expect from such skinny and serious gentlemen. It was cold on the day they arrived and I asked what they would want for their mid-morning breakfast. They said it won't matter as long as it is warm and spicy. I sautéed onions, added sliced green peppers, tomatoes and garlic, quantities of sausages and frankfurters (also sliced) a generous dash of hot peppers and served it with steamed rice. Here is spice to you. They loved it, and rinsed it off with two liters of our best wine.

They stretched out languidly in the lawn chairs (still the only furniture in the living room), enjoying perfect digestion, when one of them asked very casually if we bought a certain powder that was an essential ingredient in the mortar that was to hold together the fire bricks inside the stove. We haven't, because it was not on our list. As a matter of fact, neither of us heard of such a powder before. On Saturdays all stores close at noon, so my husband jumped into the car and took off in search of this thing. It was a miracle that he found the stuff in the third store he visited, just before it closed. Work could resume again, and was interrupted only by the next meal. They demolished a tureen of cream of tomato soup, a pork roast studded with garlic, accompanied with sauerkraut slowly cooked with caraway seeds, smoked bacon and wine, and inhaled with it a bowl of fried potatoes. They were quite short of breath by now, (S.O.B.), but managed a plate of homemade donuts in order not to hurt my feelings.

The men worked steadily and with great care, although very slowly. Each new step was discussed and evaluated. A decision was made by consensus, then it was executed with minute precision. Napoleon could not have spent more time on his strategic moves than these three, when they decided how to put down the next brick. When five o'clock came, they still worked, probably moved by the Spirit. At six there was no sign that they would ever stop. At seven I served them the dinner I planned to give them on another day. It was past ten when they left and there was nothing in the living room that even vaguely resembled a fireplace.

They did not work on Sunday, but Monday was a repeat feasting and drinking performance of Saturday, only the menu changed. They had grilled cheese sandwiches and a cold plate for breakfast; for lunch I served a spicy bean soup with enough smoked ribs in it to please three giants, a roast chicken with potatoes and grilled onions. The house started to smell as if Greece, Spain, Italy and Hungary had a culinary convention in my kitchen. But the men loved it. Between the big meals there was leisurely drinking of the quality wine.

"Look at it this way," my husband consoled me, "Even if we'll never have a stove built in our living room, we are gaining three very nice and polite family members, who seem to like us more than some of our own kin."

"Spring is almost here. Do you think I could plant something into the sand pile next to the chew toys, and make a fragrant conversation piece of it?"

Tuesday was not much better than Monday, although truthfully, there was something in the living room that started to take shape. Wednesday I could feel that exhaustion was catching up with me. The three meals I had to cook and to serve every day, even with Agnes to help, loomed large, and I was running out of spicy ideas. When I gently inquired how long it would take, they said cheerfully that it might be completed by the end of the following week. I almost passed out at the thought of twenty-one more meals. I don't know who the patron saint of kitchens is, so I prayed to the Lares and promised them garlands of garlic and hot peppers as offerings on their altar, if they would bless me with some inspiration. By Thursday the stove was slowly growing, but it could have been easily mistaken for a special altar for the Lares or Penates.

I watched the construction not only eagerly in the hope of a rapid completion, but also with total fascination. The mazes inside were so complicated that even Ariadne's thread would have been useless to help get anybody or anything out of that stove. I hoped that wood smoke has a better sense of direction than Theseus had.

But then I had a piece of good luck; or else the household spirits took pity on me. Saturday morning as I was doing a paint job on my face in order not to scare away the three knights-errant, who would appear at the door at seven, I was listening to the news. Snow was on its way, and if the weatherman could be trusted, there was lots of it coming. Nice, wet snow, that makes the roads all but impassable. And it would be coming down non-stop for days and days. Our three men drove every day one hundred kilometers coming and going on a treacherous, hilly, curving road. Even in good weather it is hard driving, but with snow and ice it could be a total disaster. Between the three of them they had one car, (although the Trabant that was made in what was East Germany once, is not considered to be a car by most people). However, they pampered this piece of plastic wonder, as they never did their wives. I am not usually manipulative, but I suddenly realized, how to wire these guys to get them out of first gear, where they seemed to be stuck for a long time.

Even before they arrived, I carried the radio into the living room so that they should hear the news without my forcing it on them too obviously. Then in the manner of a news commentator worthy of his high salary, I explained to them in fine details what they just heard. When Esther came up to the house, as she did every hour on the hour to check the progress of the stove, I prompted her to talk about the weather. She was very good at it too, and related with dramatic pauses and worried glances, how road after road was closed, and car after car ditched in the eastern part of the country. The bad weather is rapidly progressing toward our region, she panted.

I have never seen men work so fast, or eat so fast for that matter. They even begged me not to serve an evening meal, because they wanted to finish the job that day. They were not about to risk their Trabant on the slick roads, not even for the best meal I would serve them. They agreed among themselves, that this would be their very last trip to Szabar. They finally left around midnight as the first snowflakes fell. Out of sheer gratitude for losing them, we walked them to the gate. My husband put his arm around my shoulders as we walked back into the house.

"It is over and finished," I sighed. I was so busy, tense and exhausted during the week that after the mazes were completed I barely looked at the construction any more. Now we stood in front of the finished product, and I was a heartbeat away from crying.

The stove was so magnificent that my husband and I just stood there without a word. We received a piece of real art, the kind one never gets used to. Others might own a rare painting, or an antique statue; we had a glazed tile stove. My bet is that we were happier with our acquisition than they were. Later he opened a bottle of champagne and as the snow was falling ever thicker, closing out the world, we knew that the smaller world that we were creating for ourselves was beyond beautiful.

"Funny, isn't it," he finally said. "This stove was the only thing in the house that we really did not want in the beginning, but now I think it is the best part of it. Don't you agree?"

In a few weeks the weather turned mild once again, and the house was finally shaping up. The segment which was to be the apartment of Agnes, as well as the guest wing, the garage, and the winter garden were completed, discounting a few minor finishing touches. The floor was finished in the living room, the furniture and pictures were in place, and the tempo of our daily activities slowed. We slept late in the morning scandalizing Esther by this decadent habit, took Borka for long walks and read, or puttered around the house in the afternoon. In the evening we had a last glass of wine in front of the fireplace. The world beyond our gate lost its significance. We used to be always on the move to discover new places, new cultures; now we turned into sit-at-homes and had no desire to leave the house. The only exception was Héviz, a few miles from our village. We liked its gentle, *fin de siecle* elegance, the un-hurried pace and the healing water. It was no superstition after all; we did feel better and moved easier after our long soaks.

The winter garden was quickly turning into one of our favorite spots in the house and it was also the most photographed. During the late winter days the passive solar heat warms it enough, so that we usually have our lunch there. It could be bleak outside, or else snow could cover the patio, but inside we are sitting in a semi-tropical garden and cozy warmth among bushes, small trees, ferns and climbing vine. In the evening the spotlights placed among the plants lend a soft, mystic mood to it, and the gently splashing fountain soothes and refreshes. The Depart-ment of Health ought to decree that all houses located in winter zones must have a conservatory, however small. It does wonderful things to the spirit and to general health. The savings on medication and time lost from work would amply pay for the structure.

"Two years down the road and our life is shaping up exactly as we hoped it would," observed my husband as he broke another piece of the *lángos*, the crusty flat bread I just baked on the special tiles in the kitchen oven. He mopped up the last globs of sour cream mixed with salt, crushed garlic and thyme from his plate, and sighed with satisfaction.

"In order to be superbly content, some basic conditions are needed. And I have them all," he said.

"Why is it that you always get philosophical after a meal that you like?"

"Because a pleasantly filled stomach is the best friend of the brain. Notice that a starving, struggling nation never could produce any sort of advanced, lasting culture. During the last ten thousand years the best things came from areas where people were well fed. 'More-than-enough', also spelled as 'surplus' is the key to civilization. World-changing thoughts, as well as a sense of pervasive happiness can only occur when body and spirit are satisfied in their basic needs. When people have to dig for grubs and other unmentionables for the next meal, they don't have the inclination to listen to a symphony. And if there is no audi-ence, the 'takers' of culture, there are also no 'providers', or artists to offer it. Nothing is happening in that society. You got to eat in order to be productive." Food is a favorite topic and he enjoys talking about it.

"Doctors and dietitians have a very different view about nutrition," I pointed out, since I worried constantly about the arteries of this meat and potato man, who eats very little, but basically enjoys all the wrong kinds of food.

"I know, and find that very depressing. They don't want you to enjoy food, and for them a full stomach is passé. But how much do they really know? We can count ourselves lucky if they can cure the sick body. The sense of happiness is not their concern, although it ought to be, since happiness is another word for health. Happiness is the concern of philosophers, wives and mothers. And of gentlemen living a leisurely, pleasant life, like me. Doctors make it difficult to enjoy life to its fullest potential."

"Of which, good food is basic."

"Correct."

"And what are the other ingredients that insure happiness?" I asked idly. I was sure I had them down pat, but was curious about his list. He did not have to think about it.

"The pleasure of good food; the leisure to be able to do all the things I planned; independence from people and things, including money; a pleasant home that blocks out the noise of the world; attainable goals; some hobbies; health; music and books; and a great life companion," he enumerated in one breath.

"In that order?"

"The order is of no consequence. Man needs them all, and needs them equally."

"You left out the dog."

"No, I haven't. A dog, or two, count as life companion."

I was amused by his digestion-inspired sentiments and missed an important part of his statement, namely that when he mentioned the dog, a conjectural plural was hinted. I should have known better; he is not a man of idle speech. However, it was a wonderful day, and I did not feel like arguing, although I noticed that he forgot to include "friends" in his list.

Friends are very important to both of us and we lean heavily on them both in times of need and in times of happiness. We count ourselves fortunate for having so many of them, in this country as well as all over world. A few years after our house was completed and civilization became a fact of life for us too, my great treasure and joy turned out to be the computer, and through it the internet mail, which makes it possible to keep in touch with those, who live thousands of miles away on different continents. It is so very reassuring that they are only a click away from us. Phyllis and Bill from Florida, Edith from Cleveland, Minnie and Gene from Puerto Rico send me my daily doses of laughter, which often are like life-savers thrown to me. Laughter kept me afloat when things did not always work out as expected. Regina from Germany keeps me supplied with material so I can teach the village children English, which is of prime importance to them if they want to attend a good school after they complete the elementary grades. Education is valued very highly and nothing is more important to parents than a good school for their children. I'm happy that I can contribute to their success in my small way. Another Phyllis, a librarian and a discriminating reader, keeps the gray matter in my cranium alive with boxes of books she sends me. Doug in Guam, was my support system during repeated failures when I tried to find an agent for my books. When I almost lost my head during times of great frustrations and crises, Max and Jean in Palm Desert, Leslie and Ildiko in Colorado, were my all-time quadruple cheering team. When I started the program for the gifted, Max was the principal of my "home school", and my direct supervisor. He understood and fully supported the program. Without Max the program would have turned out into one of those cute, sporadic activities, heavy on units in Greek mythology and medieval chivalry. Max saw to it that I had everything that was essential for creating a meaningful program that was truly worthy of gifted students, as hundreds of children and their parents gratefully acknowledged. With his guidance and support I realized for the first time, what psychologists mean when they talk of "self-actualization." Pauline, now in Hawaii, was a solid rock and a calm corner when things were turbulent, and Debra was a true friend. There are so many more that it would be impossible to list them all. I cannot even start mentioning all the Hungarian friends who welcomed us, helped in the bad times, and celebrated with us when things went right. I guess my husband did not omit friends, but fitted them into the category of "life companions", which is what they really are.

"I am content, and have not a single wish left. Life is perfect and complete," I concluded as I cleared the table and slipped the last bit of crust to Borka.

"Life is not complete, until you have a *pumi*," my husband answered and suddenly I recalled, a little too late, his allusion to a second dog when he enumerated what was needed for perfect bliss.

The pumi, a relative to the puli, is yet another Hungarian breed. It is a small, rather ditzy-looking dog, with the uncompromising principles of a truly great personality. While Borka, the kuvasz, is a dignified, circumspect grande dame with the self-control of a saint, the little pumi is a bundle of energy, a born clown, and an unrelenting shadow of her master. The kuvasz is big and fearsome, and relies on its size and reputation to keep order around the house. The pumi compensates for size with speed, alertness and action before thought. The pumi possesses fearsome intellectual powers and is loyal to a fault. It is a working dog, and is happiest when it can organize the movements of hundreds of sheep, but can adapt to family life with equal ease. The civilized world's sad cultural loss is that the exquisite writings about animals by the Hungarian author, István Fekete, are not as widely known as the stories of Bambi or the many Walt Disney characters. Fekete's books are classics in this country. He wrote with so much love and understanding that he not only captured generations of readers of every age group, but also created a bond between man and the animal kingdom. One of his best-loved books, later made into a movie, is *Bogáncs*, the story of a pumi. If I had the power to give a great gift to the children of the world, I would make this book, and this movie available to everyone beyond the boundaries of Hungary. I believe in the power of books, and this one certainly touches that part of the soul, which shapes our very humanity and integrity.

At any rate, this was the breed of dog my husband wanted.

He is not a man given to daydreaming. When he decides on an issue, he carries it out with speedy efficiency. Within days he found a sheep farm with a large stock of dogs. It was easy enough to bid for a puppy that had the advantage of not being a victim of overbreeding. The deal was quickly made and the young farmer was satisfied. We agreed that on a given date, when the puppy would be old enough to be weaned, we would meet the farmer with the pup at one of their pastures, not far from our home.

"I'll be there for sure with the dog. If you beat me to it, just park at the roadside by the big walnut tree. My father will be there too; he is guarding part of our sheep. He is old and not very talkative, so don't get offended by his silence. It is just his way; he does not mean to be rude. I'll try to be there on time though." We knew about shepherds and suspected that they are genetically programmed to enjoy big silences and a contemplative life. They observe life around them, and probably draw their own conclusions, but seldom see the need to share their thoughts. They are definitely not given to small talk.

We were early for our rendezvous, and my husband parked under the shade of the tree, as he was instructed. We spotted the old shepherd immediately. He was lean and slightly bent, wore a black hat, a wide cape touching the top of his boots and an inscrutable expression on his face. He stood like a statue, barely moving. The sheep, kept together by a single pumi, grazed peacefully.

"Wine, wheat and peace be given us," my husband greeted in the customary way, when the shepherd moved close enough to us.

"Those we could use. And also some rain." He lifted his two fingers to his hat by way of greeting, then sunk into deep silence. The sheep decided to graze for a while near the road and the old man again assumed his statuesque pose.

It did not take long when a large, expensive car pulled up behind ours, and a young man, obviously a city dweller, jumped out of it with camera in hand, ready to take the shepherd's picture, as if he were not a human being, but a feature of the landscape. The old man regarded him with a calm gaze and straightened his shoulders proudly. At the sight of so much dignified silence the city man lost some of his cockiness, and apparently had second thoughts about thrusting his camera in the face of the old man. Perhaps wanting to ease the situation with an attempt to be polite, he started a little meaningless conversation first.

"You have some remarkably healthy-looking animals here," he said as an opener. The old man regarded his animals for a space of time, then nodded.

"The black ones are."

"And the white ones?"

"Them too."

Pause. I could see how the city man was straining to continue this conversation, but had no idea how.

"Do they eat a lot?" he finally asked.

"The black ones do."

"And the white ones?"

"Them too." The city man, not used to the sound of silence, was getting visibly frustrated.

"Why do you make a distinction between the black ones and the white ones? Is there a difference? Are they your sheep?"

"The black ones are."

"And the white ones?" This city man was terminally stupid. The answer was hilariously obvious, but he could not see it coming.

"Them too," said the shepherd quietly, then turned his attention to the clouds.

The city man whirled around, and in a flash he was in his car. He took off so fast, he was burning tires. I am sure I saw the shadow of a smile on the placid face of the old shepherd. He was not about to show up in somebody's photo album as "local color", and he won the game without losing his dignity. I hope the city man learned something.

We did not think about him too long, because the shepherd's son was moving toward us across the meadow. He carried a small black bundle of fur in his arm.

The pumi conquered our hearts instantly. She is in a class of her own as we found out even before she came to live with us. It so happened that we told our veterinarian about the impending addition to our family.

"Another dog? Are you sure? Or better phrased: are you sane?" He is a friend, so he can afford to be rude to us.

"It is a pumi."

"Ah, but that's different, of course" János said with relief. "A pumi is not a dog." Which was exactly what Fekete said about this noble little canine. As the days passed, we agreed with them.

We took her home, and introduced her to Borka. As a newcomer and of a very small size, we expected her to behave prudently and with restraint. Instead, by way of greeting, she dived from my arms and bit Borka in the nose. Borka, had she chosen to respond, could have snapped the puppy's delicate spine with a single flick of her head, but she is above such mean retaliations. She simply considered the source, which seemed pitiful to her, and shrugged. Sissi established the fact that although she was the youngest and smallest of our household, she was not negligible.

Despite the stormy introduction, they get along wonderfully. For a long time Borka imagined that Sissi was her puppy and took care of her with touching tenderness and holy patience. Sissi is happiest when she can snuggle up to her surrogate mother. I don't think she'll ever grow up, because Borka won't let her. She prefers to spoil the puppy.

This vertically challenged, peppery little dog gets royally aggravated whenever she feels that our person, or property is in danger. From the beginning, when she was still smaller than Midnight, she appointed herself as my personal guard, and in her presence I dare not shake hands with people. Not fully comprehending the gesture, she growls and is ready to attack. Anybody closer than three steps from me is suspect, and an extended hand spells danger. Just like Borka, she can't stand if anything belonging to us is touched. But while Borka, the more rational of the two, wants to see an ID and the sales slips of coats, purses and umbrellas before deciding on action, Sissi's philosophy is to shoot first, then ask questions after.

She is broken-hearted when we leave her behind even for a short while, and when we return her agitation is spectacular. She recognizes the sound of our car engine, and sobs at the gate long before the car turns in. Her little body is trembling from excitement while she runs back and forth between the two of us, barking, yapping and licking our hands. She is endlessly grateful because we returned to her. Of course, she must take a drink of water every minute, because the great excitement dehydrates her. She is just overjoyed, and tells us over and over what our reappearance means to her.

"I am overjoyed that you came back...I thought you left me...I'm so excited...this is really great...let me drink a little...and now the joy affected my kidneys...no, I don't want to go out again for fear of losing you again...well, perhaps a drop, but don't go away...this is terrific... aren't you thirsty too...? I must drink a little more ...now I gotta pee again..."

Now as a protection for suits, coats, boots and stockings, I carry a huge denim coat in the car, several sizes too large, which I don over my outfits before I enter the house to face the stormy welcome. I promise myself all the time that I'll soon train her to be more dignified, but than I keep missing the opportunity, because she is so cute in her excitement.

We chose her name not after Elizabeth, the beloved queen of Hungary and empress of Austria, whose nickname was Sisi. Our dog's name is an onomatopoeic approximation of the short little sounds she makes when she wants something. There are usually only two things she ever wants: to eat and to stay close to us. Small as she is, her appetite is ferocious and she is ready to eat at any hour, day or night. I guess her great, nervous energy burns three times the fuel that sedate dogs many times her size need.

We were so absorbed watching our two dogs that the arrival of spring was almost a surprise. Suddenly white herons were sunning at the lakeshore, and the storks were back, renovating their windblown nests. When did all of this happen? Overnight the cherry trees in the backyard turned into huge bridal bouquets. I found the garden spotlights and by the time the sun set, the blossom-laden trees were illuminated to the delight of the villagers. They were resigned to have to wait until next Christmas for another display of light and were excited about this new show. Our trees were the sensation, and people once again walked past our house to admire the shimmering blossoms in the soft light.

"Better than the pictures in the calendar. Better than a painting," an old farmer murmured as he led his grandchildren by the hand to admire such an illuminated wonder. "Funny how this plain old cherry tree can look so different in the light."

"Is it real, grandfather?"

"I think so."

The sun was warm and Béla with his crew arrived for once without a daily invitation, which truthfully often bordered on begging. They started to pave the patio with vigor and a happy song. They were also building a retainer wall between the garden and the wine cellar. The old backyard was eroding toward the cellar and we had to somehow prevent my roses and bushes to visit the wine barrels in the cellar. Maybe the retaining wall was a mistake; a drunken rose and a tipsy juniper leaning against a hiccuping cypress might have been more amusing than the functional wall.

The huge awning was put up over the newly paved patio and Joska stood at attention with spade and rake, (but minus a stern wife), in a pose for Grant Wood to paint a Gypsy Gothic. Actually he was waiting for instructions to dig the holes in preparation for the plants we ordered earlier. Things were improving by leaps and bounds and one morning I woke up and realized that I have never been happier in my life. The house was still not completely ready, but the end was in sight and it was good.

We had a superstition, more foolproof than black cats or spiders. We knew that the simple event of guests arriving, unexpected or not, would pull to the house, as if by magic, all the workers whom we have not seen in a long time. As soon as the front door bell rang announcing friends, we could be sure that craftsmen, lugging cement mixers and power drills, were breaking down the back gate. Before we could express pleasure at seeing our friends, the house would already be echoing with busy sounds, normally associated with a major factory or a shipyard. A car with a foreign license plate had a greater magnetic pull than mere local ones; but in any case the appearance of guests was sure to stimulate our various workers into action.

Minnie and Gene, who were still both employed by DoDDS in Germany, were to be our first guests of the season. Their visit was a very sudden decision, and we had no time left to send exact direction on how to reach our house. On the hastily written post-card Minnie told us that they would either arrive around seven on Saturday evening, or when delayed, on Sunday morning. This was Easter weekend with the customary holiday traffic jam, and we thought the time of arrival given by them was highly optimistic, unless they started very early. But Minnie hated the predawn hours as much as we do, and I could not imagine her getting into a car while the moon was still up. It was impossible to make it by seven in the evening, I was sure of that.

After six in the morning on that Saturday, true to tradition, Béla and his helper arrived to have an early start in messing up my life. At the beginning of time (B.C as in Before Construction) we planned a small pool in the garden. It was not just for ornamental purposes, but to be used as a dipping pool after the sauna. It was already completed, except the laying of the tiles. This would be a noisy and dusty job, since many of the tiles had to be cut to size, but the sooner it was finished the better off we were. Even in the unlikely event that our friends would arrive as planned, the mess would have been cleaned up by then, and tranquility would descend over the garden.

Half an hour after the arrival of Béla, another team came to hang the gutters on the guest house. They were expected for many weeks now, and their arrival was a historical event. I would have sooner bitten off my tongue than berated them for the unannounced arrival.

"The gutters of the winter garden must come off first," they said cheerfully after a lengthy inspection. "There is no other way we can attach the other gutters."

I gritted my teeth and smiled graciously. After all, my role in life was to cancel all private interests and plans, in order to devote myself fully to these Assorted Grand Comings. I welcomed them with a determined smile.

A short while later the painters were camping out in front of the house to give the final pale yellow touch to the stucco. My smile was waning. I was expecting two of my best friends, and now I was facing the problem of feeding eleven people, not to speak of the monumental mess they were surely going to leave behind.

I was in the midst of a beautiful, religious invocation for heavenly help, when the man from the furniture store arrived to put together the wardrobe and couch we bought weeks ago for the guest room. Both the couch and the wardrobe arrived in flat boxes and my husband was using intemperate language within hearing distance of the next seven villages, because he was not able to put them together.

"The hell with this company!" he shouted. "I didn't buy a damned kit at a reduced price. I bought two pieces of furniture from the showroom at the regular price. If I wanted to build something, I would have done so. But I wanted furniture, and not kits made for bored kids, or to be used as tests for latent intelligence. I refuse to fool with this shit any more. Let them set it up, or take it back." This is only an excerpt. He went on much longer and each utterance became more colorful and more blasphemous. He was wounded in his pride, because he could not put together something that came in a box with full instructions. In his native tongue no less.

After some initial chaos during which the various specialists yelled requests at me to provide a long list of mysterious things, everybody settled down to do serious work. I was busy in the kitchen preparing the welcome meal with great care, keeping in mind that Minnie is an accomplished gourmet cook. This heavenly idyll was shattered by the arrival of a telegram from the arboretum of Cserszeg-Tomaj, two dozen miles away. (We still had no phone and all important messages were sent that way.)

The message was short and to the point, "Plants dug out. Stop. Immediate pick-up requested." In this country the customer has to wait for weeks and months, but when the thing finally arrives, he is expected to drop everything and run to pick it up. One can argue or plead over a phone, but there is nothing one can tell a piece of yellow paper, so Joska hitched up the trailer, I turned off the burners under my welcome dinner, and we were ready to leave in order to pick up the plants we ordered. Before we left, I set the picnic table for fifteen, (just in case the workers would multiply by chow time), and asked Agnes to keep cleaning up after the various teams, and to give very special attention in the guest room, where the furniture-man was starting to exhibit rather erratic behavior.. This gentleman arrived in a suit, wearing a tie and a condescending smile. But the smile faded soon when he could not figure out how to solve the puzzle his company sent us. It totally confounded him when he had to place section A parallel to part B, after inserting part C and D diametrically to part G after part E and M were fastened perpendicularly with bolts XY as shown on diagram 5-A. It was his problem, and I was not very compassionate. We ordered a handsome couch, and not a puzzle designed by MENSA.

I told Béla where the tiles for the pool and the adhesive for it were, and gave the furniture-man a bag of nails and screws, because I know how tranquilizing it is for men to rummage among a rich assortment of small metal things. He was in great need for something to calm him down. I showed the gutter people where I wanted the valve put in the pipe, in order to catch rainwater if I wanted to fill the pool with heaven's gift. I then begged the painters to spare the window frames from the yellow goop. All in all, I felt very efficient for having taken care of all the details and eventualities.

Before we left, almost as an after-thought, I fastened two American flags to the front gate. Minnie and Gene have never visited us before, and because of the language barrier it would be impossible for them to ask for directions. If they'd got lost, the American flags would help them find us. Not that I expected an early arrival.

Thus, having covered all bases, we left for the arboretum, and calculated about an hour for the trip, and twenty minutes for loading the trailer. We should be back well under two hours. That was before we got to know the director of the arboretum.

He was a short, stocky man with a shock of white hair, and a youthful bounce in his walk. He was pushing eighty, but did not show it. He paid attention to the smallest detail of the vast operation of the arboretum, and judging by his mud-caked boots, he did not just issue directives from his desk, but tramped to every corner of the vast fields and supervised every move. He had the manners of an ambassador, the speech of a poet, and the deep serenity of the Orient. He invited us into his roomy and sunny study and started a leisurely and civilized conversation. We were a bit tongue-tied, and not nearly as eloquent as he was. Of course, he had the advantage of not having fifteen people at his home destroying his house even as we spoke.

He told us a lot, like how he was once imprisoned because he dabbled in free market practices. At that time many people wanted to buy fruit trees for their small plots around the house, but none was available. He then visited a cherry canning factory, and picked up the discarded stones, sprouted them, tended them and when they were of age, he sold them. They were snapped up in no time. There was a demand, he supplied what was needed, and made a very marginal profit, if one considers the amount of work he put in to raise the saplings from the cherry stones. At the trial he was lectured that making personal profits is diametrically opposite to everything the Communistic ideal stands for. Because of his age they were lenient, and he was sentenced to only two years in prison. But after he was set free, he found that he was a legend, a hero, with a nationwide reputation for being the "Cherry Stone Uncle." Eventually his sin was forgiven, and he was appointed director of the arboretum.

He also told us how to save our lemon trees from an early death, and what to do with an ailing ornamental shrub we had, and gave advice on how to protect our fig trees during the winter. Then he accompanied us to the trailer to say an emotional farewell to the silver spruce we bought. "You chose our most beautiful one! "(Yes. Out of eight thousand!) "Please, be kind to her," he said. I tried to remain serious. After all, we were not taking his next of kin. "Place her to her best advantage. Her beauty must be seen and appreciated from every point of the garden." I expected him to kiss the spruce, but he got control of himself and the final farewell between tree and man was reduced to a long, painful look. Then we had to trot back to his study and drink to the welfare of the trees and shrubs we bought, and only then could we start on our way home. It was getting awfully late and my husband stepped on the gas, while the precious spruce bounced helplessly in the trailer. It was not a very good introduction to its new home.

When we arrived at the house, most of the workmen were still there; as a matter of fact, they multiplied, exactly as I expected. Joska was busily digging more holes for the trees we brought, Agnes cleaned with determination, the couch stood at its appointed place, but the wardrobe still refused to be put together, although now the furniture man had two of his colleagues there to help the operation. They gave plenty of advice to each other, but none seemed to work, and as an appropriate response, all three cussed together in perfect understanding. All this made my husband feel very satisfied. As long as the company's own men could not put the thing together during an entire working day, the stigma of incompetence vanished from him. His masculinity was vindicated.

Like two excited kids, we walked out into the patio to see the pool with the blue tiles. Instead, we found Béla and Zoli, his helper, kneeling in the pool and scrubbing white foam from the blue tiles, and uttering oaths of such variety and creative turns that a linguist could have earned a Ph.D. analyzing them. The situation was grave, and it was obvious that the two usually chivalrous men were in no mood for light conversation. Neither was I. On my return I expected the jobs to be done, and everybody gone. Somebody would hang for this.

The pool is actually very small, not even seven feet long and its depth is just about five feet. The job of putting the tiles down should have been accomplished in a couple of hours. However, tile, pool and men were frothing, and not a single tile was laid.

"What happened?" my husband finally ventured.

"Nothing happened. The damned tiles slid right off the wall, that's what happened, thanks to the shit you call adhesive. May the German, who invented it, perish in hell. It's no fucking good, if you'll excuse my saying so. We applied it, and the tiles slid right off. And it foams like a damned toothpaste." He said other things too, but if I would repeat them, my computer would suffer an instant meltdown.

Horror dawned on me.

"Where did you find the adhesive?' I asked, but somehow knew the answer already.

"In the garage, of course."

"But Béla, I told you before I left, that the adhesive was right next to the tiles on the porch in front of the wine cellar."

"Jesus, so you have! I plain forgot." He looked bewildered for a moment, but true to his integrity, he admitted his momentary memory loss, and flashed me one of his charming smiles. "Then what the hell is this shit?"

"The stucco for the tile oven." Because of its unusual design, there are some areas on our oven that have to be painted. We were advised to get the special paint from Germany, as the local ones have a tendency to crack from the heat in the oven. A German friend was kind enough to track down this goop, and she lugged it across two borders for us. Béla tried to use this special, rare and fireproof material to glue the tiles to the pool wall. Béla, being a real macho man, does not read directions, even in his own langauge, but that did not keep him from being royally upset when the paint would not adhere. And I was fit to be tied.

"Don't explode, Love," my husband soothed, as he put his arms around me. "Come, let us have a glass of wine to celebrate, because you are probably the only person in the world, who owns a fireproof pool."

At that point Minnie and Gene arrived, hours before I, the house, the meal, the furniture men, or Agnes were ready for them. And yet, despite the mess, we had a wonderful visit, their first and last. Within the year the military draw-down sucked them up too, and they returned to the USA and to the experience of retired life.

The day after they arrived, I went out to the gate to retrieve the flags, but both were gone. Later that day a small boy, not more than seven years old, was passing our house and he stopped with some hesitation.

"Lady," he called, "When is the next American ambassador visiting you?"

I had no idea what he was talking about.

"What ambassador?"

"Everybody knows in the village that the ambassador came to you last night; that's why you had them flags out. We saw his big-ass car with the American plates parked in front of your house. My friends got the flags. Me, I'm too small, and couldn't reach it. But I could get it next time, if you'd tell me in time when the next ambassador is coming, so I could beat the others to it."

So Minnie and Gene were VIPs for a few days, because nobody in the village wanted to believe otherwise. The villagers felt mighty proud that such important people are visiting our backward little hamlet. I added three dozen small American flags to my shopping list, to be purchased on my next trip to the USA. If it is such a treasure to the local kids, they should have it. Let's cash in on this unexpected popularity in a world, where Americans are not everywhere so well loved.

Our friends left after a teary farewell, and soon other guests came. We welcomed them all, because they observed our simple house rule, which is that nobody should expect us to appear, entertain or serve any food before brunch. The guest apartment is a separate unit from the house, and it was built that way for a very good reason. We hate to get up early in the morning, and even if we do, we are not to be counted as fully functioning human beings at those hours. Our guests are expected to enjoy the morning solitude on their own. They may make their own breakfast in their kitchenette whenever they feel like it (I provide everything for it), enjoy the winter garden, the patio, the sauna, a selection of books and magazines, videos, or a walk in the hills, (they have their own private entrance to the apartment). As a matter of fact, they may enjoy just about everything, except our company. We are barely civil during the early hours. My husband gets a headache from the noise of my eyes blinking. I get a headache just thinking about it.

Later a light brunch is served, usually outdoors; the meal is leisurely and pleasant and by that time, so are we.

The guest, who at times takes off on her own to sightsee, or decides to take a long solitary walk, or takes an afternoon rest, is sure to be invited again. We absolutely and without reservations love company, and are delighted when we have guests. But at our age it is no longer possible to be alert for all the waking hours. We need time to regroup, and to charge our batteries. Some guests believe that it is their duty to be entertaining, and to be present at all times. Well, perhaps there are hosts and hostesses who require this; we are not one of them. We want our guests to have a good time, and they can only have it, if we too are relaxed and rested.

It is very difficult to be the perfect hostess; but it is just as complicated to be a welcome guest. Once I knew a little boy, whose professional goal was to become a guest when he grew up. I'm sure he did not know what a difficult occupation he was choosing when he was barely four. Fortunately, most of our guests have Ph.D.-s and honorary degrees in the art of being guests.

We were heading into deep spring and I was busy planning my garden. There were innumerable flats of seedlings from hopeful tomatoes to exotic artichokes. Esther tried to warn me that I would not need twenty bushes of zucchini and that seventy-five broccoli plants were pushing it, but I knew better. She advised moderation, but John Ciardi's John. J. Plenty was singing ever louder in my ears, "More! Get more!" I spent part of my days on my knees in the garden. My nails (despite the gardening gloves) were usually so grimy that I had to wash things by hand each evening, in order to make them clean enough. But I was completely happy digging in my garden all day.

One day in July, during one of those very rare occasions, when I was able to get up early, I decided to catapult my husband out of bed at four in the morning. It was easy enough, because at that time of the day he is lost to the world, and has no idea what is happening to him. A root canal could be done to him and he'd never notice. By the time he started to respond, we were already up in the hills on our property, where I was setting the table for breakfast on the deck. He sat down in a daze and attempted to drink the croissants and butter his coffee. It took some time before he could formulate his astonishment at finding himself up on the hilltop at four in the morning.

"Why?" he moaned. "Are we no longer compatible? Up to now we both hated to get up in the morning! Why this change now?"

"To watch the sunrise."

"I'm deeply devoted to sunsets," he mumbled, but this was not the opportune moment for deciding on an alternate devotion to Helios. Even in his groggy state, he understood that much.

"It is my son's birthday and I want to celebrate it in style," I intoned. The argument worked, and he sank into silence, waiting for the caffeine to do its thing.

I was pouring some more coffee, when from all the people, You-Know-Who yelled in youthful excitement, "Look at that, will you?"

A moment ago it was still quiet dark, although, the sky was slowly brightening to a steely gray, illuminated from a source that we still could not see. Lake Balaton (the big one), only rarely visible with the unaided eye from our place, was somewhere in the still dark valley. A chain of extinct volcanic mountains, shrouded in blue mist, were marking the opposite shore. The most prominent of the mountains, Badacsony, which lost its top in a gigantic, prehistoric eruption, was etched dark blue against the lightening sky.

But quite suddenly a vivid red-gold band, like a spectacular river of liquid fire, appeared at the foot of Mt. Badacsony. It was this glowing light in the darkness that caused my husband to exclaim with such excitement that I almost spilled the coffee.

His binoculars explained the magic. Even before we could see the rising sun, its rays already hit the surface of the big lake and this reflected light gave the impression of a river on fire. It was unbelievably beautiful.

In a moment, slowly and unhurriedly, the blood-red orb of the sun rose, as if emerging from the middle of the sawed-off top of Mt. Badacsony. It was simply breathtaking. To think that from a distance of some ninety million miles away a star could make such a spectacular entrance into our small world was dazzling, to say the least. And ungrateful humans that we are, day after day we slept through this unique and miraculous show. Does it pay to give spectacular gifts to mankind?

In a few minutes the sun was perched on the top rim of Mt. Badacsony and its rays flooded the dark valley, painting a golden bridge of light over the surface of the Lesser Balaton at our feet. This must have been the wake-up call of Nature, because almost instantly hundreds of birds greeted the new day. The silent hills now echoed with the songs of unseen birds. The sky turned light blue by this time, although the valley below was still dark, only the water shimmered in the light of the new day. A slight breeze came up from the lake and it shivered the last bit of sleep from the waves. The shadows dissolved in the heavenly brilliance A new day was born.

The hour was still far too early for anything alcoholic, so we toasted my son's birthday with apricot nectar and knew that it would be a good year for him, and a good day for us.

"I can't believe you did that to me," he mumbled as I was gathering the breakfast things and placed them back into the wicker basket. "But it was magnificent and we should do it again. Let's invite friends and have a predawn picnic..."

Later he was fond of telling our friends how I dragged him from his bed and hauled him up to participate in a heathen ceremony of sun worship. It always made a good story, and the list of guests, who would join us next time, grew steadily.

CHAPTER NINE

"The heads of the wheat are hanging low, heavy with grain," Árpád bácsi said. We met him during our afternoon walk in the fields. It was his mission that day to investigate the state of the wheat. "Tomorrow is the 29th of June, the feast day of Peter and Paul. Hopefully God would grant us good weather, because tomorrow the grain must be cut." We nodded at this piece of sagacity. It was pleasant to walk among the honey colored fields, the silence was satisfying, and the dogs chased each other happily.

"This new generation is besotted by the scientific methods of agriculture. Our sons believe that all the answers are in their books," he mused as he rubbed the head of a wheat stalk between his fingers. "But the saints know better. On the day of Peter and Paul the harvest must begin. Not sooner, not later. Everything at its appointed time." The afternoon breeze set the wheat into motion and suddenly I understood the line in one of my favorite poems "...the moving waves of the endless sea of wheat...". Of course, the color was no longer right, the poet must have seen it during the spring, when the fields were still green. But the motion was exactly like that of the sea.

"Have you noticed the similarity between man and wheat?" he asked us before saying farewell. "When the head is empty, it is carried high and proud; when it is heavy with substance, it is bent in humility." This was our ration of wisdom for the day.

As time passed, we learned that certain jobs or events in the life of the farmers were fixed to the feast days of saints in the calendar. For example, March 24 is the day of Mátyás (Matthew) and on this day every man with or without a fishing license is out to get a pike, which is the tastiest on that particular day. April 24 is the day of St. George. The rest of the world remembers this worthy gentleman as the dragon slayer, but the Hungarian farmer knows that this is the day to sow cucumber, zucchini and melons. It is also the day when the cattle is driven out into open pastures and the day marks the beginning of the employment period for all farm hands.

Then there are the "frosty saints" Pongrác, Szervác and Bonifác on May 12, 13 and 14 respectively. For reasons only known to themselves, they always bring cold weather with snow, ice or frost. This is a very serious matter, as I found out when I bought seeds for snap beans. On the packet the directions stated, "It is advisable that the Frosty Saints find the seeds underground, but not yet sprouted." Well, it could be a real disaster in your garden if you don't know your saints.

A few days later, on May 25 is the feast day of Urban, who is reputed to ruin what the Frosty Saints missed in the gardens. On June 8 there is Medard threatening the good farmers. If it rains on that day, behold, it will rain for the next forty days. Things will rot in the garden and tourists will stay at home, and then how would we pay our taxes? August 10 is the day of Lawrence. He is a nasty one with bad manners. It is said that one should never buy melons after his feast day, because he pees into them on the tenth, and the melons are no longer enjoyable. I suppose this was mostly true before it was possible to buy melons and other imported produce in the supermarkets, regardless of the seasons. Lawrence apparently did not know about long distance hauls from Africa, Spain and Israel; he was merely concerned with the locally produced fruit. I made the mistake of ignoring him the first year we moved here, and on a hot afternoon in late August I bought an irresistible watermelon from a vendor who was yelling his way through the village, "Buy fresh watermelons". We were salivating in anticipation. But after I cut it, we found that indeed, Lawrence was there before us. Sadly I pitched the soggy, watery, tasteless fruit into the compost pile.

Actually the saints warn about almost anything. St. Catherine's day for example is on November 25 and there is a ditty that warns: if it is cold on that day, rains would wash Christmas away; but if the day is warm and rainy, a white Christmas is assured. The duration of the winter can be foretold on February 2, and even in America we pay attention to this day, the only difference being that we transferred the weatherman's job from the saint responsible for it to the ground hog. It is also believed that if on the 24th of March Matthew finds ice, he'll break it (and the winter would be soon gone) but if he does not find any, he'll make the ice, and so the winter would be prolonged.

In time I learned that only very young children and very old people celebrate birthdays outside of the immediate family. On the other hand "name days", are big and important events, and this thing is so well organized that nobody forgets them. Every calendar is so designed that each day is dedicated to a saint of the Catholic Church, and his or her name is plainly marked, right under the date. If there is a calendar in the house, it is not possible to miss it. People having the same name as the appointed saint for the day, are celebrated in special ways, very much like birthdays are celebrated in the USA, with flowers, candy, cards, parties, gifts. Acknowledging the tendency to name children with modern names, or with names from the Old Testament, or from ancient Hungarian history, each saint shares his or her day with several other names, whose original bearers did not even exist, or were obscure and probably not very saintly.

A few generations ago names for children were not selected for their melodious quality, nor for their uniqueness, but in the hope that the developing child would emulate the character of the chosen model. In view of this, I sometimes wonder whatever motivated my father, when he chose the name Judith for me. Did he picture me in the distant future with the head of a contemporary Holofernes under my arm? With such expectations attached to me, it is a miracle that I could find not one, but two husbands. Or did my father think I would be as patriotic as the original, Biblical Judith? In this case he must be wondering in his afterlife about a daughter, who in her old age needs to be loyal not to one, but to two countries. Like the storks, I too have two homes, and have long forgotten where I belong. When we touch down at Kennedy, I clap enthusiastically with the other passengers. But when the plane lands at the Ferihegy airport in Budapest, I'm all choked up with happiness to be home again. My name, or perhaps my fate, predestined me for this duality and I'm constantly tugged in both directions.

Everybody who owns a calendar knows exactly which name is celebrated on any given day. In case somebody forgot to rip off the page on a given day, he would still be reminded a hundred ways during the day. The newspaper, the television, signs in candy shops and florists' windows all do their best. There are notes everywhere. "Today we celebrate all ladies named Beatrix and Erna", or "Angela and Petronella".

Gentlemen too are remembered. "Henry and Roland today". It is never too late to get a bottle of perfume, a box of candy or some flowers, a bottle of something for a man or to send a greeting card, or a telegram. It is amazing to me that those efficient CEOs of the greeting card companies failed to capitalize on this gold mine. I think they slept on the job. They got the initial notion all right, when they built up Valentine's and Patrick's feast days to its current frenzy, but somehow they got bogged down, and never developed the idea to its logical end. We all know that few people can keep each other's birthdays always in mind (ask any woman whose husband has forgotten hers!) but name days are public knowledge; it is virtually impossible to forget or to ignore them. The business potential behind this concept is tremendous, but the highly paid CEOs missed the boat so far.

Churches are most often dedicated to Mary, the Mother of Jesus, but there are plenty others that are named after a special saint. The feast day of the patron saint is the most important event in the life of the community. The preparations for it rival that of Christmas or Easter. Yards and houses are cleaned, walls painted, curtains washed, family graves and the church decorated. Women labor for days in the kitchen to provide for the many guests who would arrive from neighboring villages.

If the ancestors were smart, they chose a patron saint whose feast day is in one of the milder months, to ensure the success of the celebration. Early in the day, the village square is set up for the fair, which in itself is a cause for great excitement, even today, because the tents are packed with merchandise only seldom seen in the village. In the not-too-distant past, when people were less mobile, and the great shops and stores of the big towns were only half-believed, this was the yearly occasion to shop until you drop.

The bestseller on the stands was (and still is) the traditional and very large honey-gingerbread cookie, baked in the shape of a heart and elaborately decorated with sugar icing, in primary colors. The best hearts have a mirror pasted in the middle and have deeply poetic messages in white icing, such as "The one you see in the mirror now, is the one I'll love forever." Perfect happiness is to receive one of these from an admiring Adonis; its significance is about the same as a two-carat engagement diamond.

Some fairs boast other specialties too. For example Marcali, a rather insignificant little village not far from us, made its way into gastronomic history, when a baker named Ámon first offered ice cream to the delighted throngs. This exotic delicacy was often described in the turn-of-the-century romantic novels of Ms. Beniczky. Her swooning, lovesick and tragic aristocratic ladies used to tranquilize their unbalanced emotional states with portions of ice cream, served in crystal goblets by butlers in white gloves. However, ice cream was virtually unknown in the little villages, which were tucked away in the provinces. Ámon was not only familiar with literature, but also understood the psychological make-up of women. In addition he was an excellent businessman and knew that such a dish, made famous by the current bestsellers, would be a sure hit on the market. While eating the quickly melting cream, served on paper plates, the women could pretend for a short spell of time to be part of that wondrous world inhabited by the rich and the noble. It sure was worth the few coins they had to pay for the treat.

On the feast day there is a church service in the morning, and this usually includes a procession in which the statue of the saint (or the Madonna) is carried around the village streets. Often the street is covered with an elaborate carpet made of flower petals, the designs rivaling that of an Oriental rug. The devoted team of artists works on it a day and a night before the fair, and don't seem to mind that as soon as the procession reaches it, the creation is gone forever. Its only after-life is limited to the color slides made by the tourists.

Between church services and the delights of the fair, the sporting events in the afternoon, and the dance in the evening, the villagers manage to find time to consume a meal that can only be described as a gastro-intestinal endurance test. Even today, when the population is getting progressively poorer, the villagers, who produce most of their own food, still provide the feast, as it was customary in the old days.

We were invited to attend such a celebration near Lake Balaton, on July 26, feast day of St. Ann. Not only was the village church dedicated to St. Ann, but the wife of our host was named Anna, so it was her celebration too. On top of it, the day also marked their thirtieth wedding anniversary. Obviously, this called for a major production.

Tables and chairs were set up in the garden under the ancient walnut trees for about one hundred invited guests. They arrived on time, said

their silent grace, then tied huge napkins over their Sunday-best in preparation for some serious eating.

This memorable meal commenced with an incredible soup that must
have cost the lives of more chickens than a family eats in a year. Spicy,
feather-light dumplings made of veal liver floated in the golden soup, and
as far as I was concerned, it was a meal in itself. A dish, resembling
risotto followed, but was enriched by slices of goose liver, baked to a
perfect melt-in-the-mouth experience that rivaled the best *paté de foie
gras* we ever had the good fortune to eat in France. Big bowls of stuffed
cabbage were served with crusty bread, or as an alternative, chicken
paprikás with pasta for those who had a less robust appetite.

More than two hours passed since we sat down, the jugs were kept
filled with the local, heady wine, and the initial silence while eating,
gave way to spirited conversation. Well fed and content, we expressed
our appreciation to the women, who collected the plates.

"Glad you liked it," one of them answered with a broad smile. "Hope
the meal will please you as much as the appetizer did!"

"Holy Moses, she can't be serious!" my husband moaned.

But bowls of cucumber salad with garlic, dill and sour cream were
placed on the tables, along with pickles, sautéed red cabbage, bowls of
tomatoes and onions, and roasted red peppers with garlic, all delicately
flavored with a light vinaigrette. Parsley potatoes and cheese dumplings
with dill heralded the main attraction: huge platters of roasted ducks,
geese and suckling pigs. The meats were tender, the skins crisp; I never
tasted meat as good as this before. No wonder, since the roasting was
done in outdoor, ancient bread-baking ovens, built like beehives. This
method of baking gave the meats a very special flavor, which even the
most modern kitchen appliance cannot duplicate. The pigs and fowl
were homebred, ran freely all day in the orchards, having their pick of
greens, and as their main meal they were fed corn. The difference in
taste of these, and the ones we buy on plastic trays in the supermarkets
just cannot be compared. The appreciative, almost pious silence that
followed was only broken by the music of silverware hitting china in
the al fresco setting, while the sun was slowly sinking at the horizon.

Man must be the only animal that eats voluntarily past the point of
satiety.

The tables were cleared once more, to make way for the strudel, the

pride of Hungarian cooks. In some parts of Europe this delicacy degen-
erated into a heavy, pie-like dessert, its sticky filling soaking the pastry
on the underside, changing it into a heavy glob. In Hungary the strudel,
or *rétes*, is more like the phyllo in Greece. Each sheet, after it is rolled up
with the filling, must remain separate and crisp. As a matter of fact, the
very name of it in Hungarian means "layers". Since it is not possible to
roll it this thin with a rolling pin, women acquired the art of pulling and
stretching it so thin that the Sunday paper could be read through it.
Without glasses. It is said that once a girl learns how to make a proper
strudel, she is marriageable.

Some of the parchment-thin sheets were filled with cherries, or apples, nuts or poppy seeds, but there were quantities filled with dilled
cottage cheese, or sautéed, peppery cabbage for those, who like to end
their meal with a savory taste. Cakes, ice cream, huge plates of cookies
and baskets of fruits closed this midday repast that lasted until the first
stars appeared on the deep velvet of the sky.

All had a good time and the happy guests barely missed the celebrated hostess, when she failed to reappear after one of her reconnais-
sance trips to the kitchen. For all I knew, she might have collapsed somewhere between her pots and pans and the mountains of dirty dishes. But
I hoped that she had the common sense to retire to her room, where she
could kick off her shoes, open her bra and let her hair down to recuperate from producing this gargantuan meal that seemed to have no end. In
the peace and tranquility of her chamber, hopefully, she spent some
time considering how to change her name from Anna to something that
no calendar lists.

As the summer progressed, the temperatures soared, but the house
remained cool. Those thick walls did their job very well, and during the
night we searched for the covers, which we swept aside earlier. But we
liked to spend the days outside. The bamboo shoots we bought at the
arboretum grew as tall as the house; the roots multiplied into countless
new shoots, until the area around the pool turned into a small forest. It
offered a cooling, green shade. The leaves, pulled by their own weight,
bent over the mirror surface of the pool to admire their reflections. The
whispering music, improvised by the breeze among the slender stalks
and leaves, gave the illusion of far-away, exotic places. This "forest" dou-
bled as a perfect shield, long before our evergreen hedge matured enough

to serve as a wall. We could eat, lounge, or slip into the pool without being observed by those who passed or drove by on the road below our garden. The ornamental pool, originally planned for a dip after the sauna, offered a wonderful way to cool off during the hot summer days. It was also an extraordinary experience to slip into it after the evening bath or shower and come out refreshed and ready to conquer the world. This small pool is a wonderful compensation for the swimming pool I cannot have.

We established the habit of having leisurely brunches on the terrace under the awning alone, or with friends. The food is always simple, consisting mainly of salads with ingredients freshly picked from our garden. We discovered the pleasure of vine-ripened tomatoes, fresh basil and arugula, which grows so abundantly that one day it'll probably take over the entire garden, because we are powerless to control its expansionist politics. Chicken breasts in aspic, flavored with sherry, are the specialty of Agnes, while I make feather-light omelets with vegetable fillings. Sometimes I would serve cold, smoked trout with a light horseradish sauce, or pasta with a sauce that my momentary fancy would dictate. Lunch is completed with jugs of iced tea, cheese and fruit.

We lounge in the shade and talk about everything, and nothing. The world and its crazy politics do quite well without our worrying about it, and we do not understand why we felt compelled for so long to move in the fast lane. Time ceased to have a meaning for us and we learned to think in terms of seasons. The dogs, always as close to us as possible, are just as intensely lazy as we are, and on hot days they sleep on the cool tiles on the patio. In the heat Borka snores gently and Sissi, our gourmand, judging by the chewing and smacking sounds she makes, is dreaming of food. After lunch I move to the hammock and marvel about the great number of butterflies that came to visit us ever since I planted a bed of nicotinias.

Sometimes in the evening I would fill a picnic basket, take a jug of water for the dogs and we'd drive up to our hilltop property, which we nicknamed Belvedere. There is always a lovely breeze sweeping up from the lakes and in the late afternoon the deck and the picnic area are well shaded by the walnut trees. The dogs come alive and chase the butterflies up and down the ravines. It is the time to fill the goblets with wine and toast the setting sun before supper is grilled. As old age approaches, there are plenty of aches and pains, dying fires, sad farewells, and enough medications to be taken before meals to qualify the quantity as a first course, but the gentle compensations of these peaceful evenings are more appreciated than the passionate gifts of youth.

Of course, I was not idle all the time. My vegetable garden was a source of constant surprises and challenges. The soil and the climate in Szabar are so exceptional, the locals told me, that even the Creator wondered at times how He did it so well. I classified this as patriotic bragging and to the amusement of practically everyone, I planted enough vegetables to keep an army well fed and a canning factory to work overtime. Too late I learned that the proud statements of the neighbors were absolutely true. The quantities I harvested defied imagination. By August I was seriously worried that the fence posts would start shooting leaves or producing fruits. Whatever I stuck into the ground promptly came up, rearing to grow. Since I can't bear to throw away anything (not even into the compost) and since it is not possible to give away vegetables in a farming village, all summer I was preparing the bounty to be stashed away in the three freezers, and in every canning jar I could find. I also mailed quantities of my produce to city dwelling friends. Postal service in Hungary is exemplary, and whatever I would send one day was always delivered the next, still fresh and good.

Some fashion conscious women coordinate the color of their makeup and nail polish with the outfit they are wearing. But ever since I became a country wife, the color of my hands is carefully coordinated to whatever I happen to be canning (peeling, slicing, etc.) at the moment. Like the French painters, I too go through my brown, green, yellow and red periods as the summer progresses from green nuts through carrots to beets.

The worst offenders are the green walnuts, staining my hands and nails a deep, and almost permanent shade of brown, which is hailed as an especially attractive color on hardwood furniture. No wonder that this particular brown was such a favored color in the Middle Ages. A bowl of unripe nuts could do the staining job for an entire family's winter wardrobe, and the leftover brew could color the hair of the aging female members to a shade even Clairol can't duplicate.

Each year I decide not to bother with the nuts, but the final product of my labors, nuts ripened in heavy syrup, is so enthusiastically greeted by our guests, that I always capitulate. The enjoyment of it is admittedly an acquired taste, but one that is acquired very easily; much easier in fact than the art of producing them.

My rational decision to stay away from green nuts always weakens by the middle of June, the best time to pick the fruits. This is when the walnuts are getting nice and plump, but the woody shell inside the green outer-cover is not yet formed. By this time the stain on my hands from the previous year is just a memory, and then one morning, almost against my will, I'm picking the green nuts. I wear surgical gloves, but somehow by the time I fill the basket, my hands are again the color of a Franciscan monk's habit.

After washing the nuts, the tips of both ends have to be sliced off and then the nuts are pricked several times with a knitting needle. Now my hands are the color of double-roasted coffee grounds. The nuts are covered with water and kept so for eight days. Of course, the water has to be changed twice daily, and so my yellow plastic colander also turns brown. On the eighth day the nuts are placed in hot water and boiled for 15 minutes. The hot water is drained, and the nuts are placed in a cold bath for 24 hours. After this the real fun starts. The water is drained, the nuts are dried, then weighed. For each two pounds of nuts a mixture of one pound of sugar and one quart of water is cooked into a syrup. The hot syrup is poured over the nuts, and a cinnamon stick and about fifteen cloves are added, and set aside for twenty-four hours. For the next four days the nuts are removed very carefully in order not to bruise them, and the syrup is heated up and cooked for a few minutes, then poured back on the nuts. On the fifth day the syrup is quite thick and now the nuts are cooked in it for ten minutes, cooled and placed into sterilized jars. The nuts must be completely covered by the syrup, but if the process was done right, there won't be enough of it, so the jars are filled up with brandy, then set in a cool, dark place to meditate in a booze-induced, sugary state, and in the process acquire virtue, class and of course, taste.

This is the end of the procedure.

The dark brown nuts by now are so sinfully ugly that the more squeamish might have second thoughts before putting them into their mouths. However, it is a truly heavenly condiment, excellent with venison or other roasts, a unique addition to puddings or dessert creams.

Packed away in small attractive jars, it makes a much-appreciated gift to friends.

My husband's personal opinion is devastating. He claims it takes a nut to do all this to perfectly nice nuts, which would ripen on their own, if left on the tree. Also, says the Man, the brandy is quite excellent without all that nutty syrup. His argument would be more effective, if he would not eat them as fast as he can put his hands in the jar.

While I am endlessly fussing with the nuts, I have some deep thoughts about the mentality and the psychological makeup of women in general, and our ancestors in particular. This recipe hails from my great-grandmother, who raised six children in a house without electricity, running water or central heating. Laborsaving devices and convenience foods were still in the distant future, and bread was baked at home. Fruits and vegetables had to be homegrown, then dried, canned, pickled, dug in for the winter; soap cooked in the shed from unmentionable ingredients, and rugs were beaten by hand in the backyard. Whatever possessed a woman in such circumstances to mess around with green nuts in addition to her other, never-ending chores? The nuts were not a necessary item on the family table, and kids could not eat them, on account of the alcoholic content. After a hard day of work around the house, why did she insist on doing something that took many hours to complete, was not needed, and enjoyed only by a few? Was she punishing herself, or did she have a deep need to create something that was an absolute luxury? Did our ancestresses need something frivolous in their humdrum lives, or were they simply masochists? Is it just the quirk of language that "ancestress" contains the word 'stress'? Come to think of it, I am doing now exactly what they have done centuries ago. Am I reverting to their mode of thinking and feeling? Did I catch whatever was wrong with them?

As the summer progressed with its bountiful gifts, the freezers were bulging from every vegetable that grew in my garden. On the shelves, covering the walls in my restored fruit cellar, stood long rows of jars holding pickled peppers, fruit preserves, green tomato marmalade, dried mushrooms, and pots of honey. My blackened, inebriated nuts were dozing in their special syrupy rapture. Bottles of tomato juice, like so many red-coated soldiers, guarded barrels of homemade sauerkraut, mixed pickles, and sacks of onions. The bins were filled with potatoes and winter apples. Carrots, beets, celery roots, winter squash and horse-radish roots were slumbering under layers of sand and straw. Wreaths and garlands of garlic and hot pepper were strung up; wild thyme, rose-mary, dill and other herbs were suspended from the ceiling to dry. Nuts and almonds were stored in wicker baskets. It was an olfactory ecstasy to step into this treasure house of good food. I lovingly contemplated my hoarded goods, and sighed with relief, like millions of women must have done before me, ever since an absolute genius invented agriculture about ten thousand years ago. Death by starvation was unlikely to occur during the coming winter.

Since man cannot live by bread alone, or vegetables for that matter, for beauty's sake I also worked a great many hours in my flower garden. Being a confounded romantic, I like to picture myself (twenty-five pounds lighter and half a century younger) in a white, billowy muslin dress and a large straw hat, decorated with summer flowers, carrying a graceful basket (of wicker, painted white). I would daintily and dreamily gather beautiful flowers (white roses) from the impeccable garden, tended by a certified gardener, to be arranged later in my (non-existent) vases, all collector's items or antiques.

However, I don't own a billowy muslin dress, nor would I dare wear it, if I had one. Forget the huge hat with the flowers and ribbons. And realistically speaking, even by the wildest stretch of imagination, Joska couldn't be called a certified gardener.

Instead of floating among the roses, searching out the best blooms for my Rosenthal and silver vases (which I do not own now, but would certainly have if I had a billowy muslin dress and the other requisites), my so-called garden work starts each day by swinging a broom on the patio and across the walkways to counteract the nightly efforts of our dogs. The two animals are single-minded in their goal of digging and spreading good garden soil at places where it is not at all needed. They are also trying to beat the rest of the world at being the first ones to dig a tunnel to China. I'm not amused, and tell them so quite frequently. They act contrite and disappear as long as I have the broom in my hands, but I know that in the depths of their dark hearts they don't care about my displeasure.

My husband, always a dedicated spokesman for the canines, explains that I am unreasonable, and should rise above my irritation, which is very unhealthy in the heat. "The dogs have a different standard for beauty. While you find flowers and neatly raked beds charming; they think that trenches and holes are the last word in horticultural design. The problem is that you and they have different biases about what a garden ought to look like," declared the man in my life. *Nota bene*, he is not the one, who sweeps the patio and the walks daily.

"You are surely not suggesting that I should change my preferences because of the dogs?" I asked, but he merely shrugged.

"The power structure is two to one. You might want to consider giving up the effort of training them to appreciate the garden as humanoids do, and gracefully accept the decision of the majority of two." Obviously, this Pearl of Dog Owners does not find tunnels in the flowerbeds any more offensive than his dogs do.

My daughter, Andrea, has far more sympathy. Kincsem, her dog, (named so in memory of the unbeatable Hungarian racehorse of the same name; a reminder that Andrea in her youth was deeply dedicated to horses), also suffers from this canine digging habit; although the motives of Kincsem are a bit different. Her reason for digging is to carefully hide her bones, ostensibly because she is afraid that Andrea and Mike, or perhaps their children, would steal them. She is obsessed with a paranoid fear that the four of them would retire to the nightly family reading hour with her bones as special snacks. She also fears that the girls would pack them for lunch, since she thinks that the current in-thing at the Shaker Heights schools is to chew slightly used bones. Normally she is loyal and devoted to a fault, but she draws the line where her bones are endangered. Unfortunately, as soon as she hides them, she forgets the location and so spends her days frantically digging up every square inch of the garden in order to find the bones.

"Our lawn and the flower beds must have by now a solid foundation of bovine and porcine pelvic bones, femurs and tibiae," Andrea writes. "One day somebody will find them and think we are mass murderers. I can already see how the Shaker police will haul us away and give us life sentences. Kincsem, still angry about her 'stolen bones', won't say a word in our defense, but would gloat as we are dragged away in handcuffs and leg-irons. She'd then retire and write the story of her life. It would be a best- seller and make her filthy rich. She would retain a manager, a body-guard, an exercise trainer, an accountant, a butler and a secretary to answer her fan mail. And we'd be languishing in a dungeon off Lee Road, and would be buried in unmarked graves." In comparison with Andrea's prospect, a tunnel to China appeared almost desirable.

The big event of the summer was the installation of the telephone. I have long given up hope ever getting a line, but then after all, on a sunny morning the van of MATAV, the Hungarian Ma Bell, pulled up at our gate. I was as excited as the dogs, and asked about as many silly questions as Sissi would on one of her more excitable days. It is to my credit that unlike her, I did not drink constantly, so I didn't have to run to the bathroom every minute. Following the installers at their heels, I wanted to know if I'd get a push-button or a dial type of a phone.

"I hope it is a push-button," I bubbled (or babbled?) "because I hope to get a fax and an answering machine."

Both guys stopped in their tracks and laughed so hard that I was sure they'd be the ones having to visit the bathroom.

"Lady, you just wait and see what you get!" they guffawed. I was a bit suspicious. When men laugh in this way nothing good ever comes out of it.

I was right. They unpacked a huge, black box; the weight of it could have qualified it as a weapon. It had no numbers on it to push or to dial, and it was definitely not the one ET used to call home. This one had to be cranked, just like in the movies, shown late at night. The cranking would alert the postmaster, alias mayor, who then would plug in some wires in his office, provided he had time to do it. Then he would call the city with a telephone center, from where the operator would connect us to the number we wished to reach. It was a marvel of retarded technology, for which I was supposed to be thankful.

For a while we could not decide whether it was its advantage or disadvantage that it only worked during the limited business hours of the post-office. The peace of the evenings, weekends and holidays was great, but it was quite difficult to reach my family through all the time zones, not to mention their work schedules, which further complicated reaching them.

Andrea once tried to call us and she very nearly had a nervous breakdown. The US operator, who suffered under the delusion that the whole world can be reached through direct dial via satellite, was vexed.

"Ma'am, this is an impossible situation! I have been trying to get a line for twenty minutes without any results... I have no idea what is happening over there," she complained. The correct phrasing should have been, "what is NOT happening over there".

"Please Ma'am, could you explain to the American colleague not to be so impatient; we are trying our level best," the Hungarian operator pleaded. Wisely, Andrea refused to interfere. Let them fight it out between themselves; after all, it is their line, their satellite, their cranky phone. Mike, macho and efficient, took the receiver from her hand.

"Let me handle this."

It did not take long, before all operators on both sides of the ocean heard his opinion. He then slammed down the receiver, but there was still no line to Hungary.

"They are complete idiots, all of them," he fumed. "Inefficient and incompetent. Their IQ is probably lower than their shoe size."

"Peace, my master. They are all very decent, and sincerely want to help. I'm already on a first name basis with some of them, since we established friendships during the long wait. It is not their fault that they have to work with equipment found in Noah's ark, that was not only obsolete, but also damaged by the deluge."

Three days later she finally got through, but she was so excited by this success that she forgot why she wanted to call me in the first place. Not that it mattered. The exact text of this historical first overseas conversation to Hungary has been saved for posterity:

"...Hello, Mom...Hello...I can't believe that I got through...Hello? Can you hear me?...Hello...Are you still there?...Hello....Mom!...Talk to me...this is not a phone; this is a disaster...Hello?...Oh, shit..."

And then we were cut off.

Once I managed to reach her number and had the rare pleasure of talking to their answering machine. "Nobody but us books here..." it said. I was back at square one, and contemplated my son's advice of learning to make smoke signals. On official questionnaires I simply marked that we had no phone. We could never be reached on it anyhow, and I could not explain all this in the little box provided for "remarks". Besides, nobody would believe it. It was easier to say that we had no phone. It wasn't even a lie.

It took another three years before a decent telephone line was built, and we could exchange our museum piece for the real thing with buttons, redial, stored numbers, and our own retaliation to the world of Ma Bell: an answering machine.

There was only one single cool week that summer and instead of enjoying the sub-boiling temperatures, we decided to hang wallpaper in the dressing area of the first bathroom we built BC (Before Construction). The project could have waited, but I was instantly inspired, when I found a few rolls of wallpaper, bought a long time ago, heaven only knows why. It was a very sophisticated paper with well-spaced vertical stripes, and of a remarkable color combination of soft purple and forest green, with a dash of gold, on a cream background. It was just the right touch for our ostrich-like toilet.

Since neither of us knows anything about hanging wallpaper, we became instant experts, telling each other very contradictory things to do. The area to be wallpapered was not the size Architectural Digest would have considered worth mentioning, but it did not dampen our adventurous spirits. After we lugged in the ladder, the tools, the wallpaper, we squeezed ourselves into the bathroom and were so tight that we had to ration the amount of air inhaled and exhaled.

I was in charge of following my husband with the paste-dripping paper, which I carried like the train of a ceremonial gown. His job was to fit the upper edge to the top of the wall. He kept telling me, how to hold the paper, and I kept telling him how to fit it just under the ceiling. While these directions are harmless in themselves, a hint of irritation was gradually discernible in our tone, and it grew more vehement after each frustrating attempt of trying to make the paper stick.

Undaunted (but irritated), we forged ahead, but alas, as soon as we accomplished the task of spreading the paste and positioning the paper, it slid right off, with the predictability of a soufflé falling. After the fifth trial, the man with the practical side to his character suggested that we nail a wooden slat to the ceiling and hang the paper from it, curtain-fashion. I did not care for that look, but suggested using Elmer's glue instead of the paste that would not stick. He then thought we ought to give it up altogether and I promptly called him a quitter. It was the first and only time that we came close (very close) to have a fight during the entire ordeal of building our home. Fight? Did I really say fight? We were ready to walk out on each other, only we had nowhere to go.

Money, infidelity, interference from in-laws, or incompatibility of two careers are often cited as reasons for the breakdown of marriages. Our marriage was teetering on the brink, because of a striped wallpaper. What really kept us from screaming "divorce", on the spot was that actually neither of us wanted to be stuck with an unfinished house, and both of us wanted custody of the dogs.

Enter my sister-in-law with the sixth sense that tells her exactly when she is not wanted somewhere. The first words out of her mouth were, "What are you doing?" Hell, I thought that was pretty obvious. Her brother was trying to wrap me up in a strip of wallpaper a mile long and dripping with paste. And I was about to kill him.

"Won't the paper stick?" she asked the obvious according to her despicable habit. She has never seen wallpaper before, let alone hung any, but she hastened to add her expert advice immediately.

"Maybe you should dry it a bit. It looks awfully wet to me."

If I would stick some of that paste into her mouth, would it shut off her mouth-machine for a while? "Funny that it won't stick," she mused never even guessing my murderous thoughts, "because both of your dogs are practically cemented to the kitchen floor."

My husband dropped the wallpaper on my head and dived from the ladder. I picked up the unusual train of my attire and ran after him into the kitchen. There they were, both of them, looking as guilty as only children and dogs can look when they are caught red-handed, actually white-whiskered in this case. Sissi's black little face was all white and her hair stiff. The kitchen looked like the studio of an artist gone mad.

It appeared that she tried to lick the paste, which we left on the floor. But used to good food, Sissi could not believe how tasteless this new treat was. Having a stubborn streak, she tried again and in the process tipped the bowl. Paste oozed on the floor, into the rug, and under the appliances. Borka, less food oriented, merely stepped into the mess, then walked several times across the kitchen, leaving artistic footprints behind her. Having exhausted themselves with this fruitless labor and not particularly impressed by the gastronomic value of the paste, both dogs stretched out to rest, smack in the middle of the paste puddle, and were in the process of drying permanently to the floor.

The divine wrath on my husband's face was such that I could guess what the four horses of the Apocalypse would look like. I took my stance at his feet, ready to cringe, if it must be.

"*Your* dogs!" he bellowed and in his holy anger he forgot to add a few expletives, which would have been warranted in that situation.

I forgot about the wallpaper and the Apocalypse and burst out laughing. The game of "our children", as opposed to "your children" (depending whether they caused trouble, or brought home the glory) was apparently over. The name of the game in this new passage would be "our dogs" as opposed to "your dogs." For a moment he looked perplexed, then caught the implication, and he too burst out laughing.

I spent the rest of the day scraping and washing off paste from the rug, the dogs, the appliances and from, myself.

"Why didn't you ask me first?" Feri, the painter, wanted to know when my husband contacted him to hang the paper. "You can't hang paper on untreated stucco walls. I have all the necessary material and I'll take care of it next week." We forgot to ask him which next week he meant: in this season, or perhaps the next millenium.

CHAPTER TEN

Fall was approaching. The green of the trees turned a shade duskier, less vivid. The swallows and the storks already left for the south. In the early hours when the fog was still thick over the lakes, we heard hundreds, perhaps thousands of geese as they flew in great V formations. They were invisible in the mist, but their loud screeching heralded the fall.

There was only one topic now worth talking about in the village, and it was constantly discussed at the street corners, at the store, after church and at the post-office: when should the grape harvest begin? Should we start now? Should we wait a week or two? The weather forecast was never followed as carefully as in these days. Esther was in her element, because she thrives on excitement. She stopped everyone who passed her house and discussed the latest weather reports, then ran up to our house on the hour, out of breath and with a dooms-day expression on her face, to analyze from isobar to isobar the impending disastrous highs and lows in barometric pressures. The trusted saints, apparently teetotalers, were of no help in determining the best day to start the most important job of the year in this wine-producing district.

During these early fall days the nights are already cool, but the sun is still powerful, and able to ripen the grapes some more. The riper the grapes, the higher the sugar content and the better it will ferment, hence it will provide a better wine. But it could happen that during those last critical weeks one of those autumn rains would fall for a few days, even a week, and the grapes would absorb too much water too suddenly. The fruit could burst and rot. Or the weather could turn unseasonably warm and the overripe grapes would invite legions of wasps and bees. An early frost could also ruin the crop, which was tended with so much care and labor all summer. To set the date for the grape harvest is one of the most difficult decisions of the year in the life of the viticulturist.

We turned for consultations with Lajos bácsi, the vintner of our vineyard, which we bought the previous fall. The general fever of indecision was contagious and we too wondered when to start, especially since we were so new in this business.

Lajos bácsi is a charismatic, delightful person, the kind one often meets in novels or in the movies, but only seldom in real life. He is well past seventy, but has the stamina of a man half his age. Rain or shine, scorching heat or vicious wind, summer or winter, every day he covers the two miles up to the vineyard. In the beginning we used to offer him a ride in our car, but he refuses to sit "in one of those devil's machines", and prefers the walk. His private, so-called short-cut, goes through a marshy, wet area, then skirts some corn fields and a small forest, then starts climbing steeply up to the vineyards. On account of the wet areas and the ticks, he travels in high boots, and the path is so steep that in cardiovascular output it ranks not far behind a stroll up on one of the mountains in the Himalayas. But he is robustly built, his back is straight, his walk has a measured dignity and his sky-blue eyes always shine in suppressed merriment. Most of his teeth are missing, but this fact does not bother him in the least. As a matter of fact, nothing ever bothers him, and I have never seen him in a hurry, not in speech and not in action. His work gives him pleasure, and he is extremely proud of the high quality wine he produces and the way he keeps the vineyard and the cellar in perfect order. He is at peace with himself and the world.

We met Lajos bácsi during the first summer we spent at Szabar, before we even considered moving here permanently. During one of our walks we passed his wine-cellar. He was sitting in front of his neat little domain and was repairing some tool. Out of politeness we greeted him, and he invited us to sit with him. Soon he disappeared into his cellar and came out with a strange glass tube in his hand. I have never seen anything like it and was fascinated.

It was a long, slim glass pipe, open at both ends. At the top end it bulged into a sphere that could hold about a half quart of liquid. The top opening of this sphere could be plugged up with the tip of the thumb, so that the wine would not flow out at the bottom opening. It looked like a greatly enlarged transfer pipette. Our host dipped the long end of the glass pipe into the barrel, and just like a laboratory technician, sucked on the shorter, top end. Through this action the sphere filled quickly with wine. He then closed the top opening by pressing his thumb over it, leaned the contraption against his shoulder, so that the wine-filled sphere was level with his head, and was ready to pour the wine for us. But first he rinsed the glasses, by squirting wine into them. This was simply accomplished, by removing his thumb for a second from the opening; atmospheric pressure and gravitational pull forced the wine into the glasses.

"I wash the glasses in rainwater," he explained during the operation, "but I like to rinse them with alcohol to be on the safe side." After he swooshed the wine around in the glasses, he spilled the alcoholic "dishwater" on the ground, then filled the glasses again. We toasted each other and so were introduced to one of the most delightful of the villagers, and certainly to one of the best wines on the hill. It was robust, fruity but on the dry side, exactly the way we like it.

We were sitting under his apple tree on makeshift benches, and enjoyed the lovely view of the village below. Behind us his vineyard rose uphill at a precarious angle.

"My plot is steep," he admitted, "but not overly so. The rainwater does not run off it. It also faces southwest and gets the benefit of the best sunshine all day long. You now taste the stored-up sunshine in the wine, That's what gives it the deep taste."

Below us the composition of the red tile roofs of the village, huddled around the church that Buzád built, and beyond it the blue expanse of the Lesser Balaton was like one of those postcards on which the overt message is "Wish you were here", but the unsaid sentiment is "Hope you turn yellow with envy." Even without his wine and the quiet mood of that afternoon, it is a memorable place and we fell in love with it.

Lajos bácsi was an out-and-out host, and would not let us go. He made several trips into his cave and made sure we sampled his old wine, his young wine, his dry and his sweet wines. He told us in his slow, unhurried way how he built the cellar himself and showed us proudly the arrangement he invented for the harvesting. The grape collecting vats, the grape-press and the juice-collecting tub were housed in the upper part of his split-level cellar. This facilitated an easy approach for the harvesters with their heavy loads of grapes as they brought them down from the steep hillside. The freshly pressed juice flowed into the collecting tub, then with an ingenuous system of hoses it continued to flow through a hole drilled from the tub through the ceiling of the cellar down into the lower level, where he could guide the juice into the already prepared oak casks. It was neat, efficient and clean.

"I'm forced to hire all sorts of 'types' to help with the harvest," he explained. "But I cannot abide these characters in my cave. This way they can deposit the grapes above and have no call to enter my cave below."

I think he wanted to use the word 'defile' instead of 'enter'. His cave was his temple, dedicated to Bacchus, or perhaps to his own personal god of the grape, and he made sure that the 'types' never entered his sanctuary. Nobody ever got nearer to his sacred wine than the upper level, or the small veranda in front of the cellar.

In the upper level he had a small room for his own use, where he could spend the night if he so wished. However, his wife (for obvious reasons) was not too fond about this practice. He was a prudent man with long experience in marital disquiet, and liked to avoid confrontations, so whenever practicable, he made the trip back home.

"Going home depends on how many visitors I catch a day," he said with a wink. I could understand that. His wine was heady and by the time we strolled home, we felt no pain.

After we were already more or less settled in the village, Lajos bácsi had a bad accident. Some wasps decided to take lodgings in his temple. An impeccable host to humans, he was quite inhospitable to the wasps and attacked them vigorously. The wasps turned militant, retaliated viciously, and our hero had to flee from his cellar to avoid the maddened insects. In doing so, he tripped and fell, broke several ribs, was badly bruised, had a brain concussion and almost died from the stings of the wasps. He spent several weeks in the hospital.

His wife, a tall and religious type, was upset. According to some, she was royally aggravated, and called him everything except a gentleman. She, a lady from her toes to her scarf-covered head, would never say it openly, but body language and covert hissings indicated that she suspected the noble nectar of the gods to be at least partially responsible for poor Lajos bácsi's accident. The old man wasn't even out of the hospital yet, when she decided the vineyard had to go. She was up to her eyebrows with his daily sojourns and wanted it ended once and for all. She was in no mood to become a young widow at seventy-six. Roma locuta, casa finita. Rome has spoken, the case is closed.

Lajos bácsi was crushed; he was ready to turn to the wall and die. Life suddenly lost all of its appeal and the years ahead loomed empty without his beloved grapes and the slow, careful tending of them. He could not face life without the peace he created for himself in the hills, where he could take a glass of wine without having to listen to a lecture about it, or get the silent treatment as a punishment. When we visited him in the hospital, he held a long, sad monologue, mostly to justify himself.

"…so what if I drink a few glasses? It never hurt anybody. I am a decent man. My house, my vineyard, my wine are clean and impeccable. I love my sainted wife. Never beat her, even if at times I was close to it. I care for our adult children, and for the grandchildren too. I worked hard all my life. For years I made a living by shoveling earth out of the basin, which is today the Lesser Lake Balaton. Yeah, that beautiful lake could be filled with the sweat of those who dug it out. Dig, shovel, lift, fill the wheelbarrow. Then start all over again. Twelve and fourteen hours a day, six days a week. We were not paid an hourly wage, but according to the number of barrels we were able to deliver to the foreman. It was a labor God designed for the damned. Somehow I survived. In those days, when I was young and times were hard, I could not even dream of ever having a vineyard of my own. Now I have one and it is my life. Take it away and guaranteed the old pump would stop working. There are just a few years left to me, why should I not enjoy myself and drink daily from my own wine? All my life I had to drink water. Sometimes I even drank it when I was hungry. For a little while hunger can be silenced, when you fill your belly with water…" His old hands moved restlessly on the bedcover. As long as he could remember, he was never in bed during the day, and most certainly never received visitors there, clad in a scanty hospital gown. Understandably, he was uncomfortable. "I am now king in my own cellar and am respected, because I make a good, honest wine. I never add water or sugar to the juice. I know a man who puts so much water into his wine that instead of fruit flies, seagulls circle his damned barrels. Not me. My wine is pure and undiluted."

He paused again, probably recalling the smooth taste of his Riesling. I wished that I brought him some, but being forewarned about the intravenous tubes forming a network around his bed, I decided not to interfere with doctor's orders. As if reading my thoughts, he continued. "My sainted wife is unreasonable when it comes to wine, and she parrots what the doctors tell her. Cirrhosis is meaningless at my age. One has to die of something sooner, or later. It makes no difference which mischief will cut the thread of life. Something happens to people, and then they die. Hardening of the arteries, cancer, pneumonia, or cirrhosis. Or maybe a car hits them. The one thing we can't escape in life is death, and we all know this. And anyway, what would God say to me if I'd die with a healthy liver? 'Lajos, Lajos,' God would tell me and shake His head sadly. 'You did not appreciate my gifts. I placed you in one of the best wine regions of Central Europe, and you had the audacity to die with a good liver? You did not have the decency or the common courtesy to enjoy my gift. You hurt my feelings in a big way. You belong in hell.' And at once the pearly gates would slam in my face. I could not do that to my Creator, who all in all, was pretty decent to me, could I? Damned wasps. They got my sainted wife all upset and she got bent out of shape. I could still be a happy man if the wasps hadn't messed it up for me…"

After a while he left the hospital, but stopped being interested in the affairs of man, and very wisely, stopped talking to his wife.

However, being a robust fellow, he soon snapped out of his funereal mood. One evening, dressed in his Sunday suit, knocked at our door. After the preliminary small talk he presented the reason for his visit. Would we buy his vineyard? The offer was unexpected and outrageous. What on earth would we do with a vineyard? We don't know a thing about it, and we are not looking for work at our age, especially since we were still buried deeply in our renovation and addition projects. All we wanted to do was finish our house, and live happily ever after. Also, we had no money to waste on something that would be no more than a fancy. Thanks for the offer, but no thanks. His blue eyes narrowed shrewdly, for this is exactly the answer he expected.

Slowly, carefully chewing every word before saying it, he explained that his wife's heart was set on selling it. He assured us with the most serious face that there is absolutely nothing he would deny his dear wife; if she wants to sell, so be it. What is more, he took the burden of selling it from her shoulders, and would sell it himself, just to please her. For the love of her, he was ready to sacrifice everything, his vineyard included.

Now he had our attention, because we knew that he was stretching the truth way out of proportion, to the point of obscenity. He did not love her all that deeply, nor was he ready to sacrifice anything, least of all his vineyard in exchange of her tight-lipped love. Sensing our interest, good salesman that he was, he was finally moving in for the kill. He would sell us his property, vineyard, cellar, barrels, press and all, for a sum that would equal roughly sixteen hundred dollars. To be paid in cash.

I knew there would be a "but" to this extraordinary offer, and of course, there was.

"You will pay me in full," he said and twirled his hat nervously before he added his clause. "But as long as I live, and am able to work, I'll be your vintner, and nobody else. That is the clause of the deal." So that was his game. He would prove to her that he sold it, would even flash a sum of money, which would surely appear huge to her, but everything would stay as it always has been. We would pay for the day laborers he would need, provide for the sprays and the fertilizers, so he would not have any expenses that she could question. We would be the legal owners of this prize property, and each year half the wine he makes, would belong to him. As an extra precaution, he would keep his share of the wine in the cellar, out of her eyesight. For the negligible price of the chemicals and for paying the wages of the occasional laborers (a dollar an hour), we could own a prize property and about 250 gallons of superior wine each year. We weren't sure that this was the offer his sainted wife had in mind, but it couldn't be resisted.

"Won't your wife object to this arrangement?" asked my husband, whose thoughts were running on the same wavelength as mine.

"Let that be my worry," he said happily. We made the deal and were all extremely happy, with the possible exception of his sainted wife.

So now, as owners of an excellent vineyard, we too were caught up in the general dilemma of "to harvest or not to harvest", and so walked up to the hill to consult with Lajos bácsi. He was calm with the assurance of someone, who knows exactly what he is doing. The general hysterics of the village bypassed him. He brought out his wine tube, went through the ritual of rinsing the glasses, and only after we drank the contents of the sphere in the glass tube did he declare that we won't pick the grapes until mid-October.

"Fools always hurry with the grapes, only to find that the sugar content is too low for decent fermentation. So what do they do? Add sacks of sugar to the juice, but that is not enough. In addition there are all sorts of things the fake wine needs to get its color and clarity. And they call that wine! You get a royal headache from such a wicked drink. It will mess up your peristalsis for three days, and get a memorable hangover from it, which is not even caused by the wine, but by the chemicals that made it. Good wine never does that to you. We make honest wine, and not a concoction from sugar and from the products of the chemical industry." We felt honored that he used the plural. It was wonderful to hear about the wine that "we" made.

Mid-October arrived before we had our fill of the summer, then one evening Lajos bácsi arrived, dressed up, as if he was going to his own wedding. He announced that the grape harvest was to take place on the following Saturday and he already hired ten workers for picking the grapes. Our job would be to provide a noon meal and a somewhat lighter supper for the team. Nothing to it; by then I certainly had enough experience to run the kitchen of a hotel in high season.

Grape harvesting is not an easy labor, even when one is used to it. For one thing, having two legs of the same length is a real handicap when one has to stand on a wildly slanting slope all day long, fighting the real possibility of tumbling head over heels down the incline. For another thing, the body position is awkward, because most of the grapes have the perverted habit of growing at the lower part of the vine, so one has to be bending over or crouching down almost all day. Very soon the back and the legs start hurting with a pain even the Grand Inquisitor was not able to invent. The bunches of grapes are cut either with a knife, or small shears, but in either case wrist and fingers respond to the unusual exertion with a pain equaling that which is already killing the back and the legs. It is also quite hot as the sun beats down on the excellent southwestern exposure of the hill, and the poor grape-picker is so dehydrated that all the water in both lakes could not quench his thirst. But despite all these physical tortures, it is a merry occasion with lots of fun and laughter.

The women's job is to snip off the clusters of grapes and drop them into the collecting baskets. The men empty the grapes from the baskets into large wooden butts, then strap them to their backs and carry the load down the steep slope to the press. Other men keep turning the wheels of the press so the juice flows into the collecting tub. Lajos bácsi is one level below in the cave, where he directs the flow into the barrels.

I asked him about trampling the grapes with the naked feet, as I have once seen it on an episode of 'I Love Lucy'. He laughed so hard he could not speak for a spell. Later, when speech was possible again, he explained that in the old times the primitive presses would crush the seeds together with the pulp of the grape, and this would give a bitter taste to the wine. It was then more efficient for the sake of a better wine to trample the grapes. Nowadays grape trampling is done for tourists only, he said, provided they give a rich tip for the spectacle. Only the cabbage is trampled by naked feet, when it is put up for sauerkraut, but then only the men may do it, he added. However, I never know when Lajos bácsi is being serious, or when he is pulling a fast one on me. He thinks that I am especially gullible, and he likes to tell wild tales to me. He enjoyed hugely when I fell for this explanation, so I am not sure about the authenticity of his information. At any rate, because of my question, many jokes were born that afternoon. In retrospect I must admit, that they were not particularly funny, but I was the star in all of them.

The food served at the harvest is traditional in this region, and deviations are eyed with suspicion. We were not about to disappoint our team and decided to adhere to the menu to the letter. After making a show of helping to harvest, I was actually very happy to be delegated to the role of hostess, which was far easier than to fight the slope with my back bent, in the midday heat. I set the table in the shade of the old cherry tree and was busy with the part of the meal, which was entrusted to me, while my husband made the preparation for making the goulash over the open fire.

The proper spelling for goulash is gulyás, and the pronunciation is almost identical to the English version, except the digraph 'ly' is sounded like the 'y' in yellow (gou-y-ash). It is probably one of the most misunderstood foods in the world. Originally 'gulyás' was not even the name of a food. The caretaker, or herdsman of the cattle was called that. Only later did the herdsman become synonymous with the food.

Huge herds need huge pastures, and it was the time-honored custom to drive the cattle for the entire summer into open grazing areas, far from the villages, or from the estates of the big landowners. The caretaker guarded his herd with a few dogs (pumis or pulis, together with a few larger dogs, either a kuvasz or a komondor)), and a few young helpers. He had to make do what he could easily carry with himself, then store his supplies, which were very basic, in his makeshift summer shelters. Translated into Hungarian that meant lard, onions, potatoes, salt and quantities of red, hot peppers that were dried and strung up into garlands. He also had slabs of bacon, smoked sausages, cheese and bread. His meat-supply walked along with him in the form of lambs and sheep. At times other supplies were sent after him, but basically his food was extremely simple.

The food he made world-famous, the 'goulash', can be either a thick all-meat stew, or it can be a somewhat thinner dish, with potatoes added, and is eaten as a soup. It can be made of beef, but many, including us, prefer it the original way, prepared from the shoulder part of a no longer very young lamb.

The herdsman, who either lived under the stars, or had a small hut somewhere in the vast grazing land, did not have complicated implements or ingredients. His food is internationally hailed as excellent, but he cooked it without the abomination of added carrots, tomatoes, caraway seeds, bay leaves, rosemary, and heaven knows what else, which he could not possibly have at hand. Big-name cooks usually feel that something of distinction must be added to make the stew more chic. Any day I am waiting for Bocuse, or Jacques Pépin to suggest the addition of truffles and a bit of brandy to the open-air cauldron, or to decide to serve it with Beluga on toast.

But the secret of the original is not a lot of incidentals tossed into the pot, but the excellence of the ingredients, and the loving care with which it is prepared. The herdsman would sit in the gathering evening dusk with not a thing to do, except to tend his fire and his meat. It did not matter what time it was ready, but since it was his only real meal of the day, he took great care to do it just right. It is not possible to cube some meat, throw it on the stove in the company of a dozen miscellaneous items found in the fridge and in the pantry, then let it suffer until it is done, or overdone, and then call it goulash.

Actually the cooking of the gulyás is a man-thing. (According to some vicious remarks I overheard around the kitchen stoves of otherwise rather mild mannered ladies, this food is so simple to make that it is practically the only thing men are willing, or capable to tackle).

The man in my life, who is an expert on this dish, claims that the secret is in the preparation. The shoulder or lamb must be cleaned from all membranes and from some of the fat that may give it that strong flavor, which many people dislike. The meat then is cut into cubes and some lard is heated in the cauldron. (Never oil, or margarine, and while currently these fats are called the less offensive enemies to our arteries, they are no friends of the goulash. I know this is a sad truth, but I can't change it. Fortunately, very little of it is needed in the dish). Now the meat is added to the cauldron, a little a time, so that the cubes would sear first, and seal in the juices. The heat is then lowered (achieved by hoisting the cauldron a few notches higher) and finely chopped onion is added. Meat and onions are gently sautéed, until the onions are glassy. Now salt and the dried, whole, hot peppers are added. The meat is cooked over a gentle fire in its own juice, until the meat is halfway done. At this point the pot is removed from the heat and a very generous amount of high quality ground red pepper (paprika) is added. Two things are important here. First, during this step the dish should be off the heat, because when paprika scorches, it turns bitter, and its color an ugly brown. Second, the paprika must be extra fine quality. Just like Mediterranean food can be ruined when using inferior olive oil; Hungarian dishes too are ruined if the paprika is old or not of good quality. A very little water is added now and the stew is carefully tended on slow fire, until the meat is tender. And truly, that is all there is to it. I must admit, it takes a man to come up with a superb dish that takes so little work.

When it is done, it should have a wonderful red-gold color and an aroma so enthralling that I yet have to see in a Hungarian vineyard a gong to call the harvesters to the table. The fragrance is the irresistible call .

Our team sniffed into the air and appeared at the table at the exact moment when the gulyás was done. They sat down quietly, placed a huge slice of bread next to their plates, bowed their heads while saying the shortest grace I ever heard, then for the next space of time there was no other sound except the clinking of spoons on plates. When all was eaten, they wiped the plate clean with the bread and sighed in contentment.

"This was powerful," declared Lajos bácsi as he wiped the perspiration from his forehead. Unlike the rest of the team, I only had a small portion, but my gums were numb from the hot peppers. "In the sweat of thy brow you shall eat thy gulyás," he intoned religiously, and the others nodded in deep appreciation. "It ain't baby food, so it better be hot enough for our mouths to smoke."

Wine was poured and more compliments heaped on the chef, who beamed as if this was the greatest accomplishment in his life.

After the stew the traditional *túros csusza* followed. It too is a simple dish and quite a favorite around here. Tagliatelli is cooked al dente, then mixed with plenty of dry cottage cheese, doused with sour cream and heated until it is warmed through and through. Now smoked bacon is cut into fine little cubes and fried until crisp. Still sizzling, it is sprinkled on top of the pasta, together with a generous amount of finely cut, fresh dill weeds. It is a good dish, but I felt it was an anticlimax to the stew.

However, this too was put away to the last noodle; this I took as a silent compliment. There was but a short pause and we were already serving the grilled spareribs with a salad and dilled squash. More wine followed and the sighs of contentment were the best rewards for our efforts. Naturally strudel had to follow, but I was not about to admit, that this I ordered from a wonderful woman in the next village. I guess I am not marriageable just yet, because it is beyond me to pull the dough into the required thinness.

As Agnes and I were turning our attention to the pile of dirty dishes, our crew dispersed into the shady spots and in a while the bird-songs were enriched by a deep and rhythmic counterpoint as our team snored away. But in an hour everybody was up again, bending over the grape-vines.

By the time we sat the table for the evening meal, the crew picked clean the entire hillside, with the exception of the very last plant. Lajos bácsi brought out glasses of wine and the workers all stood around this last grape bush. The men removed their hats and the old vintner called for my husband.

"The work of the harvest is done. It is our custom that the master gathers the last grapes." He handed his very own, precious knife to my husband, who was visibly touched by this gesture. He cut off the last six or eight clusters, and everybody cheered. From the tray we took the glasses of wine, so cold that pearly water droplets ran down the sides of the glasses, then wished each other health and hailed the good weather that permitted us to complete the harvest. Our glasses were filled again, and we raised them to the good master, then to the good vintner and then to the good cooks. A third glass was filled to wish for a better future, to peace and to the successful metamorphosis of the juice that was now safely resting in the big barrels behind us in the cellar.

The sun was setting and the air had a little chill to it when we sat down under the cherry tree for our evening meal. Jokes were told and everybody had a good time, but exhaustion was catching up with the men and the women around the table. Soon after they finished the meal, they called it a day.

My husband drove ahead with Agnes. The car was loaded with the cauldron and the rest of the mobile kitchen, but I chose to walk with our workers down to the village. As we wound our way through the paths between the vineyards, other harvesters joined us, and by the time we left the narrow road of the hills and reached the village, a large crowd was walking, all tired, but jubilant. The church bells were ringing and we were met by a band of gypsy musicians, who accompanied us down the main street. We were all singing and laughing and felt satisfied, even dazzled, with joy at the thought of work done well.

The emotional side of my character triumphed, because despite the merry-making, I was very close to tears. A strange, unfamiliar mood swept over me, almost medieval, or perhaps even older, in character. It was basic and earth-bound, as simple and as magnificent as life itself. Summer was gone. The earth, like the good mother she is, gave us all she had, and we, greedy children, took it all. She was bare, but our fruit cellars and larders were filled, and in the many tiny wine caves in the hills, the juice was fermenting and ripening all the way until Christmas, when the new, young wine would be timidly tasted to get an inclination about its character. The summer was a good one…would the wine show it? If it promises to be good… But it must be good; it always is good. The kids need new shoes and the wife needs a coat…the price of fuel has gone up again…the taxes…and a pig or two ought to be bought… the tractor needs new parts… But the wine, the good wine will pay for it all.

I didn't work all summer in the vineyard as they have. I was spared the labor of hoeing, cutting, cropping, binding the vines, spraying, or even harvesting. The wine, which would soon be murmuring toward maturity in our cellar, was only a chance hobby for us. But during that long walk home, I could understand the dependence on the soil, and on what it produces. It was a love-hate relationship, as old as agricultural history is — and I could see why. The soil first gives them the means by which to live, and then it kills them, slowly and painfully. Working the soil is not just a job or an occupation for them; it is something more basic. It is a cradle-to-grave relationship of deep personal meaning, of total dependence, of pain, disappointments, exhaustion, small triumphs, and ultimately death.

These people work, pray, hope and receive so very little in exchange for it all. They bend their heads gently and work patiently as long as they have the strength to do it, never cursing their fate for being so frugal with its gifts to them. And the most amazing part is that despite poverty and failures, they have the gift to carry their fate with dignity., and what is more, they have discovered the secret of inner peace. Their needs are simple, and they are willing to work hard to achieve them.

My background and aspirations are so different that I might as well have come from a different planet, yet I felt close them. We were sisters and brothers, having a common mother, the good earth. This rare experience reminded me that the rapidly progressing civilization is bent on sweeping away this very basic human interrelation. We are becoming lonesome in the heady forward rush, and the needs of others touch us only when their troubles are catastrophic.

I was too emotional and too tired to sort out what I felt, but the difference between buying and producing dawned on me. I knew without doubt that back home in the USA I have never felt close to tears in a wine-shop when selecting bottles from the richly stocked shelves for my dinner party (unless I happened to look at the price sticker). I did not choke up with gratitude or love, when I chose a head of lettuce or a sack of (pre-scrubbed) potatoes in the supermarket. Nobody was ever observed talking lovingly to a bunch of radishes at the food emporiums. Shopping there was a common and natural task. Like every mentally stable housewife in those stores, in my former life I too was merely selecting ingredients for supper, and was not thinking about living things that had to be nurtured for months. There was nothing mystical or sacred about it, not even at the end, when the cashier asked me if I wanted paper or plastic sacks for my purchases.

A few years have passed since then. I no longer have to decide whether a tree should be cut down to provide my paper sack, or whether I should choose plastic bags, which enjoy eternal life, and would stay here piled as high as the highest mountains, long after life has ceased on earth. In this new passage of my life I have been using for my shopping trips the same wicker-basket for which no tree had to die and no permanent garbage will remain after it lost its usefulness. Cutting off the branches from the willow to weave the baskets makes the tree stronger and healthier, and after the basket falls apart of old age, it will return to the earth as good compost. Some necessities do push us into being thoughtful and noble; God grant us that we preserve our humility and never shelve this new environmental consciousness.

Getting back so close to the earth freed some emotions buried very deep in my complexities. It was astonishing how uncomplicated these feelings are, but at the same time fundamentally important as they touch all the dimensions of a long forgotten past. Walking in the gathering darkness, I was not just as an aging woman on the threshold of the twenty-first century; I became the link between the past and the future. Suspended in time for a little while, I realized that I could look back into the past and understand our ancestors and their ways, but having been placed in a privileged position, I could also reach forward and be part of the future. As I understood this new role, I was already anticipating the day when I would show my grandchildren that food does not grow freeze-dried, canned or packaged, and that a brussel sprout is not really a cabbage that was manipulated into a smaller size by genetic science. I long to show them that luxury, convenience, and amusements are wonderful, and one must never minimize their importance, but I would also point out that these things are not natural rights, enjoyed by everyone. They need to see that happiness is relative, and that when the superficial layers are peeled away, it is possible to find beneath those things the real content of life.

A full moon was rising over the lake. God's world seemed infinitely peaceful, enriched with the deep meaning, which we humans crave all our lives. The answers, to at least some of our existentialist questions, were suddenly not quite so incomprehensible and unattainable.

CHAPTER ELEVEN

In late October the last visitor of the season was Susan, my only sister. She flew from the US to Budapest, then took the train and we picked her up at the station, a few miles from our home. We were excited about her coming and planned it for weeks, especially, since I owed her for something she did for me after I was promoted to the administrative position.

Shortly after my promotion, my husband and I flew home to Cleveland for a visit. My mother, Susan, Andrea and her two children were waiting for us at the Cleveland Hopkins airport. After the enthusiastic, whirlwind greetings, we retrieved our luggage and were directed to follow the tribe down the escalator and up again where the taxi stands are. In my excitement I did not pay much attention where we were going.

"Is this something new?" was all I asked. "Each time I come home, this airport changes."

"Well, Cleveland is keeping time with the changing world, and it gets better all the time. Andrea's van is parked quite a distance, so we are taking the shuttle to it."

As soon as we arrived at the curb, a pale gray stretch limousine pulled up, like a ghost from a magnificent, make-believe world, known to me only from heresy and Hollywood productions.

"Sure, I was promoted, but I have not yet reached the limo category," I exclaimed laughingly. At that moment the uniformed driver stepped out of the limousine, and opened the door for me.

"Welcome home, Madame," he said, just like in the movies.

I don't believe I have ever been quite as surprised as then, or laughed as heartily, as we stepped into this magnificently elegant vehicle. I love my crazy family, because they never tire of thinking up surprises to make life more fun. Laughter has a high priority with us; dull moments are rare and quickly remedied. "We'll be drab enough after we die; let's have fun, while we still have a pulse," is the family's motto.

My mother leaned back elegantly, as if she always traveled in a luxurious limousine, then sighed with pleasure. "I actually hate to ride in a car, but this is wonderful. I wish our house would be in the next state, to prolong the pleasure. And think of it, we don't even have to be in a funeral in order to ride in it!"

So now it was our turn. A highly polished, streamlined carriage, drawn by four horses, its driver smartly dressed in the picturesque, traditional garments of the Hungarian coach driver, was waiting behind the train station. He and his coach were the big tourist attraction during the summers, but now after the season was over, it was relatively easy to hire him to be our version of a chauffeur -driven limousine. Susan's squeal of enthusiastic delight so scared the four horses that they all but took off without us.

The day was glorious, a last generous gift of the departing season. The leaves already turned color, and the sun shimmered gold on the branches. There are few things as relaxing, or as visually satisfying as riding in a horse-drawn carriage. Everything is in slow motion and so many things that cannot be seen from the window of a speeding car, become delightfully obvious and familiar as viewed from the leather-covered comfort of an open carriage. I handed her a scarf and my husband opened a bottle of champagne, as we moved on, slower than any moving thing on the road. I'm sure that we were giddy from the experience and not the alcohol.

During the lovely, lazy days that followed, we spent long hours talking and recalling memories. We have reached the age, when the future plans are no longer as important as they have been years ago. What tomorrow would bring is certainly only half as interesting as our past has been.

She talked about my children and grandchildren and I listened hungrily to the details of their lives, of which I knew less than she did. She was always a good friend to all my children, and now she gladly played the surrogate grandmother role to Andrea's children. They, for reasons known only to themselves, decided to call her "Gamma Dudi". It is probably a baby-talk version of "Grandma Susie", but the name stuck to her.

She talked about our mother, whom she showers with love and attention, and attempts to compensate for my absence. I was deeply grateful for having a sister, who can generously love the family that I more or less abandoned.

Susan told me that my children were doing very well. I knew that, but it felt good to be reassured. Like so many parents in my age group, I do not fully understand what my children's jobs are. When I was young, girls got married, or if they hankered for a profession, it was a choice between teaching, perhaps medicine, secretarial work, or the nunnery. Or they could go into the service jobs; there were always openings for hairdressers, seamstresses or milliners. My children have long outgrown my limitations. They hopscotch across the USA in their business suits, and carry their laptops, briefcases and overnighters with the same ease I carry my wicker basket. The electronic language they speak, I do not comprehend. Sometimes I wonder, whether we are residing in the same solar system.

At one point my son was deeply hurt, because I could not fully grasp what his work was all about. He believed that the phenomenal ignorance I exhibited, was a lack of interest on my part. As a little boy, he cherished the fantasy that his mother was omnipotent. She could kiss away his hurts, and was brilliant enough to help with long division. As an adult, he realized that she was not really the Wonder Woman he thought she was, but felt more comfortable accusing her of disinterest, rather than admitting his mother's cultural limitations.

Christina, being a woman, is very supportive, and attempts to correct my ignorance. Although not an educator by profession, she believes that everybody, her mother included, is educable. In this spirit she attempts to inform me of her doings, never doubting that I'm smart enough to comprehend such passages in her letter: "I returned from San Francisco and started working with our new Decision Support Group." (Is she kidding me? Where was *my* support group when I had to make decisions?) "The Group is responsible for supporting ad-hoc type reporting that is outside the normal reports that our on-line system provides. We used Supercalc as a spreadsheet package and Easytrive as a simple programming language. Both of those main-framed packages..." My eyes glaze over at this point, and I think with nostalgia back to the long-ago day, when we gurgled and cooed to each other, and we both understood what the other was communicating. And than it struck me too that I prided myself at one time to be computer literate... I am as obsolete as yesterday's floppy disk.

Andrea, after being a stay-at-home mom for more than a dozen years, is back on somebody's payroll, and judging by the miles she puts behind, and seeing her reserved parking place at the office, I assume she is doing something important. I don't even understand her title. She does mysterious things when she travels to faraway cities, but at least I can spell the name of her company. She still finds time for some volunteer work, like teaching Sunday school.

"...I am great teaching the Old Testament," she writes. "I love all the revenge part, but am less successful with the 'Jesus loves the little children' tales. And then this offering the other cheek really galls me. Try that in downtown Cleveland and you'd probably end up in the city morgue. Get real. My daughters are getting trained in Korean martial arts, and I keep a monster dog, who'll probably eat us out of the house. So I gloss over the meek parts and get back to Jezebel. At least that's real." I guess I know why she is so successful in the business world.

In my letters to them I report about our shrunken world. I write about our spectacular sunsets, the sound of crickets, the swallows nesting under our eaves, the walks with the dogs. I write about sipping a glass of wine in the gathering dusk with the man I love, and the peace I feel in the wonderful spot we created for ourselves. I try to explain to them our efforts to sum up the reasons for our existence and our attempts to come to terms with our complexities, and our decisions for choosing the life we have.

When Susan left at the end of the week, uncharacteristically, we became emotional and we both cried. We have never before made an issue of our partings. We have crossed and recrossed the ocean so many times that we lost track of the number and were used to it. Our farewells were always light, always with a laugh and a breezy, "here we go again". This is how it should have been now, but something very painful slipped into the good-bye. The self-control, of which we were always so proud, left us. We clung to each other and wished we would never have to part. Ever. I feel ungrateful, because I was showered with rich gifts during the last twenty years, and had no business asking for one more thing. I have everything. But it does have a price and it does hurt to have to pay up.

"A person of noble spirit never cries, when he has to pay the bill," Árpád bácsi told me the other day by way of his weekly contribution to my moral education. I do not consider myself to have a particularly noble spirit, but it is a nice goal to have in mind.

We tore off two more pages from our wall calendar and suddenly it was December. The sky was a dismal steel gray and the clouds could not decide what to do. The north wind tried its best to convince us that winter has really arrived. The birds puffed up their feathers to keep warm, and sat sullenly on the branches of the cherry tree. I threw my huge alpaca shawl around my shoulders, but was chilled to the bones during the short run to the gate, where I picked up our mail. I took my place again near our blazing fire and sunk into the delight of reading the letters. Christina sent a box of books and packed some catalogs as well. "I know how you miss books, and then life is not really complete without junk mail, is it?" I touched the books with a sensual pleasure that always overpowers me at the sight of books. (Andrea, fully aware of my weakness, loves to tease me when she is heading for the library, "Mom, do you want to come along for a little touchy-feely?"). I glanced at the catalogs. What strange riches, what treasures there are over the ocean! I am almost forgetting how life is in the Land of Plenty. How fortunate that I live here! There are too many wonderful things to buy in the USA, and I would probably end up being very poor there, because I could not fight the temptations. It is relatively easy to be frugal here, when one can walk into a store and not desire a single thing.

We received the first Christmas cards, among them a very cheerful one from my mother. Not once, not even between the lines, does she ever let me feel that she too is hurting from the geographical distance I put between us. Time and time again, after my regular visits back home, I leave her standing in her doorway, infinitely frail and vulnerable, waving after me. The last impressions of her are always that of a smiling face, a cheerful glance, a light wave of the hand, reminding me of a butterfly fluttering in the wind. She acts as if I am just running out to get something from the grocery store down the street. "Come back soon!" she calls after me, and for a second I hesitate. She was born in 1911, just how long can she be waiting for my next return? I do not know what she does or what she feels after she closes the door and goes back into her empty house, but she smiles to the very end to make the parting easy for me. I put down her card, because I was fighting tears.

I did not recognize the handwriting on the next letter, and had a hard time recalling the face that went with the name of the sender.

She sort of considers, she writes, that they would drop in on us and spend the holidays in Szabar. "No definite plans yet," the letter says, "we are still debating between the Canary Island, skiing in the Alps, or flying to Israel, but we thought it would be fun visiting you instead. Your hills are lovely, so I hear. We could do a little cross-country skiing; the guys could go hunting. There is a thermal lake nearby, right? That would be super. I also heard that you have a sauna. It would be such a romantic, cozy Christmas. We are all excited about this idea, including the kids. Because of the iffy weather conditions, we won't drive, but you could pick us up at Budapest. Do you have a problem with that? Our plans aren't finalized yet, but I'll drop you a card with the time of our arrival…"

The absolute nerve of her! What makes her think that we don't have our own plans for the holidays? And who is she anyway? I had a hard time recalling her and was sure that she did not belong to our circle of friends. And even if she would be welcomed here, how dare she expect to be picked up? My very own sister opted to take the train from the capital. We don't exactly live in a suburb of Budapest. Whenever we go to the capital, we never drive, but take the train, because coming and going takes nearly six hours, even if the road conditions are good and the traffic is light. Are people born insensitive, or do they learn to be so on the way through life?

Borka was stretched out and snored gently, and Sissi, in her comfortable digestive pose was a study in contentment. Holding the unpleasant letter in my hand, I stared into the fire. I too love the winter mood and the tranquility. I love the dark mornings when we sleep late and only the freshly brewed coffee of Agnes could get us out of bed. I love the brunches, served in the winter garden among my plants, while the world is buried in deep snow outside. I love the long afternoons in the study, where I would either write, or curl up under the mohair throw with a good book, until my eyelids grow heavy and I fall asleep on the couch. I love to try out new and intricate recipes or to indulge in my passion of baking bread. The walks in the falling snow with our dogs are wonderful, as are the evenings when we decide not to cook. Instead, we would go to the small inn that stays open even after the tourists have long departed. We order good, homemade comfort foods, and eat in the congenial company of the locals. I love our winter life.

What I do not love is being used by people I do not even know, and who plan to use our home as a conveniently located winter hotel.

My husband looked up from his paper and saw my contemplative face, which he learned to respect the same way sailors respect the signs of a gathering storm. I handed him the letter, which he scanned rapidly.

"Are they friends?"

"No."

"Did you invite them?"

"No."

"Do you like them?"

"I don't even really know them! I can't even remember her husband's name, let alone those of her kids."

"Do you want to operate a hotel during the holiday season?"

"You know, I don't."

"Could you spend ten days without your dogs?"

"Maybe."

"There are then two options. First, we could shoot straight and tell them to go to hell. Freeloaders like these deserve the word. But there are two things speaking against this. The first one is your well-known squeamishness on seeing corpses left behind on the battlefield. Not that it would be possible to hurt such pachyderms in any of the conventional ways known to civilized people. The second thing speaking against such a direct solution is that they are not one-of-a-kind jerks. There are loads of them lurking out there. All through the holidays you might find some-body at our doorstep, who most likely got our address out of the phonebook, and who is not visiting us because of a deep love for us. If these manipulators get the hang of it by word of mouth, we are lost. We need to put a stop to this nonsense before the habit start."

"Therefore…?"

"Therefore, here goes option number two. We need to establish the fact that we have a life of our own. We are not appointed to serve the chance tourist. Don't even answer these people, such uncouth idiots don't deserve the price of postage stamp. Instead, let's escape. You de-serve a break, and we haven't been up in the capital for ages. We'll over-dose on culture, while successfully avoid unpleasant confrontations with jerks, or a very probable capitulation on your part. Believe me, the word will get around that we are not world-class suckers. In addition, by using this escape technique, we'll save our energy and hospitality for the friends we really want."

As always he was right, and in a few days we were ready to leave our house for a short while.

CHAPTER TWELVE

And so it came to pass that we did not spend that Christmas at home, but took the train up to Budapest. We know a lovely woman, who rents the lower apartment in her split-level home on the Buda side of the twin city. Whenever we stay in the capital we rent the cozy little place, which in addition to the convenience of a home, also offers the most spectacular view of the River Danube and of the Parliament Building.

We installed ourselves, and acknowledged with gratitude that she turned on the heat long before our arrival, and placed evergreen boughs in the vases. This was home, away from home.

We slept late and I cooked breakfast, which we ate in the tiny kitchen, while admiring the best view in the world, as far as we are concerned. Later we walked miles window shopping, browsing in bookstores, drooling over antiques, and having a wonderful lunch of cream of mushroom soup and a spinach quiche baked to flaky perfection. We ordered a bottle of Hárslevelü, an absolutely lovely, fruity wine, before embarking on a cultural extravagance.

We spent most of the afternoon up in the royal palace, which now houses the paintings of Hungarian artists. We stayed mostly in the rooms with the classical works, and merely nodded to the neo-modern, with the polite coldness one would greet a casual acquaintance. At the risk of sounding lowbrow, I have to confess that I can't comprehend what the very modern artists are saying, (or even why they are saying it). It follows that what I don't understand I usually don't like. My aesthetic development came to a screeching halt at the period when painting stopped representing even a vague impression (or at least a subjectively sensed mood) of the real thing. But as we entered the palace, it was, from all the things, a modern, (but still representational painting), that took my breath away. Right at the first landing there it was: a huge canvas, mostly in orange tones, by the impressionist painter Csontváry.

We both stopped and exclaimed simultaneously, "Taormina", because it was so unmistakably that. Never before did I have such a strange and intensive experience evoked by a painting. Despite the washed out, blurry lines and the unusual coloring, I was suddenly transported there. I could again smell the spring flowers, see the smoke of Mt. Aetna, the blue of the lovely Bay of Naxos, and the breath-taking Greek-Roman theater with a stage setting that no other theater in all the world enjoys. And I could recall the flavor of the frutti di mare; see the stand at the corner, where a vendor was selling lemons, still on the branch. I was back at the hotel Monte Tauro and saw us eating breakfast on our balcony among the orange trees, which bloomed in huge tubs. Through the painting, I could see and hear the entire miracle that is Sicily.

"How about that!" my husband exclaimed.

"Yes, how about that? I'm, actually homesick for the place." I never before wanted a painting so much.

On other days we went to see movies during the day, and visited theaters at night. We caught up with the latest from Hollywood. I guess one has to speak several languages in order to really appreciate the fun of hearing David Niven, Robin Williams or Barbra Streisand speaking in another language, in this case Hungarian. Stage and movie stars don't earn a great deal in Hungary, so they grab any work that comes their way. Speaking the parts in foreign movies is always a welcome extra income, and because they are professionals of the highest degree, the synchronization is perfect. I think even the stars would get a real charge hearing "themselves" speak in Hungarian. But of course, the voice is miles away from the real thing. Way back in college I had an outstanding professor in English literature. Before the semester was over, he turned the entire class into devoted fans of Shakespeare, and at least in my case, this love lasted an entire life. He also had the most pronounced drawl from the Deep South that my north-central ears ever heard. Imagine Hamlet, King Lear or Macbeth with that accent! The element of surprise when we heard him was similar to seeing and hearing "Good Morning, Vietnam" in Hungarian.

One afternoon we saw an avant garde, artsy film, which was praised by the critics and which was, as far as I was concerned, just terrible. It was confusing, depressing, pointless and so very subjective that probably even the shrink of the filmmaker could not fully explain. I did not understand the plot, the intent, or the symbolism, or anything, although we stayed to the end, unlike most of the handful of viewers, who had more sense than we did, and left before they would lose their minds. I even read the credits at the end of the film, but it did not help to comprehend it better.

When we left the movie house, I was disturbed and vaguely resentful for having squandered a lovely afternoon on it. I was dissatisfied with myself for having reached the state of mental deterioration where I couldn't understand or accept a creation, which was hailed by the critics as culturally advanced and mature. My husband, who has a very relaxed point of view in life, and who trusts his own instincts and judgments far more than I do mine, laughed at me.

"Why does it bother you? Why do you feel compelled to admire horseshit? As far as aesthetic quality or intellectual content, or the non-language used, the film belongs in the stables, or the dung pile. You didn't like it, because it sucked. I don't know about the idiot who wrote the review either, but I have a pretty good idea who would write such an adulation for such a pot of crap, and I can also guess why."

But I was still somewhat uneasy. My youth, my figure, my face, my career have all gone down the drain; my only assets left were my brains and my education. But apparently these two were on their way down the same drain. Was I getting really dull? Were art and the new thoughts out of my reach and scope? I don't understand or appreciate modern art, can't read a modern poem, hate confusion and hated the movie. Despite my husband's rational reassurances, I could neither understand, nor ignore the experience. The movie was full with random flashes of unexplained and vaguely scary scenes, smears of paint (perhaps blood?) that must have had some meaning for somebody. There were repeated close-ups of doorknobs turning, clicking, unclicking, and there were undefined sounds in the background, as if coming from an institution of mentally challenged people, who were way past all controls. There were people, who did not seem to be part of the plot (if there was a plot, which I doubt), who kept running in and out of alleys, up and down staircases, chasing or being chased without any apparent purpose or reason. I was mentally exhausted from this crazy jumble of impressions that resembled a vast mental garbage dump. What was it all about? Or maybe I should have asked, 'brother, what did you take before you made this?'

After the show we went to the magnificent New York cafe. As soon as we sat down at one of the marble tables, the confusion I felt earlier disappeared and I felt whole again. The very atmosphere of the place and the wonderfully mingled fragrances of coffee, vanilla, toasted almonds and other good things made us feel good. This was our world. Understandable, predictable and stable. The door knobs were of bronze, polished shiny by constant care and long usage, and they only turned when a waiter came through the door with a tray full of earthly delights. It is what the doctor ordered for ruffled nerves.

The New York is not hell-bent on showing life the way it must look to a junkie on a bad trip. It does not try to interpret, explain, or alter the way things are. It does not try to be avant garde, or falsely old-fashioned. It is not looking for an identity through grotesque mind games, because it has no need for it. It already has an identity.

The New York simply is, and it exists in its own nearly perfect world. It has been here for a long time. It has seen women in long and short dresses, artists hungry, or padded with success, authors discussing or defending their work; their portraits cover the walls in the upper gallery. On its velvet chairs lovers were swearing eternal everything to each other, which rarely lasted the season. Beautiful society people told flamboyant lies without any apparent shame. But its atmosphere never changed. Not for the brown shirts, and not for the red or the black ones. Its name changed several times, but its essence remained. All, who enter through its graceful portals, have the vague impression that the long lost, refined and carefree times are magically preserved among the exquisite columns and elegant seating arrangements.

So many things are wrong with the world today; or perhaps in this day of instant communication over the globe, we are just better informed about the many ills that we inherited along with the good things. At any rate, romantic idealists, such as I, cling to a nostalgic dream , a yearning for a time and place where things are nice, safe and civilized, where personal honor, human dignity, and culture are facts of life. Such a Shangri-la probably never existed, but still we dream of a place, where it would be safe to walk on the streets at any hour, and where children would live in complete homes, and get lots of love so they could develop into full human beings. We long for a place where the written and spoken language expresses ideas and emotions, and is not used as a weapon that carries insults, profanities and the means for brainwashing. We long to find a place, if only for a short time, where the ambience is defined by refinement rather than money, where vulgarity and violence are left behind at the coat-check with the umbrellas and overcoats. We crave for a place, where life is conducted pleasantly, in slow motion, with style and grace. It is a homesickness that drives us toward the never-land of peace and order, of quiet enjoyments and optimism; toward things that we need to have, even if it only lives in our fantasy. But the New York, this landmark edifice, is capable of offering for a short while, the illusion that things are whole and unblemished.

There is only one New York cafe in all the world, and the visit there would be imperfect if one would be chained to a long and austere list of "thou-shall-not", created by a doctor whose first commandment is 'thou shall not have pleasures through any food whatsoever.'

We looked at each other, took a deep breath, then ordered *puree de marrons*. With whipped cream, rum, and sprinkled with shaved chocolate. It is such a highly sensuous food that it borders on the scandalous to serve it in public. While eating, it is best to turn the back toward the other guests, so they cannot observe the sinful rapture on the face; after all, the New York is synonymous with decorum. I ate it slowly, delicately, letting the chestnut cream melt in my mouth to make it last longer. After I die, I want to go to a heaven where they serve this *gesztenye püré* at least once a day, on doctor's orders.

Every evening we went to see a play. We both love the theater. My husband, because it was his profession and his passion for a quarter of a century, and I, because I had so very little of it in my life. Opera came once a year for five days to Cleveland and the price of the tickets for the five us broke our budget for three months. At the time I lived there, the local theaters were just starting to achieve the outstanding reputation they now enjoy. (Our unbelievable experience was to see the Cleveland Playhouse perform at Budapest in the late nineties.) But back then, for us, occasional and not very well-heeled visitors, the matter of attending had to be seriously considered before splurging.

Our only indulgences were the performances of the Cleveland Orchestra with George Szell conducting at Severance Hall. Our seats were way up in the nose-bleed section, located so high that my acrophobia reared its ugly head just seconds before I could sink with shaking knees and wet palms into my seat. Understandably, I refused to leave my seat during intermission, and after sitting two and one half-hours in the rarified atmosphere above the tree line, I went home suffering with swollen ankles and parched skin.

As an extension to Severance Hall, our other fling was Blossom Center during the summer, usually on a blanket that we shared with the ants. Even so our concert tickets were usually severe budget-benders. But in Hungary our tickets at choice locations in the theater cost far less than the parking fee we used to pay in Cleveland. Being able to attend the theaters was like reaching heaven without having to die first.

But the staggering selection offered every night in Budapest made us insatiable, and we were like children in a candy-shop, wanting it all. The theaters were sold out, every night, but fortunately my husband still had enough pull to obtain tickets, when apparently none were left.

After the performance, we usually went backstage to meet old friends and colleagues (his), whom he had not seen for two decades. Each time there was a stormy, emotional greeting, and then we always ended up having supper with them somewhere.

A whole new world opened up for me and I never quite got over the seductiveness of it.

I find it fascinating to walk through the labyrinth of halls and dressing rooms, or through the darkened stage, which now looks so very different from the fantasy world that was illuminated by the floodlights just a few moments ago. I love the smell, the cables on the floor, the requisites all over; I love the backstage chaos, which is never perceived by the audience. I love looking at the flimsy stage sets and cheap costumes, which during the play looked so wonderful through the magical projection of the artists. Perhaps in a former life I was connected with the theater.

I have never met actors personally before, and I was awed from the very moment I entered their dressing rooms, where I no longer could recognize them, because they looked so different in their robes and the makeup washed off. Most of them could not, or did not want, to eat before a performance, so they were usually hugely hungry, and ready for a serious meal in a nearby restaurant.

If there were any spouses of the actors with us, they were as quiet as

I was. It was not their world, nor mine, and we were closed out from the moment the shoptalk started. Groups of theater people (including my husband) just like any other professional group, have the obsession to talk about their craft. Doctors like to discuss that lovely gallbladder which was almost bursting with a stone as big as maybe a walnut. Bankers talk about investments and the Dow Jones. Teachers talk about the last staff development meeting; dancers are concerned with raked stage floors and the choreography that requires acrobatic skills that would be more at home in a circus; actors moan about poor scripts and eccentric directors.

While they discuss and argue I have a chance to look at them and never tire of it. Even after years of exposure to the best in this field in Hungary, I never quite lost my romantic fascination for them. When a prima donna appears at our table, without her makeup, often not even particularly well dressed and visibly fatigued from the performance behind her, she still seems to me special and different. I can never look at her as I do at any other human being, say a librarian, a dentist, or a computer programmer. To this fan, she would always be admirable, in a class of her own, and definitely not of this world. Actors radiate that extraordinary aura of make-believe, that divine magic of being able to compose themselves into something totally different from what they are. They are the magicians with the power to reduce me once again into a child, who is endlessly fascinated by an improbable tale, superbly told.

Well fed and light-headed on a cultural high, we hailed a cab and returned to our hilltop residence, snug with the belief that we are the chosen favorites of gods.

Our landlady invited us for the Christmas Eve celebration and the festive supper later, but being familiar with the local customs, we politely declined. December twenty-fourth is a close family affair and we were not about to intrude. Instead we wanted to see a movie, then have supper somewhere in the neighborhood. We were going to end the day by attending midnight mass at the Coronation Church, right next to the Hilton on the hill.

The plans were beautiful, but the city and the weather were not cooperating. After we left the movie house, practically the only adults in the swarm of children, we found ourselves alone on the street. In Hungary Santa Claus, because of his religious origin, was metamorphosed into a politically and ideologically correct Father Winter figure (Télapó) during the years of Communism. In this great transformation some Christmas facts were mixed up, and for a while the confused children were told to expect the generous Old Man on Christmas Eve.

However, in Hungary Santa Claus, (alias St. Nicholas, a venerable bishop who might or might not have existed many centuries ago, hence the red garments he still wears in the department stores today) was traditionally celebrated on his proper name day, on December 6. The night before his feast day, children place their carefully polished shoes in the windows of their bedrooms. (Because boots have an undeniably larger cubic area, the smarter ones prepare boots instead of shoes!) Then during the night Santa Claus stops by the windows and fills up the shoes with sweets, oranges, nuts and very small presents. Misbehaving children only find a piece of coal and a switch in their shoes. So much for the sixth of December.

But Christmas is a different story altogether. According to the pre-Communist traditions, on Christmas Eve legions of angels descend from heaven to decorate the Christmas trees in the houses and bring special presents for children to celebrate the birthday of Baby Jesus. Since mortal children may not see angels (although in my opinion they alone are innocent enough to communicate with the heavenly decorators) parents send them to obliging grandparents while the celestial throngs do their Christmas magic in the house. If grandparents are not available, the movies will do as babysitters, and traditionally all theaters were obliging by putting on very special programs for children. (For example, *Bogáncs*.) This is why we were practically the only adults watching the movie that evening. But as soon as the show was over, the children sped off with the velocity of sound (at least) to check out whether the angels had already visited their house while they were at the movies. We were alone on the street.

Snow was coming down hard, there was no traffic to speak of, and everything was closed, including the restaurants we tried. Budapest is a city, where eating is taken very seriously and this was an unusual and totally unexpected situation. We are not big eaters, but as soon as we realized that there would be no supper, we acted like Pavlov's dogs, only in reverse. At every "closed tonight" sign we salivated and I haven't been that hungry in months. Apparently the city left while we were at the movies. Our vision of a cozy, well-planned evening was dissipating, as was our prospect of finding a taxi to take us to the other side of the city where the big hotels and the possibility of food were.

"We need Robert here." I mumbled.

"Robert who?" Apparently hypothermia was setting in. The cold was already confusing his memory and his thought processes.

"Robert, like in son-in-law. Our son-in-law. Christina's husband."

"I get it," my husband sighed sadly. "But he is in Atlanta." And so he was.

Robert is a man of many talents, not the least of which is his ability to divine a good restaurant anywhere, any time. As surely as an Australian aborigine seeks (and finds) water, he too follows his instincts and comes up with the perfect place anywhere, not excluding the middle of the Sahara desert, where he would get the best table with a splendid, panoramic views of the sand. Even Chaucer was familiar with men like Robert, as is evident from the line "He knew the taverns in every town". Having no children, but two very demanding careers, Robert and my daughter eat out more than at home. Even as our starving bodies were slowly covered by three feet of snow, they were probably deliberating what to choose at Hedgerose Heights, or making serious decisions at Pano's and Paul's, or feasting on a lobster at Anthony's Antebellum Plantation, without a single compassionate thought for us. Just thinking about it, I started to salivate again.

Finally we spotted a street vendor as she was packing up her portable kitchen. Her menu was definitely not three-star quality, but we bought her last grilled chicken and the three pickles left at the bottom of her glass jar.

"Did Budapest die tonight?" inquired my husband as he was paying her.

"On Christmas Eve? You bet. I'm the last person to clear out of here. Tonight you won't find a cab, or a restaurant. Even the trams will only run sporadically. In a very short time, this city will be so quiet you'll hear a snowflake fart."

We thanked for the information, and clutching our greasy booty we shivered until a tram finally appeared. The only other passenger on it was a man in an advanced state of inebriety.

"I was waiting for a tram, but forgot the number I have to take," he explained, although nobody asked him. "I think I have to take number six... or maybe sixty-six." He spoke with a slur, so that it sounded like 'shixty-shix' and breathed such powerful stuff that I was in danger of getting drunk by just inhaling the air. If there is such a thing as passive smoking, then passive drinking too might be possible. Striking a match could have set the car on fire. " Maybe it wasn't shix that I had to take," he said as he continued to search in his muddled brain. "Now I get it. I have to take either number five, or number nine."

"You hit the jackpot, man" my husband told him. "This tram is number fifty-nine."

"So much the better," he mumbled and belched with a powerful echo. "At least I don't have to make a decision. As long as this is both five and nine, I'll get there one way or another." In a moment he was snoring, oblivious of the world around him.

Merry Christmas. I don't know who was waiting for this fellow traveler, sitting on the wrong tram and probably heading in the wrong direction, but I suppose somebody was not very amused that evening in the snowbound city. To this day when someone does something irrevocably stupid, we just nod and say "fifty-nine" and people glance at us with looks usually reserved for the mentally challenged, because they can't comprehend what is so funny about a number.

At long last we arrived somewhere in the vicinity of our apartment, and huffed and puffed our way up the hill in the rapidly accumulating snow. It has been a crazy decision to leave our lovely house in Szabar and trade the festive meal I would have cooked at home for the sad pieces of grilled chicken, already cold. My regrets were belated.

Tacked to our door was a note from the landlady. "You just discovered that tonight it is not possible to dine out in this city. We'll light the candles on the tree at eight, and I'm serving supper at eight-thirty. See you five minutes before eight. I'd hate to use force."

Her family, consisting of a husband, two sons, their wives, three grandchildren and three elderly relatives, was already waiting in the dining room when we came upstairs. The living room door was closed and the youngest child's teeth were chattering from excitement.

Sharp at eight, the living door swung open to reveal in the darkened room the Christmas tree in its candlelit, glittering beauty. For a moment everyone was silent, awed by the sudden sight of so much loveliness. Only the sparklers, fastened to the ends of the branches, hissed. I looked at the children and understood why our landlady has gone to so much trouble. As all first rate photographers know, there is hardly anything more beautiful than the huge, surprised eyes of children, shining with joy and wonderment. It was the big event of the year for them, and it was written all over their little faces.

To tell the truth, I was just as awestruck and enchanted by the sudden magic of the tree. For a second I was almost ready to believe together with the children, that angels had done it, because I saw nobody near the tree to light them, yet all the candles and sparklers were going at once. Even more amazing was that the tree did not catch on fire.

Our hostess started to sing a Christmas carol and the rest joined in. The sparklers spent themselves meanwhile, but the candles were still burning and I panicked when I realized that each child would recite a poem, as their contribution to the festivities. Fortunately none was as long as the "Night before Christmas," no pun intended. We said a short prayer, which on my part included deeply felt thanks for the fact that the house was still not in flames. I have seen evergreen branches burn in our fireplace and the ferocious rage of it cannot be forgotten. We sang one more song, then to my endless relief, the candles were finally blown out.

We toasted with champagne, wished each other a happy holiday and then sat down to the traditional fish dinner. The children glanced with barely contained excitement toward the tree and the gifts under it. But self-discipline is valued above all, and they had to wait until the end of the meal, which was heavenly (the angels should have stayed for a bite) and no doubt far too long for the eager youngsters. Sympathizing with their impatience, as soon as supper was over we thanked our hostess for the invitation and slipped out, to leave the family alone for the enjoyment of opening the presents. Our hostess accompanied us to the door.

"I have a surprise for you," she smiled as if she had not given already a wonderful gift by including us with her family. "I know you want to go to midnight mass, but as you found out, there is hardly any transportation this evening. In this snow and at your age it would be a cardiovascular extravaganza to attempt the climb uphill to the Mátyás church.

However, there is a special microbus service tonight. Pick-up and delivery is just around our corner. I warn you though, the church will be packed, so leave early to get a seat."

This was indeed good news. The snow was still coming down, as if it decided to bury the entire city. The roads were increasingly more difficult, and the church was a long distance away, up on the hill. She was quite right; this midnight walk in deep snow would not have been for us. We were just about ready to give up our plan, when she told about the bus.

Hungarians always call this church incorrectly and lovingly, "Mátyás" (Matthew), although the church is actually dedicated to the Madonna. My wild guess is that perhaps half the population does not even know who the patron saint is; it is always remembered as the church of Mátyás. It is probably one of the few Catholic churches in the world that is associated with a person, who was not a saint by a long shot. Mátyás, or King Matthew, a shining example of justice, wisdom, worldly polish, superior education, enlightenment, and plain human goodness, had the church rebuilt about five hundred years ago, and in doing so he transformed it into a national treasure. His second marriage to the elegant, highly educated and thoroughly Renaissance Beatrix of Naples took place with singular pomp in the newly restored church. Ever since, through the centuries, it was the site of great festivities, including the coronation of kings, thus pushing the imposing cathedral on the Pest side of the city, across thee Danube, to a mere second place in importance.

We did not take the first bus. The temperature was falling, and the prospect of waiting in a cold, empty church was not terribly inviting. Mindlessly, we ignored our landlady's warning. By the time we arrived there, it was so crowded that we had to squeeze ourselves in sideways to find a spot where we could plant both feet on the floor. It would have helped if we had smeared petrolatum on our coats to facilitate sliding. In the end, using what we knew about the psychology of earthlings, we found two seats. For many years I was alternately a student, a teacher, or a lecturer, and so I am familiar about people's disinclination to sit in the front rows, with the possible exception of buses and trams. In this respect churches are no different from lecture halls, and we found our seats in the first row.

"Isn't there a passage in the Good Book about how the first ones shall be the last ones?" inquired my husband, already planning our exit. "By the time we get out of here, the last bus will have left."

"So what's wrong with the Hilton for one night? It's next door."

"Nothing. As long as not everybody else has the same idea for a solution."

The service was unforgettable, as we knew it would be. It was one of the reasons we have decided to spend Christmas at Budapest. To be quite honest, the throngs at the midnight mass at the Mátyás are not there for the purely religious experience only. May I be forgiven for having said so, but under the guise of devotion, many attend the service to listen to the music, sung by some of the best voices in the city. The organ of truly majestic dimensions is complemented by a full orchestra, and the midnight mass is undoubtedly one of the outstanding musical events of the year.

The enjoyment of the music is greatly heightened by the visual beauty of the church. The walls are covered with intricate designs, painted with gold and the muted colors of ancient, enameled jewelry. As the walls shimmer in the soft light, the church emanates a mystic, somewhat oriental mood. One almost expects a miracle to happen. The altar and the sanctuary practically disappear under masses of flowers, forests of evergreen boughs, and hundreds of candles. Their fragrances mingle with that of incense to sweeten the air.

It was a supreme gift that we could be there.

The music first teased with gentle wisps of angelic interpretations, but as it gained strength, the angles withdrew into the sacred shadows that shroud the upper regions of the church under the vaulted arches. Joy and passion took over; the triumph over the hopeless condition of Man was announced with all the stops pulled in the organ. The crescendo of unrestrained emotions rocked the soul, and filled the empty spaces between the bodies of people, then rose into the dizzy heights of the church where the angels were hiding. Near-revelation surfaced, clinging to the ghosts of almost-formed ideas; the soul was overpowered by a wealth of half-formed thoughts, and by strange insights. Dazzling passions bubbled up from the subconscious, waiting to be transformed into rational ideas and recognizable emotions. The joy was boundless and real. We became one entity with the hundreds of strangers, bound together by a magic energy, created at the beginning of time, and spelled out again two thousand years ago. And this energy was not fabricated out of fashionable esoteric fantasies, or of electrical or magnetic power fields, but was created out of the only force that makes life worth living: love.

The service ended when chorus, soloists and worshippers all sang the national anthem together with the passion unique to people who were finally, after half a century, free again in their own country. Men and women cried openly, because they were relieved, or happy, or triumphant. Or perhaps just very grateful. The church, built by the great renaissance king of the country, was the most perfect place to express this all-consuming joy at the rebirth of the nation.

After it was all over, we waited in groups for the buses. The snow was still falling heavily and it muffled all sounds, covered all dirt; it was indeed a silent and holy night. Our dark overcoats were soon covered with the soft white stuff, and we smiled at each other with open happiness, secretly glad that we had to wait for the bus and so could prolong the magic feeling we just experienced. We were standing around like a well designed stage group, waiting for somebody to make a grand entrance and to dramatically speak the words of a great denouement. And the words were finally spoken, when the silver-bell voice of a young child said loud and clear, "Mummy, Christmas is wonderful. I wish it would never end."

The frantic preparations for the holidays were forgotten, irritations and pre-holiday conjugal tensions vanished under the falling snow, and good will was palpable.

"This is what you ought to write about," remarked the man in my life as we were boarding the bus. "At one point in his hectic life, Man took a wrong turn somewhere, and ended up on a road that does not lead anywhere. Christmas became a season for obscenely long and expensive wish-lists, mad shopping, constant reminders of how many more shopping days are left, culminating in office parties, followed by inevitable disappointments, bankruptcy and hangover. More suicides are committed than on any other day of the year, and half the population is so overworked and stressed out that there is nothing left but be hauled away with blue lights and sirens, straight into the intensive care unit, long before the turkey hits the table. We forgot how to celebrate. But tonight we saw a different set of values that make a celebration dignified and tranquil."

He finished his little sermon, visibly happy to have found the secret formula to provide mankind with the much needed spirituality. I responded with a holiday smile and debated whether I should, on this blissful and holy night, shatter his peace of mind with the truth, or whether I should let him hang on to his innocent illusions. But then I remembered the dark shadows under the eyes of our hostess, the barely hidden pain as she raised her aching, overworked body from her chair at the end of the meal. I remembered the small packages she placed under her perfect tree, and the lovely black gown she had the energy to put on for the festivity. And millions of women all over the globe were doing exactly what she has been doing that night, in order to make a holiday memorable for those they love. Men know so pitifully little about the really important things, and sometimes it is necessary to point out the facts of life to them. Even if I could not tell it to all the men in the world, it was to be my special Christmas mission to enlighten at least this one, my husband. I owed that much to my sisters of all ages, all colors, and all religions, who are regularly and unselfishly working their buns off all over the planet, to make a holiday special for their families.

"Darling," I intoned snuggling up to him. "What makes you think that cleaning the house for the holidays, then without the convenience of a car doing major food shopping for the three days while the stores would be closed, decorating a fantastic tree, putting presents under it, then cooking a fabulous meal for fourteen, setting a festive table and then cleaning up the mess after it —would be void of stress, frenzied overwork and frazzled nerves? Have you not noticed that she was half dead when we left, and that she declined to come up to the Mátyás for the mass, even though it was she who so enthusiastically recommended it?"

And so, on this most silent of all nights, I managed to have the last word.

EPILOGUE

Before I started this book, I already decided to close it at the time the house is completed. We reached that point and this is the end of the tale. The book was not meant to be a biographical account of our intimate life, nor was it designed to show the complicated national or local politics of the country that adopted me. I am not qualified to do that, nor would it fit within the framework and the style of this writing. But I did make copious notes of what I observed, and of what I heard.

From time to time Hungary, or Hungarians, emerge briefly in the news, but so very little is known about them that by the time the first commercial is flashed on the screen, the interest has flickered away. The point is that it scares me that the inhabitants of this world know so little about each other. Perhaps it is the tell-tale sign of my otherwise secretly kept pathological obsession, but I am convinced that as the world is shrinking and as we are increasingly more dependent on each other, we need to know how the other fellow lives. It is important to understand how he is affected by the great alternating waves of destruction and progress, commonly known as war and peace. How else could we ever come close to preventing the worst that can happen to us?

In my blackest moods I despair that universal peace only exists in the dreams of the idealist; but surprisingly there are times when I wake up like a raging optimist, and then I can almost believe that peace is just around the corner. On those days I think that the secret to achieve this goal is to simply know each other better. If we knew our fellows, we could perhaps learn to like them, and maybe then we wouldn't hurt each other quite so much. For this reason I included in my account many of the conversations and episodes I encountered. I have the naive hope that through sharing the somewhat bewildered and confused thoughts, the painful memories, bitter disappointments and daily struggles of people, who were just emerging from Communism that lasted almost half a century, some understanding could be born. While it is true that millions of European tourists visit Hungary each year, many Americans are not even sure about its location, and often confuse Budapest with Bucharest. I hope that this writing is a small step toward getting acquainted.

But basically this book is not political, nor sociological; it is not even a travel book, although it touches on all that. Its aim is to tell about our enforced move, and the house we built after the rubble of both was cleared away. It is about going through a passage when we no longer expected one, and about our trepidation to accept the unavoidable. Ultimately it is about the joy of discovering that neither losing a job, nor early retirement, nor illness, nor a total change can kill the life force that we all inherited at the beginning of our lives. Because of this, the book is not a personal, private account. The problems we faced are unfortunately not at all unique; far too many share it. The very readable report published by 'The New York Times': The Downsizing of America (1996), is an eye-opening account of millions of Americans, who are losing good jobs even as these pages are turned. They, just like us, are facing gigantic problems at an age when little can be done to salvage their career, indeed their future . Hopefully our experiences, and what we got out of them, are reassuring and encouraging. Heaven knows, we could all use a little optimism. Life stops when the heart stops beating, and not when we reach a certain age, or when fate decides to do us an ugly turn.

As is the case with so many "previously unpublished authors", I too had to accept endless rejections. Years have elapsed between the completion of the book, and the writing of the Epilogue. Many things have changed during the interim. The country is no longer the fumbling, emerging, almost backward place we found when we moved here more than ten years ago. Democracy is being absorbed gradually, and people are looking with renewed hope into the future. Finally there is a good, honest and stable government in Budapest, with a young, vigorous, enlightened leadership. Victor Orban, the Oxford-educated head of state, is offering new hope to the country, and is guiding it into the right direction.

Things have changed on the national and personal levels. We no longer face the ridiculous problems we encountered when we moved here. But it is also a sad fact that during the long stretch of time since I finished my account, many of the people mentioned in this book have left us. Esther's advice to have a black dress for all seasons, proved prophetic.

As I edited the book recently, I often faced the problem with the grammatical tenses. So much of what I wrote ten years ago should already be in the past tense. Perhaps not past perfect, but definitely past. And even now, events follow each other so rapidly, that as soon as I put down a fact, it becomes obsolete, history. If I would write the book today, it would probably have a different tone. But what I wrote was very true in the beginning of the last decade in the millenium.

At any rate, the house has been finished and we think it is beautiful. Despite all the frustrations, the disappointments, the illnesses, and despite the distance and the separation from our families, we are truly happy in it. It is more than just a house, more than a place to live in. It is part of us.

Imre Makovecz, the genius of Hungarian architecture, often talks about "organic architecture", which is the true meaning of the unique, breath-taking buildings he creates. (The world had a taste of his singular creativity at the Seville Expo '92; Makovecz designed the Hungarian pavilion, which received rave reviews.) Our house does not have the daring design of Makovecz (unfortunately), because our pocketbook was tailored to less lofty and less expensive ventures. But I often feel that our house too is "organic". It evolved out of our life, our needs, and it was made for living, for growing and changing and was designed to be always close to nature. It accommodates the seasons as we wander from one spot to the other as the weather dictates. We sit by the fire, when the winds howl outside, have lunch among our exotic plants while the snow falls gently, or sit on the patio under the awning, or next to our tiny pool when the temperatures soar. Like a thing come to life, our house understands us, teases our fantasy, and offers a spot for our changing needs and moods. We can always come back to it, close the door and instantly all pain and all disappointments fall away, and our energies are recharged. It is a fortress that shields us from the ugliness of the world, and in this sense it is truly organic.

Sometimes I imagine that it is like the castle of Sleeping Beauty. (Fairy tale history has it that the legendary castle was probably located at Sababurg, Germany. It is now a hotel.) As a child, I was fascinated how she slumbered in it for a hundred years and how that most potent kiss of all history woke her. I loved to read every little detail about how the immobilized court came to life like a clockwork wound up once again. The bustle of the day resumed, without the disorientation and trauma a time warp of a century would cause. I laughed when the cook simply finished the intended slap aimed at the little helper, who stuck his finger into the cream a hundred years ago. Beauty did not act surprised about the "modern" look of the prince, although I'm sure he was dressed differently than her courtiers were. Fashion does not stand still for a century. I never really considered that during her long sleep the world outside the castle must have changed, and that she and her court were in for some serious adjustment problems, and perhaps in need of a good shrink. Like all children, I delighted in the permanence of the make-believe world. Her safe sleep became my personal security.

But as an adult, blessed (or cursed) with an analytical mind, I saw the situation from a different point of view. In times gone by, I was especially intrigued by the rose-hedge around Sleeping Beauty's castle, because it prevented anyone from penetrating the compound. I now realize that the thorny wilderness was not a bitter curse, or a malicious act of Nature, but it was a blessing. The fairy, who installed it, apparently had a better understanding of the world, than her colleagues did. The living, impenetrable wall offered supreme protection to the Princess, and to all, who shared her life. Without that thorny hedge, legions of adventurers, research scientists, talk-show hosts, paparazzi, biography writers, Hollywood, boulevard magazines, the news media and worse could have penetrated. Left unprotected, more likely than not, she would never have woken from her century-long sleep. The hedge closed out the world and its aggressive representatives, and protected her from it all.

I have mostly ornamental beans on my garden fence, but thinking of the Princess, I also planted some symbolic wild rose bushes at our boundary line. We live in a gloriously selective isolation, which is perhaps the last of the real luxuries in this overcrowded century. Friends get through the hedge, without even noticing its existence, but enemies meet the same fate as those, who tried to penetrate into the castle of Sleeping Beauty. For further reference, see the original story, preferable the one written by Perrault.

We no longer are surprised when friends, coming for an evening or a few days, also feel the magic of the place. Ours is a very simple house from the outside, and from the street it appears much smaller than it really is. Once an author friend, Géza Cséby, wrote into our guest book: "Your house is serious and substantial from the outside. It has no frills or ostentatious displays, its simplicity is uncomplicated and dignified. One could even pass it without taking notice. The house shows its real beauty, its wonderfully rich spirit to those only, who are invited to enter. I feel honored and enriched that you opened the door for me and let me feel the magic." Even Makovecz could not do better than this.

But again, perhaps it would be wiser not to say such outlandish things, lest someone would overhear it. The good, God-fearing people in our medieval Szabar would be truly scandalized if they heard that inanimate objects, such as a house, have spirits and magic. If they knew about the invisible fence around our property that keeps evil out, they would probably no longer greet me with a smile and a kind word when I am working among the bushes and flowers on the front lawn. They might brand me as a witch, and go out of their way while doing their errands, to avoid being near this strange house.

My husband assures me that I don't have to fear witch-hunts in this country. Exactly one thousand years ago Hungary was forcibly converted to Christianity, he tells me. Soon the last vestiges of the beautiful, ancient religion were gone, and the men and women, who performed the dignified rituals, disappeared. Gone were the venerable shamans, (*Táltos* in Hungarian) and those magnificent women, who seemed to have a sense of the future, knew herbs intimately, and could cure the sick. Once they were trusted and respected, but almost overnight, they dropped into a cultural void. The word, Táltos, is still remembered, but only as a name for particularly fine horses. With Christianity came the fear of the Devil and his coworkers, the witches. The first recorded witch trial was not until 1330 in Spain, and it took almost a century to reach all of Europe, where at the height of this frenzy, on a single day in Quedlinburg, Germany, 133 'witches' were sent to their deaths, after unimaginable tortures. But Hungary has not a single record of inquisition; either there were no witches here, or else they were left alone. Two things saved the women of this country. One was the ancient law, very unusual and extremely advanced at that time, namely that self-incrimination was not evidence enough to earn the death penalty; hence, torture made no sense and was not a necessary tool in trials. This law effectively disposed of the Inquisition in this country. The second woman-saver was a truly enlightened king in the eleventh century, Kálmán, who earned the sobriquet *'Könyves'*. This attached name means that he was learned; he was one who knew books. I suspect he also had a little shaman blood flowing in his veins, because quite uncannily, a couple hundred years before the witch trials became serious business on the Continent, he wrote into the law under paragraph 57 : *"De strigis vero quae non sunt, nulla questio fiat..."* (At that time the language of the law was Latin). Translated: witches do not exist; therefore no question (no mention) is necessary. As a consequence, there were no witch trials, which in my opinion were first invented by men, as a convenient and inexpensive alternative to divorce.

In view of King Kálmán's enlightened declaration, I suppose it would be safe for me to talk about magic without the fear of being extradited to Rome for a belated *autodafé*. Yet, it is better to be safe than sorry; therefore the rose hedge in front of the house is just that: a plain old hedge of *rosa rugosa*, and no mention needs to be made of the invisible, protective wall. As the good king said, *"...nulla questio fiat..."*

Life is good. Not perfect, but good. Too much perfection smacks of otherworldliness and death. Of course, from time to time in its unaccountable perversity, life would throw us a curved ball, for which we are not ready. But then, who is? I yet have to hear the exclamation, "Thank goodness, this misfortune came just in time; we were eagerly expecting it and are ready for it." But we don't complain about the bad turns, and somehow they get resolved, or go away, or we simply accept the inevitable. I even learned to laugh about my book's innumerable rejections, and once we threw a party to celebrate when I hit a round number of returned slips with the uniform message, "sorry, you obvious have talent and tell a story well, but I'm afraid, it is not for me." Géza's wife, Erika, baked a cake in the form of a book, and wrote on it with red icing, "This book isn't for agents. It's for readers." She baked a note into the cake and sliced it so that I got the piece with the message. It said "We love you and keep our fingers crossed for you."

As I was concluding this book, I could not ignore the passions, the fanatic hatred and the incomprehensible angers that were boiling south of the Hungarian border. Glancing out through our beautiful arched windows, I wondered about the slowly dissipating white stripes in the sky. I did not know whether the planes that made them were just friendly people-movers, or if they were flying with a frightening military mission. Once, when I was supervising Joska, who was working in the garden, I heard a distant rumble and my heart skipped a beat, while I tried to decide what it was. It could have been a sonic boom, or an explosion from a nearby stone quarry. But the former Yugoslavian border (now Croatia) is awfully close to Szabar and I feared that what I heard could have been the distant verification of the insanity that would not only cause untold tragedies there, but could even threaten our precarious peace here. The unthinkable was no longer just an abstraction.

I try to be philosophical and remind myself that we all have to accept a certain amount of trouble in our life. That was part of the birth contract. (Which we probably never signed.) But war and other atrocities are certainly more than just mere "troubles", and I doubt that it is possible to ever get over the inherent inhumanity. There seems to be no limit to the horrors that people can do to each other. In case we forgot this, Kosovo and Chechnya just reminded us again. And who can tell what the future holds? Man has astounding powers and resources. Will he ever learn how to harness hatred?

At the time of this writing that particular "trouble" is more or less resolved, and phase two had begun. What was destroyed is now being built up again. It was always so. Throughout the written history of mankind, wars were fought, towns and villages destroyed, civilians murdered, torture chambers activated, and heads rolled. As soon as all the damage was completed, peace treaties were engineered. Former enemies became allies and friends. After the dust settled and the last fire was put out, Man habitually and enthusiastically cleared away the rubble and built up what was leveled, only to be destroyed again in the next confrontation. The bereaved families were always left on their own to get over their losses as best as they could; the grief was their very own. It was always so and this makes the future somewhat frightening. History does not show that Man had become much tamer, kinder or more peaceable during his otherwise spectacular evolution.

And yet, life is still good, at least for us, and I pray a lot that it stays that way. We greet each day as a precious gift, because time is not standing still. We are all heading toward that great mystic event, our single, magnificent encounter with the supernatural that will finally reveal the absolute truth about life after death. Most of us have learned how to live, but there is little preparation, or briefing on how to exit bravely, or at least properly. Ultimately we'll have to pass the threshold from here to there on our very own and do it totally alone, dying being the single most private act in the life of a mortal. The excitement of finally knowing what is behind the door is somewhat dimmed by the very finality of the event. We are not permitted to shop around, or to step back from the deal if we don't like what is offered. No user's manual, no guarantees and no refund. And no choice.

But I feel that most of us learn the lesson by the end, which is almost primitive and commonplace in its simplicity: in the long run, we get just as much out of life as we are willing to put into it. For most of us nothing is really free. Nobody hands us the prize and the roses, unless we work for it with everything we have. Nobody can make us happy; the power to generate happiness is deep inside us. And so is the power and talent to love and to endure.

And even that is not always true, and the last century showed us a staggering number of examples where this was painfully not so. It takes so little to be singled out for the worst fate there is, and the victim cannot defend himself, because his fate was sealed before he was born, and he had no choice in choosing his parents. Being born with a skin color different from the local preference, or becoming part of a family with a different religion, or being born at the geographically wrong location, or at the wrong time in history, or just being born into a family that is gravely challenged culturally, morally or economically, is quite enough for absolute disaster. We often hear about the few, who despite all the odds made it, and gloss over the millions, who simply could not get ahead. So very many of our brothers and sisters, due to no fault of their own and despite their desperate struggles and bravery, were destined to be passive toys in the hands of a horribly evil spirit. Their inhuman agony, their loneliness, and the injustice that was meted out to them, cries to the heavens above. These are such mind-boggling facts, which cannot be comprehended, forgotten, forgiven or prayed away. Mankind was always amazingly inventive when it came to creating horrors, but I do believe that the last century of the second millenium was worthy of Satan himself.

Not because of merit or excellence, but due to sheer luck, we were able to avoid that unimaginably painful fate. We can't be thankful enough for that.

There is nothing more to add. I bow my head in humility, because we were so lucky. In retrospect, our sufferings were minor, and we got back all of our investments; in the end, a handsome interest was even added to it. And we always had love and hope.

The End

ISBN 1553697413

9 781553 697411